W9-AAZ-776

Jewish
Holiday
Traditions

Jewish Holiday Traditions

Joyful Celebrations From Rosh Hashanah to Shavuot

Linda Burghardt

CITADEL PRESS
Kensington Publishing Corp.
www.kensingtonbooks.com

CITADEL PRESS books are published by

Kensington Publishing Corp.
850 Third Avenue
New York, NY 10022

All Kensington titles, imprints, and distributed lines are available at special quantity discounts for bulk purchases for sales promotions, premiums, fund raising, educational, or institutional use. Special book excerpts or customized printings can also be created to fit specific needs. For details, write or phone the office of the Kensington special sales manager: Kensington Publishing Corp., 850 Third Avenue, New York, NY 10022, attn: Special Sales Department, phone 1-800-221-2647.

First printing July 2001

10 9 8 7 6 5 4 3 2 1

Printed in the United States of America

Library of Congress Control Number: 2001091894

ISBN 0-8065-2206-2

To David, Amy, and Katie,
with love, laughter, and latkes

Contents

Introduction   3

The Holiday Cycle   10

PART I: FRESHNESS AND FERTILITY

1. Rosh Hashanah: Gateway to Renewal   19
2. Yom Kippur: To Begin Anew   39
3. Sukkot: Heaven Under the Stars   58
4. Simchat Torah: Dancing With Joy   79

PART II: SWEETNESS AND ABUNDANCE

5. Hanukkah: Holiday of Lights   101
6. Tu b'Shevat: The New Year of Trees   123
7. Purim: The Book of Esther   144
8. Passover: The Road to Freedom   163

PART III: WARMTH AND RENEWAL

9. Yom Ha'atzmaut: Israel's Independence Day   187
10. Lag b'Omer: An Island of Song   205
11. Shavuot: Festival of Weeks   223
12. Shabbat: A Day of Rest and Retreat   243

Appendix A: Blessings for Shabbat and the Festivals   265
Appendix B: Secular Dates of the Major Holidays   269
Glossary   271
Recommendations for Further Reading   281
Acknowledgments   283
Index   285

Jewish
Holiday
Traditions

Introduction

FROM THE FIRST MOMENT the doorbell rings to the time the last guests put on their coats and head for the car, your holiday party is the center of their world.

If they feel comfortable in your home, it is because of your welcoming embrace. If they eat heartily, it is because of your culinary skill. If they feel warmed by Jewish tradition, it is because of your ability to lead the rituals.

Achieving all this may strike you as a daunting task, and the truth is, you are right. But Jewish hospitality is both an art and a craft, inseparable from Jewish history, lore, customs, poetry, food, love, laws, and the people who create them. And because of this, much of what you need to know you already have mastered without necessarily being aware of it.

Everything else you need to know to succeed as a holiday host is in this book. Everything, that is, but the one ingredient only you can supply: that profound stamp of individuality so deeply honored in the Jewish tradition. Fortunately, you already possess that in abundance.

This special quality, together with the processes, plans, and procedures you will find in these pages, will take you from the first scratch mark on the shopping list to the afterglow of success, guaranteed to last long after the final dish is washed and put away and the final gesture of praise accepted.

We live in many worlds at the same time—the worlds of physical dimension, of intellectual movement, of spiritual depth. And our many hungers are satisfied at once by only a very few events in our lives. One of these, and perhaps the most profound of all, is the celebration of the Jewish holidays.

But where exactly do you start? What would Sarah, Rebecca, Rachel, and Leah do?

They would begin by mastering the basics of hosting, and then gain a thorough understanding of the beauty and complexity of each individual celebration within the holiday cycle.

And so will we.

Throughout this book you will find out how to build your menu around each specific Jewish holiday, prepare both traditional and innovative dishes, time your courses, select music and wine, decorate the table, create crafts to involve young children, organize the required rituals, and even choose the appropriate fresh flowers to enhance your home's ambiance. But first, it is a good idea to go over the basics common to all holiday celebrations and see what hosting choices will set you on your path toward a successful party.

Making a Game Plan

Dinner party or buffet? Hired help or not? Homemade dishes or ready-made? If the answers elude you, the first thing you need to do is find a notebook and a quiet place to think.

A simple bound notebook similar to the kind kids use in school is a good investment, because you can keep your notes all in one place and refer to them easily the next time you plan a similar party.

If you use any outside services, you can staple or tape in the business card of the vendor for easy reference in the future. You can jot down quantities of food and drink that worked for groups of different sizes, note which flowers wilted halfway through the evening, and whether music enhanced the conversation or overpowered it. You can also attach bills to help you determine your expenses for this party and make a budget for the next one. It is also a good plan to write down who in your family did what task and how it worked out. Will you assign different roles next time, or help family members refine their skills in one particular area?

Start by making spaces in the notebook for the type of event, the time of day, the time of year, the guest list, and the menu. Leave room for the photographs you will take of the table after it has been dressed. Note whether any of the guests have any particular allergies or dietary restrictions. There is no sense cooking a silvertip roast for your vegetarian aunt and uncle, for example, or a whole whitefish for your cousin who cannot handle bones.

How Much Do I Serve?

Knowing how to determine the right quantities of food to order and cook is an important part of the planning for a party, and figuring out correct portion sizes can be tricky. Every host feels some anxiety over having enough food to serve and fears that fatal error of underestimating their diners' appetites.

As a rule, for appetizers you can figure about two ounces per person. If you are serving salad, half a cup is the average amount; a generous soup portion is six to eight ounces per person.

When it comes to the entrée, the serving size depends on the type of meat or fish. For boneless meat, such as prime rib, six to eight ounces per portion is fine. One four-pound chicken cut up will serve four people. If you are serving boneless poultry, figure four to six ounces per portion.

For fish, the average serving size varies from six ounces if it is boneless to eight ounces with the bone. For dessert, count on two to three ounces per person for pudding, pies, cookies, or soufflé.

If you want to make sure you have enough of everything, pretend there is one extra guest coming to dinner and plan on an additional portion of each item. Few families mind tasty leftovers from a gala event.

Making a Timetable

There are three important days to a party—one week before, one day before, and the day of the party itself—and several tasks to do on each one. If you take care of the chores assigned to each day, it will help you keep that all-important sense of control.

One week before, make sure you confirm the guest list, write out the menu, and begin to purchase nonperishable items like paper goods, wine, sugar, canned food, and soda. Buy or borrow any special equipment you might need, such as extra folding chairs or the food processor that will cut down some of your prep time. Now is the time to prepare any foods that you plan to freeze.

The day before the party, purchase all but the most perishable foods, check that plates, flatware, and glasses are clean and unchipped, plan the seating arrangements, cook the foods that will keep overnight, and set the table.

On the day of the party, shop for the flowers, fish, salad greens, and bread, and put white wine in to chill at least two hours before the guests are scheduled to arrive. Measure out the coffee, set it aside and finish the last-minute cooking.

The Role of Ritual

Are there any specific religious rituals surrounding this holiday? Note them on a separate page. If you will need to research them, indicate where you will find the material or whom to ask for a reference.

If you are making a Passover seder, for example, it will be helpful from year to year to know how to prepare the seder plate and even where you stored the Haggadahs. Write it down! After twelve months the exact location of the books will have long fled your memory.

Culinary Culture

The time of year is important in determining the menu, because you will want to consider seasonal produce and take advantage of what is available at your grocer's. It is also a good idea to save meaty stews and hearty dishes for winter, for example, since summer cooking tends to be lighter.

When planning your menu, think about freezer, refrigerator, and oven space. Only have one oven? Choose foods that all cook at about the same temperature so they can be made at once.

If you need extra space, you might be able to borrow cold storage space from a neighbor or use a portable ice chest. In the winter, if you have a back porch or terrace, you can use it to cool cakes awaiting icing or store soda, wine, and juice.

Make friends with your freezer! That means cook ahead and freeze whenever you can. The fewer things you leave for the last day, the calmer you will be when your guests arrive.

If you are fortunate enough to have an outdoor space available to you, use it from late spring to early fall for dining al fresco. Food always seems to taste better outside, and the look of lanterns and seasonal greens can go a long way toward making simple fare seem exotic and elegant.

For larger dinner gatherings of over twenty people, you might want to consider serving two entrées so your guests will have a choice. But if this is too difficult, a simple way to add variety is to offer two or three vegetables and starches.

For a traditional dinner party, plan on four courses—the appetizer, salad, entrée, and dessert. If you want to expand your menu to six, you can do so by adding soup and fish. In general the earlier courses are smaller and grow in size and intensity of taste as the meal progresses.

Plan your menu with care, and beware of new recipes when cooking for guests. Always try out new recipes on your family first before adding them to your holiday menu. A private mistake is much easier to recover from than a public disaster.

The Guest List: A Good Beginning

Whenever possible, invite a mix of guests, and not a great many at once. Realistically evaluate your table and chairs, the size of your dining area, your kitchen space. Squeezing in extra people can add to the intensity but also will raise noise levels and decrease elbow room.

Look for the perfect balance and stick to your decision. Don't let yourself be pushed into agreeing to anything at the last minute that didn't seem like a good idea when you had the leisure to think about it.

To Hire Help or Not

Realistically evaluate the workload and consider whether you want to hire help, particularly for the clean-up end of the party. Family members and friends may offer help in good faith yet at the last minute find themselves drawn into the ambiance of the event, leaving you with no extra hands.

Keep in mind that you have as much right to have a good time as your guests. So if you need help preparing the food or packing it away, or to help serve the soup while you are needed to make the sauce, don't deny yourself the extra luxury.

A Warm Welcome

Jewish hospitality starts with a firm handshake, a hug, and a friendly greeting at the door. While "hello" or "welcome" are always fine, it can be very nice to greet guests with "good yom tov," "good Shabbat," or "shana tovah," depending, of course, on the occasion. "Shalom" is always right, and lends an appropriately Jewish touch to the gathering. Warmth is a keystone of a welcoming house and is always the best way to begin.

It is also a good idea to pay attention to what guests first encounter when they enter your home. Are intruding pets safely out of range? Are

Timing Is Crucial

What type of party do you have in mind, and at what hour will it take place? Brunch is usually served between 10 A.M. and 2 P.M.; lunch can run from 12 to 3. Making a tea? Schedule it between 3 and 5, a cocktail party from 6 to 8. Traditional dinner parties go from 7 to 9 in the evening, while dessert-only get-togethers generally start about 9 P.M.

cooking smells limited to the kitchen? Are unpleasant views set off behind a screen or a closed door?

Because music and light draw people toward them, it is useful to plan how to use them to make your home pleasant and welcoming and to create the traffic flow that suits your party. A softly lit foyer and a bright living room will make guests instinctively move toward the living room area. When it is time for dinner, lower the living room lights and raise the level of music in the dining room, and your guests will know what to do.

Your Role as Host

And finally, make sure you have plenty of time to dress and calm down before the doorbell rings. If possible, aim to have the entire last hour before the first guest arrives to take care of yourself. Build the hour firmly into your plan and you are more likely to see it materialize.

As the host, you are in charge. It's that simple. Remember that you have the ability to blend art, grace, and culinary skill with your knowledge of religious ritual. You have the edge. Use it.

The Holiday Cycle

CREATING A CELEBRATION for the Jewish holidays connects you to your family and your tradition in a way nothing else can. In Judaism, it is a simple truth that religion, food, and entertainment are intertwined like the three inseparable braids of the Havdalah candle.

Properly presented, the food you serve and the ambiance you create enlighten the spirit of the holiday. But at the heart of each holiday is the deep sense of sanctity and renewal that forms its spiritual core. Offered in its own unique way, it is this sense that transcends even the comfort and satisfaction you offer your guests, and provides the power that connects them with the heritage of their ancestors and the dreams of generations yet to come.

Rosh Hashanah: Gateway to Renewal

The dates of Jewish holidays vary every year because they are determined by the Hebrew lunar-solar calendar, not the secular system we use in everyday life. And so Rosh Hashanah, which means literally "head of the year," falls sometimes in September, other years in October.

Rosh Hashanah occurs on the first two days of Tishri, the seventh month of the Hebrew calendar, and signals the beginning of the most holy days of the year, the ten Days of Awe. It is during this period that we search our souls in anticipation of the divine judgment that will be rendered on us, determining whether or not we will be inscribed in the Book of Life for yet another year.

In addition to prayer and introspection, Rosh Hashanah is a time of deep joy and hope for the future, a time to share apples dipped in honey with the people we love in the hope that we will all enjoy a sweet year.

Yom Kippur: To Begin Anew

Prayer, charity, and self-evaluation mark the period between Rosh Hashanah and Yom Kippur, the day on which our fate for the coming year is sealed. By the time we have reached this most solemn day of the year, Jewish tradition commands us to have asked forgiveness of those we might have wronged as we try to atone for all our sins.

Yom Kippur is a solemn day of fasting and attending services, a day to put aside our physical needs and devote ourselves to our spiritual side. To prepare for this, we often share a special meal with family and friends the night before, making sure to finish before sundown, then break the fast the next evening after the shofar is sounded in the synagogue, signaling the start of a new beginning.

Sukkot: Heaven Under the Stars

While Rosh Hashanah is celebrated at the start of the seventh month, Sukkot falls exactly two weeks later and lasts for seven days. The holiday is named for the sukkah, the temporary hut that sheltered our ancestors during their forty years of wandering in the Sinai desert, the time between the Exodus from Egypt and their arrival in the Promised Land.

In later times, when farmers left home to gather food from their fields, they lived in similar huts. Thus the holiday commemorates the difficult times our ancestors lived through as they journeyed from slavery to freedom and also honors the harvest. We follow this tradition by building sukkahs at home and at the synagogue, decorating them with fruits and vegetables, and eating our meals there, under the slatted roof, with the sky for a canopy.

Simchat Torah: Dancing With Joy

Two days after Sukkot ends, Simchat Torah begins. Simchat Torah means literally "rejoicing with the Torah," and it is traditionally a time of great joy.

The day marks the end of the reading of the Torah, and the beginning of its reading too. The Torah scroll is rewound, and both the last verses of Deuteronomy and the first ones of Genesis are recited, showing that the reading of the Torah never ends.

But first, we pass the Torah from one to another and dance with it, feeling its weight and experiencing the excitement it engenders as the procession winds around the synagogue led by children carrying paper bags that congregants fill with candy.

Hanukkah: Holiday of Lights

For eight days in the darkest time of winter, candles are lit, latkes are eaten, songs are sung, dreidels are spun, and children are enthralled by the story of the Maccabees. It is Hanukkah, and what began as a minor festival in the holiday cycle has grown into a major celebration.

The holiday commemorates a miracle that took place two thousand years ago when oil that was sufficient to burn for only one day lasted for eight. It happened during a time in history when the Jews in the Holy Land were ruled by a cruel king named Antiochus, who threw the Jews out of the Holy Temple in Jerusalem, demanded they worship the Greek gods, and killed those who disobeyed. A group of rebellious Jews banded together to fight the Syrians under the leadership of a farmer and his five sons, the Maccabees. We recall their victory every year by lighting the menorah with its eight branches, and eating foods cooked in oil.

Tu b'Shevat: The New Year of Trees

Spring in Israel is a joyous time, and it is marked by a holiday known as the New Year of Trees, or Tu b'Shevat, which falls on the fifteenth day of the month of Shevat, usually in February. A relatively minor holiday, it is nevertheless a happy one, embraced most warmly by those with a love of nature. It is sometimes called the Jewish Arbor Day, celebrating the season when blossoms open and vineyards and orchards turn green.

This was a significant time in ancient Israel, with its agricultural base, and became important again in modern times with the creation of agricultural settlements in Israel in the late 1800s, when it once more became necessary to plant trees to rebuild the land. Tu b'Shevat is celebrated with a seder celebrating fruits and wine.

Purim: The Book of Esther

A holiday of raucous exuberance, Purim celebrates the triumph of Esther and Mordechai over Haman, an ambitious and deceitful official of Persia who plotted to kill all the Jews. Lots were drawn to determine on which day this would take place—Purim is the Hebrew word for "lots." Esther, who was married to the king, risked her life to reveal the plot against the Jews and told him that she herself was Jewish. Instead of hanging Mordechai, the king killed Haman.

A carnival spirit pervades this celebration, in which we read the Scroll of Esther, make noise, and eat hamantaschen, a comic, cookie-pastry rendering of Haman's three-cornered hat. It is traditional to exchange food and sweets packed in baskets with friends and neighbors.

Passover: The Road to Freedom

Passover celebrates our ancestors' escape from slavery in Egypt three thousand years ago and commemorates both the unending universal quest for freedom and our obligation to care for those in need. Falling as it does in the early spring, when new life is awakening in every green bud, it reminds us of our duty to regard the future with hope.

An eight-day holiday, the celebration of the Exodus is traditionally marked by a seder on the first night, sometimes another on the second, and often a third on the last night of the festival.

During the seder the story of Passover is read from the Haggadah, which literally means "retelling." The table is set with wine, matzoh, and the six traditional symbols of the holiday, and the story of our flight to freedom is relived once again.

Yom Ha'atzmaut: Israel's Independence Day

In 1948, on the fifth day of the month of Iyar, the State of Israel was established, and every year on May 14, huge celebrations in Jewish communities throughout the world commemorate the creation of the modern-day Jewish state.

While this holiday is patriotic and not religious in origin, it is a popular festival to celebrate because of its deep meaning for Jews throughout the world. In Israel the day is marked by parades, fireworks, music festivals, and family barbecues, much the same way we celebrate the Fourth of July in the United States. Outside of Israel, Jews revitalize their strong sense of identity with the Jewish homeland with special festivities.

Jewish communities in the United States often hold parades, enjoy lively sessions of Israeli dancing, run songfests, and watch Israeli films and live entertainment. Most performers begin or end their shows with a rendition of "Hatikvah," the national anthem of Israel, which literally translated means "the hope."

Lag b'Omer: An Island of Song

Lag b'Omer, which nearly always falls in May, brings a day of sanctioned festivity to the solemn period between Passover and Shavuot.

In ancient times, when Israel was mostly an agricultural nation, our ancestors celebrated the beginning of the grain harvest every year by offering a measure of barley in thanks. *Omer* is the Hebrew word for measure or sheaf. The offering took place on the second day after Passover, and then, after fifty days, it was time to offer two loaves of bread made from the first wheat.

Traditional Jews observe this interval as a period of semi-mourning, commemorating the destruction of the Second Temple and the fighting and concurrent epidemic that took place at the time. But on the thirty-third day of the Counting of the Omer (Lag b'Omer, for short), the epidemic miraculously ceased, and so we celebrate this one uplifting event that occurred in the midst of destruction.

Shavuot: Festival of Weeks

Shavuot is said to be the wedding anniversary of the Jewish people, with the Torah as the marriage certificate between the Jews and God.

Celebrated on the sixth and seventh days of the Hebrew month of Sivan, this beloved holiday first developed as a celebration of the wheat harvest and later grew to embrace the choicest early fruits of the season. It is celebrated every year in late May or early June. The word *shavuot* means, literally, "weeks," as it occurs after the seven-week period during which the *omer*, or measure of grain, is counted.

Shavuot is best known as the time when the law was given, and is a celebration of the day God gave the Torah to the Israelites gathered at the foot of Mount Sinai.

Shabbat: A Day of Rest and Retreat

Shabbat, the oldest of all the Jewish holidays, means "rest" in Hebrew. In the Jewish calendar, Saturday is the last day of the week, and so the familiar story of God creating the world in six days and resting on the seventh comes home to us in a most basic way. It is on Saturday that we seek a day of peace and harmony, set apart from the frantic work week to bring us renewal of both body and spirit.

Several rituals attend Shabbat, including lighting the candles at sundown, saying blessings over the wine and challah, and sharing a leisurely meal together with friends, family, and welcome guests. Because ancient law did not allow fire to be lit on Shabbat, tradition required that all food be fully prepared by sundown on Friday. This gave rise to many slow-cooked dishes, originally kept warm over the embers after the sun went down.

Shabbat ends when three stars appear in the sky, signaling time for the Havdalah service, which bids goodbye to the light of the Sabbath and brings with it wishes for a good week.

PART I

Freshness and Fertility

1

Rosh Hashanah: Gateway to Renewal

On the first day of the seventh month there shall be a solemn rest for you, a holy gathering proclaimed with the blast of a ram's horn.

—Leviticus 23:24

Sweet Beginnings

THE ANNUAL CYCLE of the Jewish holidays begins with Rosh Hashanah, which marks both the start of the Jewish calendar year and the anniversary of the creation of the universe. This sacred and beloved holiday is two days long and falls on the first and second days of the month of Tishri, in September or early October in the secular calendar. Because of its joyous nature and its ability to touch the Jewish soul, it is the only holiday celebrated for both days in both Israel and throughout the world.

Rosh Hashanah, however, is a holiday with duality at its core. On the one hand, it is a solemn festival, one in which we turn our thoughts inward to examine our actions of the past year. Yet on the other hand, it is a big celebration commemorating the birthday of the world, marked by the twin traditions of festive visits to friends and family and menus heavily laden with sweet foods. Many cooks deck their tables with foods that represent optimism for a sweet future. Honey, raisins, prunes, carrots, and apples are culinary reminders of hope for the coming year.

The best-known ritual of the holiday is the sounding of the shofar, which is blown several times during the synagogue service to awaken in us the need to examine our deeds of the past year. Rosh Hashanah ushers in the most sacred time of year, the High Holy Days, or the Days of Awe, a period of intense prayer and introspection that ends ten days later on Yom Kippur.

The Origins of the Holiday

Although Rosh Hashanah means, literally, "head of the year," it takes place at the start of Tishri, the seventh month of the Hebrew calendar, and not Nisan, the first. To understand why this is so, it is important to look at what is happening to the earth at this time of year.

In Israel the first rains have fallen and the soil is being plowed for the winter grain. In ancient times, when the agricultural calendar took precedence over all the others, this was the time of year business dealings were made and when sabbatical and jubilee years began. Thus it naturally became the start of the year.

In the Bible, Rosh Hashanah is called Yom Teruah, the Day of the Sounding of the Ram's Horn. It was not called Rosh Hashanah until Talmudic times, somewhere between 200 and 500 C.E. While it was always a festival day, historians do not always agree on what exactly was being celebrated. Many scholars believe Rosh Hashanah was originally a Near Eastern coronation festival celebrating God, the King, who created the world.

Rosh Hashanah Celebrations

Although the majority of Rosh Hashanah rituals take place in the synagogue, the New Year holiday is also a wonderful time for home and family celebrations. Tradition tells us to visit one another on the afternoon or evening of the first day and enjoy a festive meal replete with sweet dishes.

At formal celebrations, it is customary to serve a main course of fish, often with the head left on, to symbolize the "rosh" or head of the new year. Some people believe this expresses the hope that the New Year will see Jews at the head of the nations of the world.

Jewish lore says that at the time of Noah, before the flood, fish were the only animals considered free of sin, which is why they were permitted to live and flourish in the flood when all other animals perished except those rescued by Noah. Fish, especially sweet fish, are closely associated with immortality and fertility, symbols of our hopes for abundance in the New Year.

No bitter or sour dishes are permitted on Rosh Hashanah. Some hosts go so far as to remove the salt shakers from the table and replace them with sugar bowls or honey jars, which they keep on the table throughout the meal.

The most popular and widespread culinary tradition at Rosh Hashanah is a festive round of sliced apples and honey before the meal begins. Guests dip the apples into the honey and offer each other good wishes. It is customary to say, "May it be the will of the Almighty to renew us unto a good and sweet year."

The Journey Within

Together with Yom Kippur, the two days of Rosh Hashanah are the holiest days of the year. They are also the most difficult to fully understand, since the holiday does not commemorate a historical event, an agricultural festival, or even a celebration of the season.

Instead, Rosh Hashanah celebrates something very personal: our ability to grow and change. On Rosh Hashanah, we become keenly aware of our ability as human beings to affect our own fates through thought and action. It is a time for introspection, prayer, and self-examination.

As we look at what we have done in the past year, we concentrate on our belief in human potential for improvement. It is a holiday that requires much effort, but our work is invisible. It goes on inside each of us as we wrestle privately with our consciences over our deeds in the past year, knowing in our hearts that not all those deeds deserve our approval.

Ultimately we hope to achieve a turning away from our past selves toward our better selves. Through a process of inner change, we atone for our misdeeds and find ways to improve. This process begins on Rosh Hashanah, triggered by the first heart-rending blasts of the shofar.

The Story of the Ram's Horn

The shofar, which is an ancient trumpetlike instrument, is considered to be the world's oldest wind instrument and is mentioned in the Bible as central to many ritual observances. Once upon a time it was sounded at the new moon and at all festivals and celebrations. The Bible tells us it was blown at Mount Sinai to mark the giving of each of the Ten Commandments, and used by Joshua during his conquest of Jericho.

In ancient times the shofar heralded great moments, calling people to the town square for the coronation of a king, the ascent of a queen to the throne, or the gathering of the army in wartime. It was also used to sound the alarm in times of crisis.

There are many stories about the meaning of the shofar blasts. The Talmud says the shofar is blown on Rosh Hashanah to confuse the devil to keep him from harming the Jews during this fragile time of judgment. The great Jewish philosopher Moses Maimonides referred to it as a call to repentance on this important holiday. To many, the shofar is the voice of Creation itself, proclaiming God's wish for us to heed our own heartfelt promises and find renewal through honest introspection during the Days of Repentance.

The shofar is traditionally made of a ram's horn, though it is acceptable to use the horn of a gazelle or antelope or any other kosher animal except a cow or an ox, as these are reminiscent of the golden calf at Mount Sinai. The sound from the curved horn of a sheep or mountain goat is considered clearest and most potent.

Some scholars believe the ram's horn is preferred because its curves remind us of the human heart, which is bent in humble repentance at this important time. Others say it is symbolic of the substitution of a ram for Abraham's beloved son Isaac, whom God commanded Abraham to sacrifice in the Torah portion read on Rosh Hashanah. For this reason the ram's horn has become a symbol of the faith of Abraham and the Jewish people.

A shofar is made by boiling the horn in water until it softens, then hollowing out the inside and flattening it slightly. After that the mouthpiece is shaped, and the horn is put aside to harden.

The Shofar in the Synagogue

The only biblical ritual required on Rosh Hashanah is the blowing of the shofar, whose blasts are made in a long-established pattern, with the alternation of long and short notes interspersed with quavering sounds. It is the most primitive sound any of us hears rendered in a modern setting, and many people feel it emits a strange, compelling power, sounding much like wordless cries of pain and longing. Others hear in it a primeval call proclaiming the birthday of the world. Still others interpret its sound as a prayer to God to forgive their sins. Yet whatever its specific meaning, the shofar remains a multifaceted symbol, at once recalling past events and making us look to a Messianic future.

Before the shofar is blown at Rosh Hashanah services, many rabbis recite Psalm 37, which proclaims that one day the shofar will announce God's divine sovereignty over all people throughout the world.

Jews are biblically commanded to hear the shofar at Rosh Hashanah, and to many people the mournful blasts symbolize our prayers for renewed life in the year to come. The three sounds—*tekiah*, one long blast; *shevarim*, three short blasts; and *teruah*, nine staccato blasts—are each separate and distinct yet able to merge together in a powerful and ancient pattern. This pattern pulls our attention inward toward prayer and soul-searching, the first step in the difficult process of inner change that characterizes the Days of Awe begun on Rosh Hashanah.

Making the Most of the Holiday

Like all Jewish holidays, Rosh Hashanah begins in the evening of the day before its official start. The exact date is determined by the new moon nearest the beginning of the gathering of the fruits in autumn, symbolizing a new year of rainfall and fertility. We usher in the holiday at nightfall by lighting festival candles and saying the appropriate blessings (see appendix A.)

Evening services are held that night, and many Jews prepare a festive dinner after their return from the synagogue or before they go. Others prepare an afternoon feast served after morning services the next day. The holiday is sober but not somber, and though our thoughts turn inward, our actions call for festive meals with friends and family.

The Book of Nehemiah tells us to celebrate on Rosh Hashanah: "Eat rich food and drink sweet wine, and share with those who have none." This admonition can take any form—from entertaining large groups to holding intimate luncheons or dinner parties with close friends.

Many people celebrate the holiday by sending greeting cards with the message, "May you be inscribed for a good year." An ancient Babylonian legend tells us that on Rosh Hashanah God opens two books of destiny and writes in the first, the Book of Life, the names of all those completely righteous people who will live another year. In the other book he inscribes the names of the completely wicked who will perish in the next year. But those whose names are written in neither book have a future

Rosh Hashanah

The primitive blasts of the shofar reverberate through holiday services with a power unmatched in any other synagogue ritual. Since ancient times its strange and compelling sound has signaled the promise of renewed confidence and hope for the future.

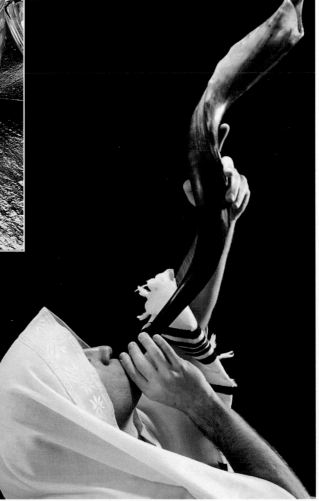

Rosh Hashanah is a time to search our souls and find peace within ourselves by examining our thoughts and deeds of the past year. We eat sweet foods like apples dipped in honey to help ensure that the coming year will be sweet and bountiful.

PHOTOS © BILL ARON

Yom Kippur

On Yom Kippur, the most solemn day of the year, we read the story of Jonah from the ancient Torah scrolls. Jewish tradition teaches us love and tolerance, just as Jonah learned to honor the people of Nineveh, though he did not fully understand them.

At the synagogue, the chanting of the Kol Nidre prayer touches the heart and opens it. The haunting melody is inexpressibly sad yet uplifting at the same time, and the slow lament is chanted three times, canceling all unintended vows and making them void.

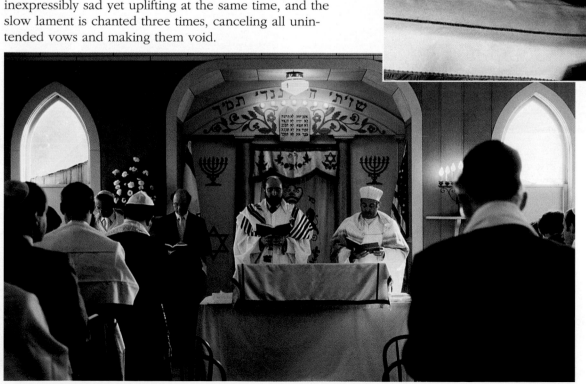

This seven-day holiday is named for the sukkah or temporary hut that sheltered our ancestors while they wandered in the Sinai desert searching for the Promised Land. Decorating our own sukkah at home provides us with a joyful place in which to eat our meals with the open sky for a canopy.

Fruit, vegetable, and flower decorations all combine to make our sukkah the perfect place in which to rejoice in our security as we celebrate the harvest. Each evening before dinner, we light candles and recite blessings to show gratitude for our safety and fulfillment.

Sukkot

At Sukkot services, congregants parade through the synagogue carrying samples of the four species of plants that celebrate the bounty of the harvest: the *lulav*, a tall, green, date-bearing palm branch; the shiny myrtle leaf; the delicate willow; and the *etrog* or citron.

Star of David New Year's Cards

Materials Needed

White card stock
Scissors
Tissue paper in two colors
Felt-tip markers
Square sheets of paper, about 8 × 8 inches
Pencil
Craft glue

Directions

1. For the card, cut the card stock to form a rectangle measuring 5½ × 11 inches. Fold in half so you have a 5½-inch square card.
2. Cut one equilateral triangle measuring 4 inches on each side from each color of tissue paper.
3. Paste one triangle on the cover of the card, then turn the other upside-down and paste it on top to form a Star of David.
4. Inside the card, use the markers to write "May your year be good and sweet," or "*L'Shanah Tovah.*"
5. To make the envelope, take an 8 × 8-inch sheet of paper and lay it down in a diamond shape with one point facing up. With a pencil draw a square inside the triangle reaching to the sides and centered within them.
6. Fold three sides in on the lines and glue them down, leaving sufficient space inside the envelope for the card.
7. Insert the card and fold down the flap. Address, stamp, and mail.

that can go either way, depending on what they decide in their self-evaluation during the ten Days of Awe. On Yom Kippur, the Day of Judgment, all the names will be written and the books will be closed.

The message is that those who open their hearts to their misdeeds of the previous year and promise to live a better life can change their fates. New pages of life are to be written, new chapters lived. More than any other concept, this idea most deeply embodies the meaning of Rosh Hashanah.

Some people call Rosh Hashanah the Holiday of the Second Chance, believing it offers them a unique opportunity to resolve to improve on their pasts and strive to become better people.

Sending cards can be more than a way to keep in touch with friends; it can be a method of mending broken bridges with estranged friends and family. The holiday turns us away from what has been to what can be, and it is a time to tell people you have hurt that you are sorry and to ask forgiveness. It is also a time to offer forgiveness to those who have hurt you.

Many beautiful cards are created around these themes, and you can make your own or purchase a wide variety of messages that say it for you. After Rosh Hashanah is over, save your cards and use them to decorate your sukkah.

Rosh Hashanah Traditions

To honor the past, many people visit the graves of relatives and friends in the weeks before Rosh Hashanah. It is also customary to go apple picking, gathering your own fruit for the apples-and-honey course at your holiday dinner. You might consider enhancing the holiday by picking extra apples and donating them to a local food bank or homeless shelter.

Just like on the secular New Year, it is customary on Rosh Hashanah to make resolutions that one will try to keep throughout the year. It is appropriate to promise to treat people better, give more *tzedakah*, or study more Jewish material. To help you keep these resolutions, consider posting them on the refrigerator where you are sure to be reminded of them each day.

Many people wear new clothes on Rosh Hashanah as a way of symbolizing the inner work they are doing to start anew. Buying new clothes can be a simple and effective way of renewing ourselves and our souls. Dress is, after all, an outward reflection of what is going on inside. Some people wear white on the holiday to symbolize purity and divine forgiveness.

A Visit to Flowing Waters

Perhaps the most intriguing of all Rosh Hashanah traditions is one called *tashlich*, which is based on concepts first expressed in the Book of Micah. The word *tashlich* is Hebrew for "you shall cast away."

On the afternoon of the first day of Rosh Hashanah, some Jews go to the seaside or a river and, while reciting prayers, empty their pockets of crumbs, throwing them into the flowing water as a way of casting off sins and broken promises.

Ancient rabbis did not approve of this practice, as they felt it absolved people of their sins too easily. Instead they expected people to go through the difficult steps of the soul-searching process: identifying their transgressions against both God and other people, gaining an understanding of why they were wrong and promising not to repeat them. Yet the practice continues in popularity today, especially in very traditional communities, usually in conjunction with the more difficult inner work and not as a replacement for it.

Festivities at Home

The two-day Rosh Hashanah holiday provides many opportunities for home-based celebrations and parties. You can invite guests to dinner on

Honey Plate and Apple Dish Placemat

Materials Needed

Scrap paper
Pencil
Felt-tip markers (assorted colors, including black)
Transparent plastic dish, about 6 inches in diameter
Clear lacquer spray
Red and green construction paper
Scissors
One large sheet of self-stick laminating plastic or clear plastic contact sheeting
White glue

Directions

1. On scrap paper use the pencil to draw several designs that you might like to see on the honey plate. Try drawing Jewish symbols like a menorah, a kiddush cup, or a challah, and also try drawing different-size bees. Decide on the theme for your plate, and copy the drawings in black felt-tip marker. Draw on both the inside and outside of the plate.
2. Color in the drawings with colored markers.
3. Spray the entire dish with clear lacquer to set the drawings and make the plate washable so you can use it from year to year.
4. On a sheet of red construction paper, draw a circle with a notch on top to look like an apple. On the green paper draw a stem and a leaf. Cut out these shapes.
5. Cover the red and green apple parts with laminating plastic on both sides and cut around the edges to fit. Assemble the apple by gluing the stem and leaf to the top of the red circle.
6. Place the apple placemat on the holiday table and put the honey dish on it along with a plate of sliced apples. Stand a small jar of honey and a honey spoon on the dish.

the evenings before the first and second days or to midday festivities on the days themselves.

This is a time to set the dining room table with your crispest, whitest cloth, fresh flowers, and your best dinnerware. If you are feeling particularly creative, you might make a centerpiece of branches set in florist's foam with lady apples attached to the tips by a few squirts of a glue gun. Grape vines wrapped around napkins could secure silverware and decorate pristine white plates with the natural beauty of the season.

You might consider hosting an open-house buffet on the first day of the holiday, inviting people home for a festive afternoon gathering after services. Your menu could range from cool, crisp salad to warm, succulent fruited chicken sitting atop a sterno flame on the sideboard.

For the traditional apple-and-honey appetizer, try something new: a tasting of flavored honeys. You can buy them ready-made or mix them yourself. Flavors range from cinnamon, mint, and alfalfa to orange blossom, eucalyptus, dandelion, and black locust. In addition to apples, many people dip bits of challah in honey, hoping to doubly ensure a sweet year.

Invitations to a Rosh Hashanah gathering could be made using red construction paper cut into the shape of an apple, or yellow paper with a honeycomb drawn on it. Even a bee-shaped card could lend the right spirit. If you want to give favors to guests, you might send them home with a small bag containing a jar of honey and a honey spoon.

Whether you select a sit-down dinner, formal luncheon, or a buffet, these dishes will reflect the joy of the New Year:

Round Challah With Raisins
Vegetable Soup
Baked Salmon in Cream Sauce
Shanah Tovah Noodle Kugel
Carrot and Yam Tzimmes
King David Honey Cake
Sweet Honey Taiglach

Baked Salmon in Cream Sauce

Salmon is both a hearty fish and a delicacy at the same time. Its fleshy texture makes it perfect for many kinds of saucy accompaniments, yet lightly spiced it stands alone with the dignity of its naturally fine flavor. This baked variety is simple yet elegant and goes well with traditional holiday noodle kugel.

1½ pounds salmon fillet, cut into
    6 equal pieces
½ teaspoon salt
¼ teaspoon pepper
4 tablespoons butter
2 small shallots

¼ teaspoon finely chopped dill
1 bay leaf
1 cup light cream at room
    temperature
6–8 sprigs of parsley

1. Preheat the oven to 350° F.
2. Sprinkle the salmon with salt and pepper on both sides and place in baking dish.
3. Melt the butter and pour over the fish.
4. Slice the shallots and mix together with the dill and drizzle over the fish.
5. Add the bay leaf and bake for 15 minutes.
6. Remove from oven and pour the cream over the fish. Continue baking for 15 minutes more.
7. Arrange neatly on a warmed-up platter and garnish with parsley.

Yield: 6 servings

Shanah Tovah Noodle Kugel

Jewish cooks have been passing down kugel recipes from mother to daughter for centuries. Noodle kugels come in all varieties, from low-fat to rich and creamy, from tart to extra-sweet. This recipe, perfect for Rosh Hashanah, gets a lift from fruit for sweetness, light texture, and satisfying goodness. You can put all the ingredients together a day ahead, refrigerate overnight, and bake just before serving.

4 eggs	1 tablespoon lemon juice
½ cup sugar	1 teaspoon powdered cinnamon
4 ounces butter or margarine	2 cups cooked wide noodles
½ cup white raisins	¼ cup breadcrumbs
3 large apples, thinly sliced	

1. Preheat the oven to 350° F.
2. Beat the eggs and mix in the sugar slowly, beating until fluffy.
3. Add the butter and stir till creamy.
4. Mix in the raisins, apples, lemon juice, and cinnamon. Stir together and add the cooked noodles.
5. Pour into a well-greased casserole dish, about 9 × 13 inches.
6. Sprinkle with breadcrumbs and bake for 50 minutes or until lightly browned on top.

Yield: 6–8 servings

King David Honey Cake

In biblical times, honey was a precious commodity used in drinks, main dishes, and many medicines. In a verse from the Book of Samuel, King David gave each man and woman in Israel a sweet cake "after hearing the sound of the horn." Thus it has become customary to serve honey cake on the first night of Rosh Hashanah and at other happy occasions.

4 cups flour	2 tablespoons brown sugar
¼ teaspoon salt	¾ cup white sugar
3 teaspoons baking powder	4 ounces butter
1 teaspoon baking soda	1½ cups honey
¼ teaspoon ground cloves	½ cup brewed coffee
¼ teaspoon nutmeg	½ cup chopped almonds
1 teaspoon cinnamon	Heavy cream, whipped, for garnish
4 eggs	

1. Preheat oven to 350° F.
2. Sift together the flour, salt, baking power, baking soda, cloves, nutmeg, and half the cinnamon.
3. Beat the eggs and add the sugar one tablespoon at a time, until the mixture is light and fluffy. Then add the butter, honey, and coffee.
4. Stir in the flour mixture and add the nuts.
5. Butter and flour a 9 × 12-inch baking pan, pour in the batter, and bake for 55–60 minutes. Serve with whipped cream sprinkled with the remaining cinnamon.

Yield: 6–8 servings

Sweet Honey Taiglach

Culinary traditions at Rosh Hashanah call for sweet dishes for a sweet year, and honey is used most often to enhance the entrées, side dishes, breads, and especially desserts that make up the best-loved Rosh Hashanah menus. These doughy confections, drenched in honey syrup, are almost as much fun to make as they are to eat. They offer a perfect way to end a holiday meal.

3 eggs	¾ cup sugar
2 tablespoons oil	½ teaspoon powdered ginger
2 cups flour	1 teaspoon vanilla
¼ teaspoon salt	¾ cup chopped filberts, almonds,
½ teaspoon baking powder	or walnuts
2 teaspoons sugar	¼ cup confectioners' sugar
1½ cups honey	

1. Preheat the oven to 350° F.
2. Beat the eggs and then add the oil.
3. Sift together the flour, salt, and baking powder in a bowl. Add the eggs and oil and mix into a soft dough.
4. On a floured board, shape the dough into a twisted rope about the thickness of a pencil.
5. Cut into pieces about ½ inch long and place on a well-greased cookie sheet.
6. Bake for 12–15 minutes or until lightly browned.
7. To prepare the honey syrup, mix together the honey, sugar, ginger, and vanilla and cook over a low flame for 5 minutes, stirring constantly to keep the mixture from burning.
8. Add the nuts and the baked dough and cook for 5 more minutes, stirring frequently.
9. Pour into a large chilled bowl and let cool.
10. When the mixture is cool enough to handle, shape into balls about 2 inches in diameter.
11. Sprinkle with confectioners' sugar.

Yield: about 25 balls, or 8–10 servings

On the second day of Rosh Hashanah, many people serve pomegranates instead of apples and honey. This is because this biblical fruit has many seeds and is seen as a symbol of fertility and abundance. One's good fortune should be as plentiful as its seeds, as should one's good deeds. When serving the pomegranate, it is appropriate to say the traditional blessing, "In the coming year, may we be as rich and replete with acts inspired by goodness and love as this pomegranate is rich and replete with seeds."

Holidays and Challah-days

Jews believe that what we eat has a lot to do with what we become. So on Rosh Hashanah we eat foods that are sweet in hopes of bringing a sweet year, foods that are round to ensure our living through the cycle of the year, and foods that are abundant to create fruitfulness and prosperity.

While our Friday-night challah is traditionally elongated and formed into braids, our fat, fragrant holiday challah is shaped into a spiral and graced with raisins and other dried fruits for Rosh Hashanah. It is made with an extra measure of sugar and eggs for additional richness. This rounded challah symbolizes a full year and a long span of life, and represents continuity and the endless cycles of the year.

The Rosh Hashanah challah can be braided and then made into a circle, or divided into a braided circle topped by a smaller circle. Another choice is a twisted spiral made into a circle with the end of the spiral on top, symbolically reminding us of our hopes for an ascent to heaven.

In addition, the challah might also take the shape of a ladder, which represents our wish that our prayers ascend to heaven. Or it might be shaped into a bird, a traditional symbol of mercy honored at this season when we are each being judged for our deeds in the previous year.

Many cooks like to make their own challah, and recipes and techniques abound. But for those who have the will but not the time, a handy shortcut for this essential holiday food is to ask your local baker to sell you the dough after the first rising. This way, you can have the pleasure of shaping it in your own way and filling your home with the unique and delicious scent of baking challah—in half the time or less.

Other Rosh Hashanah Specialties

Vegetables that are symbolic of fertility, abundance, and prosperity are especially popular at the holiday table, especially those that contain many seeds. Pumpkins, onions, turnips, gourds, and beets all grow rapidly in the early fall and are usually ripe by Rosh Hashanah. And all can be made into a wide variety of excellent side dishes.

Leeks are customarily eaten for luck, and large winter squash is cooked to express the hope that the guests at the holiday table may grow in fullness of blessing.

Foods should also be colorful and sweet, of course, which makes dessert a special feast all its own. In fact some hosts who are planning open-house parties call for guests to arrive at four o'clock and serve only dessert and coffee. Along with honey cake, vanilla crescent cookies, and chocolate truffles, a traditional Rosh Hashanah favorite is *taiglach*, a cookie-candy confection made by dropping balls of dough into hot honey.

When You Are the Guest

When visiting friends and family at home or meeting them at the synagogue on Rosh Hashanah, it is appropriate to say, "*L'shanah tovah tikatav*," or "May you be inscribed for a good year." This greeting, however, should not be used after Rosh Hashanah has ended, as it could imply a belief that the person is not completely righteous and must use the remaining Days of Awe to repent sufficiently to have his or her name written in the Book of Life.

If you are invited to Rosh Hashanah dinner, the perfect gift to bring your hosts instead of flowers is a jar of honey or a bushel bag of freshly picked apples. For variety, try special seasonal apples like Winesaps, Red Delicious, Jonathan, Cortland, or Gala. You could also purchase a sampling of honeys as a gift. If you can't find an appropriately decorated assortment, you can dress up a plain honey jar from the supermarket by covering the top with a small swatch of plaid fabric and securing it under the rim with a pretty ribbon or a length of raffia.

High-Spirited Craft Projects

Everyone enjoys synagogue services better when the words and concepts are familiar, and the best way to accomplish this is to read the prayerbook before you attend. The special holiday prayer book, the *machzor*, is worth purchasing so you have it handy to study when you have a few moments of free time before Rosh Hashanah begins. Once you have your book, the best way to make it really yours is to personalize it with a cover.

To do this, take the time to find appealing paper. Heavy-weight, solid-color gift wrap paper with a shiny finish can be purchased from the novelty card shop in your neighborhood and decorated with simple markers or even decals once it is folded into place. Or to keep it simple and add a touch of solemnity, hand-letter your name or print it in script on a computer and paste it on the cover.

Children will enjoy making a challah cover to dress the special round holiday loaf. Simply take a man's white handkerchief and a box of felt-tip markers and draw a Star of David in the middle, colored in with blue marker. At each corner draw a Jewish symbol—a set of candles, a kiddush cup, a challah, the tablets of the law. With a green marker connect the four corner drawings with twirling vines drawn along the edges of the cloth. Let dry and use to cover the challah while it is being blessed.

It is easy to make your own New Year's cards. Early in the fall gather small fresh flowers that appeal to you. They can be anything from roses and snapdragons to dandelions and daisies. Press them between sheets of

Bee Mobile

Materials Needed

Scissors
Yellow cellophane
Jumbo cotton balls
Tape
Black felt-tip marker
Thin string or monofilament
Wire coat hanger

Directions

1. Cut seven pieces of cellophane into 3-inch squares. Place two cotton balls in the center of each cellophane piece, one behind the other. Shape into a rectangle, wrap the cellophane around the cotton balls and tape closed underneath.
2. With the marker, draw three stripes across each bee and then draw two eyes.
3. On a sheet of cellophane, draw a set of wings shaped like a flattened barbell. Cut out seven sets and tape them under the bees' bellies.
4. Tie a length of string about 8 to 10 inches long around the center of each bee. Attach the other end of the string to the coat hanger at varying lengths. Hang near the dish of apples and honey at your dinner table.

waxed paper by placing them under a heavy book. When they are quite flat, paint the backs, stems and all, with white glue and paste them to the cover of a standard sheet of typing paper folded in half twice. Inside write "*L'shanah Tovah*," or "Happy New Year." Insert in an envelope, address, seal, stamp, and mail.

A Book of Hope

Because Rosh Hashanah is a holiday that emphasizes introspection and soul-searching, you can enhance the experience by creating a diary to record your personal thoughts. Make entries starting on Rosh Hashanah and continuing through the Days of Awe to Yom Kippur. This can be a family project, with time together set aside each day for writing a few lines. Make sure everyone understands that what is written is private.

Simply buy a cloth-covered blank book, available at all bookstores, for yourself and each family member. You might call it "Sweet Beginnings" and decorate the title page with apples, honey, bees, and flowers. In it write about what you want to change about yourself in the coming year and how you plan to do so. Record the names of people whose forgiveness you are seeking, and those to whom you have offered forgiveness yourself.

Most important, try to honestly face up to your mistakes. Remember that no one will see the book but you. Make sure you record the date for each entry, including the year. It will make an important document to review later on, when you have moved on in life and forgotten that you did not always possess all the wonderful qualities that you now take for granted.

2

Yom Kippur: To Begin Anew

*The tenth day of the seventh month shall be your day
of atonement, a day to search your soul, a sacred day
on which you shall practice self-denial.*

—Leviticus 23:27

Toward a Better Future

YOM KIPPUR IS A HOLIDAY about values, especially the Jewish values of self-discipline, empathy, belief in the power to change, and hope. We are biblically mandated to practice self-denial on this most holy day of the year, and our tradition translates this to mean fasting. When we fast we show we are masters of our desires and can overcome our physical needs to reach higher spiritual planes. When we are hungry, we are more likely to feel for the millions of people in the world who suffer deprivation. And when we are attuned to our inner selves and at one with humankind, we are able to reach a state of repentance and reconciliation.

Yom Kippur, which means literally "day of atonement," is a time of joy and solemnity, purification and penitence, a day on which we concentrate on our past so we can make our future better for ourselves, for our community, and for the larger world, the human community. When the shofar is blown at the end of services, concluding an intense day of personal cross-examination, we leave the synagogue with renewed confidence and hope, knowing we have done our inner work and are ready to start anew.

The holiday falls on the tenth day of the month of Tishri, bringing to an end the most sacred Days of Awe that begin with Rosh Hashanah, in late summer or early fall. The twenty-four-hour fast begins at dusk on the ninth of Tishri and ends the following evening, when three stars can be seen in the night sky.

On the tenth of Tishri the sages say that Moses came down from Mount Sinai carrying the second set of tablets of the Ten Commandments and told the Israelites that they had been forgiven for the golden calf incident. Ever since that time, the day has been observed as the Day of Atonement.

A Feast for the Spirit

On Yom Kippur, nearly the whole holiday is spent in solemn prayer at the synagogue. From sundown to sundown, it is a time to make things right, a day in which we hope to get in touch with all that matters: love, friendship, kindness, forgiveness. The hope is that fasting will free us from all material concern and make us experience physical vulnerability, so that we can concentrate on the spirit and rise to a higher ethical level. The simple yet difficult act of fasting places us in a humble state where we hope to gain insight into ourselves.

Yom Kippur can be a complex holiday to try to explain to children. There are no costumes, no sing-along melodies, no candy to collect from grownups in cute little bags. But the ten days between Rosh Hashanah and Yom Kippur can be a time of family closeness, an opportunity for serious discussion in which we face each other and ask for and grant forgiveness. If things have gone wrong in the past year, if family members who want to be close have grown apart, this is the time to bring them back together. On Yom Kippur we are pardoned for sins against heaven, but for sins against other people we must apologize ourselves. All disputes should be settled before fasting begins.

Two special meals frame Yom Kippur, one at either end of the fast. It is considered a mitzvah to eat well before the fast, and we eat the pre-fast meal before sunset, then spread a fresh white cloth on the dining room table, placing a Bible and prayer book at its center. If the family has many Jewish books, it is customary to set one at each place at the table instead of dinner service, to show that this is a day devoted to study and prayer.

If there are beloved family members whom we wish to honor with a memorial candle, this is the time to light it, placing it on the table with the prayer books. Yahrzeit candles should be purchased well ahead of Yom Kippur to make sure that the traditional anniversary candles are in stock on this day of heavy demand. The family then departs for synagogue services to hear the haunting Kol Nidre service.

After services the next day, we break the fast with a light meal, most often consisting of tempting varieties of egg dishes, cheese, fish, challah, bagels, fruit, and pastry. It is common practice to invite people who are alone to join your family at home in breaking the fast.

How to Honor the Holiday

Many people visit the graves of loved ones on the days preceding Yom Kippur, often when they are feeling the most reflective and introspective. It is a time to think about the contributions these people have made to our lives and how our behavior honors their memory. Often we are moved to make a donation to the temple in their names as a tribute of remembrance.

It is common to offer charity before Yom Kippur begins, honoring an age-old cornerstone of the Jewish value system. For children it is also a

Memorial Yahrzeit Candle and Holder

Materials Needed

An empty glass jar about 4–5 inches high
Paraffin wax from the hardware store
6-inch candlewick
Transparent craft glue
Paintbrush
Glitter
Felt markers

Directions

1. Wash the glass jar both inside and out and wipe it dry. Place enough paraffin wax in the jar to fill it up almost to the top.
2. Fill a pot with 2–3 inches of water and heat on the stove over low heat. Place the jar with the wax into the hot water. Insert the wick down to the bottom of the jar, leaving about ½ inch showing on top, and let the wax melt around it.
3. When all the wax is melted, use tongs to remove the jar from the water and let cool. When it is comfortable to handle, paint the jar with glue, and sprinkle lightly with glitter.
4. With felt markers draw simple lines around the top and bottom rims of the glass jar to give it a finished look.
5. Light the candle for a close relative at sunset on the eve of Yom Kippur. The candlelight shining through the glitter will look very lovely and ethereal.

fine idea to create a tzedakah project, where small change is collected and donated to a selected cause. It is also appropriate to visit someone who is ill or housebound, or volunteer for a day in a soup kitchen. The message of Yom Kippur is not only to become a better person, but to make the world a better place.

As on Rosh Hashanah, many people like to wear new clothes to Yom Kippur synagogue services. This is symbolic of the new state we will enter at the end of the holiday when our soul is freshly cleansed. It is also traditional on Yom Kippur to wear white, the color of purity and innocence, a time-honored tradition that reflects the spirit and mood of the day and an appropriate color for a day when we rid ourselves of wrongdoing.

Even the rabbi and cantor are likely to don special white robes worn only on the High Holy Days, deck the ark and the bimah in white, and dress the scrolls of the Torah in white. Some people believe we wear white because we are attempting to try to resemble angels. It is also customary to wear shoes of human-made material instead of leather, in deference to a day of gentle thought and prayer in which no animal must be slaughtered to provide us with food or clothing.

Another beautiful Yom Kippur tradition takes place immediately after breaking the fast, when we drive the first nail into the sukkah, a symbol the world over of God's protection. This act shows the continuity of the holiday cycle and the strength we gain from once again allowing our bodies to be nourished by food. Four days after Yom Kippur we will begin the joyful Sukkot festival.

It is customary on Yom Kippur to greet friends and family with the Hebrew words, "*Gemar hatimah tovah*," which means, "May you be sealed for good in the Book of Life." There is an old saying that tells us, "Yom Kippur is the day on which God gets up from the throne of judgment and sits down on the throne of mercy." When we hear the shofar blast at the end of services on the day of Yom Kippur, the book is closed and all the names that are to be inscribed and sealed have thus been entered.

A Day of Observance

While fasting is ordained, it is not necessarily mandated for everyone. Children under thirteen are not expected to fast, though common practice today is to give them smaller meals than usual or encourage them to skip breakfast or lunch entirely to get a sense of what fasting is like. Pregnant or nursing mothers do not fast, of course, nor do the frail elderly or the infirm.

Ancient rabbis believed that when people fast they have two hearts: one for themselves, and one for all the other people without enough food, but when they eat they have only one heart. This is another way of saying that on Yom Kippur, when we are weakened by the fast, we are more open to the suffering of others through our higher spiritual awareness.

It is considered a mitzvah to join the congregation in worship on Yom Kippur. Doing so draws us into the circle of the Jewish community and strengthens our ties to each other and to the values we share. Our fast becomes a public experience, something we do in common with other Jews. This is thought to promote corrective action more effectively than private contemplation.

It is also biblically mandated that we hear the shofar blast to usher in the year, which we begin with a clear conscience and a cleansed soul. A long, steady note signals the end of Yom Kippur and the start of another beginning, a new year, a renewed self. This meaningful symbol of Yom Kippur ushers in feelings of relief and exhilaration at the end of the day. For children, it is a special part of the service, one they look forward to and remember most clearly from year to year. It is worth finding out in advance what time the shofar will be blown to make sure children are present at the time.

In some congregations, everyone goes outside and blesses the new moon at the end of services. Minds and hearts turn from Yom Kippur to Sukkot, from fast to feast, from empty to full, and the cycle of the year continues.

Blessing the Children

A wonderful family custom that has grown in practice among all branches of Judaism is the blessing of one's children on the evening before Yom Kippur. This usually takes place after the pre-fast dinner and just before the family leaves for Kol Nidre services. Often there is an air of hush and expectancy at this time. Children should gather at the holiday table, the boys and girls in separate groups. Place your hands on your children's bowed heads. For girls, we say, "May God make you like Sarah, Rebecca, Leah, and Rachel." For boys, "May God make you like Ephraim and Menashe." (Ephraim and Menashe were Jacob's grandchildren, the two sons of Joseph.)

Then continue for both boys and girls: "May God bless you and keep you. May it be the will of our parent in heaven to plant the love of God in your heart. May you wish to study the Torah and its commandments. May your lips speak the truth and your hands do good deeds. May you be inscribed for a long and happy life."

Embraces naturally follow the blessing, and the family, warm and suffused with closeness, steps out into the evening to enter the world of Kol Nidre, the haunting melody and sacred words that clear the slate between each person and God. From the introductory ritual of Kol Nidre on the eve of Yom Kippur to the farewell of the shofar as night falls the next day, we will be taken on a journey after which we will never be the same.

The Power of Kol Nidre

More people attend Kol Nidre services than any other service during the year. At the synagogue, everything is white, even the flowers on the bimah. The chanting of Kol Nidre, the most well-known and powerful prayer in the entire Jewish liturgy, is meant to touch the heart and open it, stirring the spirit like the shofar, reflecting God's majesty and the strength and frailty of human beings all at once and welcoming back all who have

Homemade Shofar

Materials Needed

Construction paper
A flexible party horn, like the ones used on New Year's eve or at
    birthday parties
Cellophane tape
Black felt-tip marker

Directions

1. Choose a color of construction paper that you like and wrap it around the horn; then tape it neatly in place.
2. With black felt-tip marker, write "For on this day atonement shall be made for you," on the shofar. This is a quote from the Bible establishing the tenth of Tishri as Yom Kippur.
3. Bend the end of the shofar to make it look more like a ram's horn. Put a small piece of tape at the bend to keep it in place.
4. Blow the shofar at the break-the-fast meal to honor the end of the holiday. Make one for each of your friends and have fun making a lot of noise!

transgressed. It is a prelude to the day of Yom Kippur, the climax of the whole season, the holiest day of the Jewish year, the Sabbath of Sabbaths.

Literally, Kol Nidre means "all vows." Inexpressibly sad notes float in the air as the music begins, augmenting the high level of emotion in the often filled-to-overflowing synagogue. More than anything else, Yom

Kippur is about forgiveness. Some believe that the haunting Kol Nidre melody ascends straight to heaven, and if they are repentant it will take their prayers along.

We have put things right with our family, friends, and neighbors, repaired damage, forgiven hurt, accepted blame, and made peace with ourselves. All that remains is to ask God's forgiveness. On this night throughout the world, Jews are immersed in a richly endowed experience of history and faith, underscored by the shared notes of Kol Nidre. The slow lament in a minor key is chanted three times, first slowly and softly, then faster and louder, until the third time it is as full-bodied and rousing as can be.

The words are not in Hebrew but in Aramaic, the vernacular of the Jews following the Babylonian exile. And Kol Nidre is not actually a prayer but a statement, a special liturgical formulation and an actual legal formula for the annulment of vows. Its intent is to cancel all unintended and unfulfilled vows made in the previous year.

Kol Nidre is over a thousand years old, referred to in the writings of Babylonian Jewish scholars as early as the eighth century, yet its origins are shrouded in mystery. The melody was probably written in the fifteenth century by a group of Marranos, the hidden Jews of Spain who were forced to officially renounce their Judaism.

The Marranos, as they were called, secretly continued to observe Jewish law and customs. In Kol Nidre, they begged God to forgive them for making vows they could not keep and release them from promises they were forced to make while pretending to be Christians.

The prayer cancels all unintended oaths and unfulfilled promises to God and makes them void. It also welcomes back into the fold all Jews who have strayed during the year. Today, when Jews are not forced to embrace another religion yet nevertheless find themselves having slipped away from Jewish law and practice, Kol Nidre can be a deeply moving, powerful experience. On Yom Kippur eve, Kol Nidre brings them back to thousands of years of tradition.

Culinary Customs of the Holiday

For a day on which the central ritual is fasting, it is certainly an irony that food traditions abound on Yom Kippur. And although the holiday is solemn and holy, the meal on the night before is most often festive in character. We are, in fact, commanded to eat well on the eve of Yom Kippur to make the fast more meaningful and significant in comparison, just as on Yom Kippur it is important to feel hunger pangs to remind ourselves of the difficult task of atonement.

On the eve of the holiday the table is set as it is for any Shabbat or holiday meal, with a white tablecloth, the best crystal and flatware, and fresh flowers as a centerpiece. The setting is the formal dining room, with the chandelier shining brightly and fancy napkins and napkin rings gracing the table.

Tradition tells us what to eat before the fast. Dishes are to be relatively bland and underspiced, simple soothing food that will not provoke thirst on the day of Yom Kippur. Many cooks avoid fish on this night for this reason. The most common entrée is chicken, usually stewed, boiled, or roasted, or a Cornish hen or turkey. Moses Maimonides, the Spanish philosopher and physician of the thirteenth century, is believed to be the first Jew to recommend poultry soup for the sick and weak, and traditional chicken soup recipes are highly recommended for Yom Kippur eve.

Many cooks serve *kreplach*, a soft dough pocket filled with meat, either floating in the soup or fried and eaten as a side dish. The meat is said to denote God's stern justice, the soft dough God's compassion.

A round holiday challah dipped in honey is a staple of the Yom Kippur eve table, as are green and yellow seasonal vegetables or carrots and simple rice dishes. Many cooks serve no dessert, a plan designed to ease digestion during the fast, while others offer a fruity finish to the meal such as simple baked pears and apples or plain cookies or loaf cake.

A traditional Yom Kippur eve menu might include:

Holiday Honey Challah
Mild Hummus on Spinach Leaves
Yom Tov Lemon Chicken Soup
Roast Chicken With Barley Stuffing
Braised Parsnips and Carrots
Pears in Vanilla Meringue
Lemon tea

Ancient Rites and Modern Practice

In Judaism, all practices have a purpose, and the rituals that define Yom Kippur have great moral force. Yom Kippur, the day of reckoning in which we come face to face with ourselves, is based largely on ethical content, representing Jewish thought at its highest. Our belief is that the day should lead from thought to deed, from looking closely at our inner ideas to changing the way we act. In ancient times primitive ceremonies, which were most likely carryovers from pagan beliefs, were enacted to fulfill this goal.

Today we use speech in an effort to create a new world, but what we now express in words was often acted out by our ancestors in ritual. One of the most prominent Yom Kippur ceremonies was called Kapparot, from the same root as Kippur, or "atonement," performed on the morning of the holiday and created to expiate the sins of Jews and ward off evil. The central idea was to transfer one's sins to an animal, then kill the animal in order to cleanse one's soul. Men would take a live rooster and swing it around over their heads several times while reciting Hebrew prayers, sending their sins into the chicken's body through this act. Women would do the same with a hen. A pregnant woman was mandated to swing both a rooster and a hen, one after the other. The fowl was then slaughtered and the meat given to the poor.

Mild Hummus on Spinach Leaves

Hummus is a flavorful Middle Eastern paste of ground chickpeas that has become popular in the United States as American palates have grown more sophisticated. Tahini, a staple of this recipe, is a ground sesame paste readily available in many supermarkets and specialty food shops. Israeli recipes are especially appropriate for the High Holy Days but may be enjoyed at any time of year.

2 cans (20-ounces each) chickpeas	¼ teaspoon salt
1 cup tahini	¼ teaspoon paprika
¼ cup olive oil	Spinach leaves
1 clove garlic	8 pieces of pita bread
½ cup lemon juice	

1. Drain the chickpeas and place in food processor along with the tahini, olive oil, garlic, lemon juice, salt, and pepper.
2. Process until smooth.
3. Separate and wash the spinach leaves and remove the stems.
4. Place 2 spinach leaves and 1 piece of pita bread on each salad plate, spoon 2 tablespoons hummus on each leaf and sprinkle with paprika.

Yield: 6–8 servings

Yom Tov Lemon Chicken Soup

This silky soup is made ultra-smooth by the addition of eggs, which are blended to enhance the creamy texture. The technique that makes this work is based on adding the warmed chicken soup to the eggs a little at a time instead of dropping the egg mixture into the hot stock all at once, which encourages curdling.

¾ cup orzo or alphabet pasta   ½ cup lemon juice
4 cups chicken stock   ¼ teaspoon salt
3 eggs   ½ cup croutons

1. Boil the orzo in the chicken stock, reduce the heat and simmer for about 10 minutes, until the pasta is cooked.
2. In a bowl mix together the eggs, lemon juice, and salt.
3. Remove the stock from the fire. Pour ½ cup of chicken stock from the saucepan into a small bowl and let cool.
4. One tablespoon at a time, ladle the stock from the bowl into the egg mixture, stirring frequently.
5. When the eggs and stock are well mixed, pour the mixture into the cooled saucepot containing the remainder of the chicken stock.
6. Heat slowly, mixing constantly.
7. Pour into soup bowls and garnish with the croutons. Serve immediately.

Yield: 6 servings, 1 cup each

Roast Chicken With Barley Stuffing

Simple, comforting foods on the eve Yom Kippur make sure the next day's fast will not be worsened by excessive thirst or undue digestive stress. Years of tradition have proven roast chicken to be a good choice for nourishment and ease of preparation. For cooking times, plan on 20 minutes per pound but don't feel bound to stick to the minute. A little extra cooking enhances both the flavor and texture of a roast chicken.

1 cup pearl barley	½ teaspoon salt
2 cups water	¼ teaspoon pepper
1 fresh young roaster,	½ teaspoon paprika
about 6–7 pounds	2 ounces warm water

1. Preheat oven to 350° F.
2. Measure 1 cup of pearl barley and place in saucepan with 2 cups of water.
3. Bring to a boil, uncovered, then cover and simmer on low heat for 35–40 minutes, until all the water is absorbed.
4. Let cool about 15 minutes.
5. Wash the chicken both inside and out and pat dry, then sprinkle very lightly with salt, pepper, and paprika.
6. Spoon the cooked barley into the cavity and place chicken on rack in roasting pan.
7. Roast in medium oven for 2–2½ hours, until fork inserted in thigh brings out juices that run clear.
8. Remove chicken from pan and add one-quarter cup warm water to roasting pan.
9. Mix drippings and water together and pour into gravy boat.
10. Remove barley from inside the chicken and place in serving bowl.
11. Cut chicken into pieces and arrange on warm platter.

Yield: 6 servings

Braised Parsnips and Carrots

Whenever possible, buy carrots and parsnips with their tops on, choosing those with bright green leaves. This ensures freshness, flavor, and texture, and if you compost vegetable scraps, the tops will provide you with much useful material. The brave of heart might chop the greens and add them to vegetable soup. This satisfying side dish could become a family favorite, holiday or not.

1 pound carrots	⅛ teaspoon ground ginger
1 pound parsnips	2 tablespoons margarine, melted
1 cup water	1 tablespoon parsley
¼ teaspoon salt	

1. Preheat oven to 350° F.
2. Peel the carrots and parsnips and cut into rounds ¼ inch thick.
3. Place in baking dish and add water, salt, ginger, and margarine.
4. Cover with aluminum foil and bake about 50 minutes, until tender when pierced with fork.
5. Uncover and cook 10 minutes longer, until lightly browned on top.
6. Remove from oven and sprinkle with parsley.

Yield: 6 servings

Today we eat chicken the night before Yom Kippur as a testament to the power of the Kapparot ritual and donate tzedakah to the temple in honor of departed loved ones. As the ritual began to fade, Jews were known to place a few coins in a handkerchief and give them to the poor instead of offering the slaughtered chicken.

In Temple times, when the chief rabbi alone fasted as a representative of all the Jews, a goat was selected by the high priest for the central Yom Kippur ritual. On its horns a scarlet ribbon was tied, its head was then covered by the rabbi's hands while the sins of the Jewish community were confessed and thus symbolically placed on its shoulders. The goat was then sent out into the wilderness to perish, carrying the community's sins away with it.

A scarlet ribbon tied to the Temple gates was said to turn white when the goat met its death, a sign that the sins of the Jewish people had been forgiven and the New Year could begin with a clean slate. This "escape goat" became the scapegoat we know today.

The Story of Jonah

In the synagogue on the day of Yom Kippur, services take a prescribed route, traveling through Yizkor, the memorial service, and Al Het, the confessional prayer in which the whole congregation admits to wrongdoing and asks for and receives forgiveness as a community. Central to the theme of forgiveness is the story of a storm at sea, read from the Book of Jonah during afternoon services as the Haftarah portion of the holiday.

Jonah was a prophet, someone chosen to speak the word of God, but he was a reluctant prophet, refusing to obey God's order to go to the city of Nineveh and tell the inhabitants to repent for their sins. Nineveh was a city of Gentiles, and Jonah was afraid of them. He didn't believe them capable of repenting, and he didn't believe them worthy of God's forgiveness. So he ran away where he thought God could not find him.

He fled by ship to a city named Tarshish, but a wind came up and roiled the sea into a mighty storm. The other sailors blamed Jonah for the

Friendship Bracelet

Materials Needed

40 silver 1-inch-long safety pins
Package of small multi-colored glass or plastic beads
10 inches of thin elastic
Scissors

Directions

1. Sort the beads into colors and design a pattern based on the assortment. A simple arrangement would be one clear, two reds, one blue, two reds, one clear.
2. Thread the beads onto the pointy part of the safety pin, filling it up as much as possible and repeating the pattern as often as necessary.
3. Repeat step 2 with each pin.
4. Cut two lengths of elastic about 5 inches long. String one length through the tops of the pins, the other through the bottoms. Tie each elastic into a loop to fit your wrist.
5. Give the bracelet to a friend, perhaps someone with whom you recently made up or as a way of apology or forgiveness.

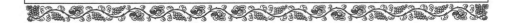

bad weather, and they threw him overboard as a sacrifice. Immediately the sea became calm.

Jonah, however, was swallowed by a great fish. For three days and three nights he was imprisoned in the belly of the whale, finally promising to do God's work and go to Nineveh. When he arrived there, he convinced the king to turn the people from their evil ways, and the king proclaimed a fast to show God his good faith.

God forgave the people of Nineveh, but this made Jonah angry. Why had God not destroyed the evil city? he demanded. But God explained that it was right to show pity toward people who repent, and that God's love was not confined to the people of Israel alone but to all humankind.

After the Fast

The last prayer of the Yom Kippur service is called Neilah, which literally means "closing" and refers to the gates of heaven, symbolizing our last appeal to God's mercy. Then the shofar, with its one steady note held as long as possible, signals the closing of the Book of Life and the end of services. It is time to break the fast at the most special meal of the year.

Break-the-fast foods are served for their restorative powers, their symbolic significance, and their ease of preparation. Usually break-the-fast dishes are dairy, most likely because white symbolizes the theme of purity that is so relevant to the holiday, but also because dairy foods are easy to digest on an empty stomach. It is also traditional to have some pastry, including coffee cake and a variety of strudels.

Many hosts serve herring, whitefish salad, and smoked salmon, because fish helps return the mineral and salt content of the body to normal after a day of dehydration. Often deviled eggs show up on the break-the-fast table, along with dairy casseroles, assortments of cheeses, and challah, bagels, and pita bread. On the table as a centerpiece you might place a shofar, which will speak eloquently about the events of the day without, for once, making a sound.

Planning for guests at a break-the-fast gathering entails careful thought and preparation days before the event to prevent overtaxing your own unfed self. Most hosts find a buffet works best, and often an informal group affair in which guests help serve the meal is most efficient.

If all the dishes are prepared in advance and day-old bagels are rejuvenated in the microwave or toaster oven, feeding a crew of extended family and close friends can be a festive event. Make sure to allow yourself a cup of strong coffee or a quick sugar lift from selected pastry before devoting yourself to your guests. You will not be a cheerful host if you are uncomfortable, so an immediate snack upon homecoming and before the serving begins is highly recommended.

If everything is to be served at room temperature, you might set out the buffet before you leave in the morning, then just come home, fling open the doors and eat. A glorified brunch featuring lox and bagels, varieties of cream cheese, herring, and kugel is gaining in popularity because of its ease of preparation.

Here is a menu to follow for a satisfying break-the-fast buffet. It is built on a base of delicacies that can be bought already prepared and artfully arranged for an appetizing presentation:

Chilled Juices: orange and pineapple
Fish Platter: smoked carp, lox, whitefish salad
Dairy Plate: sliced gouda, cream cheese spreads, deviled eggs
Breads: assorted bagels and whole wheat pita
Fruit Platter: sliced pineapple, strawberries, melons
Pastries: honey cake and assorted rugelach

3

Sukkot: Heaven Under the Stars

On the first day you shall take the fruit of goodly trees,
branches of palm trees, boughs of leafy trees and willows
of the brook, and you shall rejoice before God for seven days.

—Leviticus 23:40

Celebrating the Harvest

SUKKOT BEGINS THE SEASON of rejoicing in our security. Unlike the soul-searching uncertainty of the High Holy Days that have just passed, Sukkot emphasizes safety and fulfillment, encompassing the longest and happiest holiday season of the Jewish year. It also offers us an annual chance to enjoy the outdoors and recall that people are part of the natural world, as it takes us back to a time when we lived closer to the earth.

The holiday comes exactly two weeks after the first day of Rosh Hashanah and just four days after Yom Kippur, from the fifteenth to the twenty-first of the Hebrew month of Tishri, in September or early October in the secular calendar. It is celebrated for seven days in Israel, and either seven or eight outside the Holy land. There are three *mitzvot* or commandments connected with Sukkot: to live and eat in the sukkah, to gather the four species of the land of Israel, and to rejoice in the happiness of the holiday.

The only prescribed ritual is to say prayers and light candles on the first night of Sukkot, a very good time to hold a celebratory party. Building a sukkah offers you a full week of opportunity for inviting guests and being invited as a guest. Dining under the stars creates a moment of poignancy in which we experience nature at the time of year when both the warmth and the light are fading. But although the soft summer air is being crowded out by crisp autumn breezes, Sukkot enables us to enjoy the outdoors just a little longer before the turn of the season sends us indoors.

A Way to Express Our Thanks

The original purpose of the Sukkot festival was to show appreciation for the harvest. Meals were eaten in the sukkah, a small, temporary hut decorated with fruits, flowers, and leafy branches. One theory holds that they were built to commemorate the temporary shelters lived in by the Israelites when they fled from Egypt and had not yet coalesced into the Jewish people. Other scholars say that the huts come from our agricultural background and that they provided temporary housing while our ancestors brought in the harvest in ancient times.

Most likely, both explanations are correct. After forty years in the desert, the Jews finally reached the Promised Land and became farmers, settling down to grow wheat, grapes, and olives. In early fall it was time for the harvest, and the farmers needed to live near the crops to pick them if a sudden storm should start. So they built small huts of wood in the fields, and these sheltered them while they gathered the crops.

Along with Passover and Shavuot, Sukkot is a major pilgrimage festival. In ancient times people would travel day and night from all over Israel to come to the holy city of Jerusalem for sacrifices and special rituals, bearing offerings of animals, grains, fruit, oil, and wine to the Temple. During this time, the people once again lived in temporary huts or sheds, another reason we honor the sukkah on this holiday.

When Sukkot Is Celebrated

In Israel, the first two days of Sukkot are days of mirth and gladness, sacred holidays when no work is allowed. In the United States, Reform Jews celebrate the first and last of seven festival days; Conservative and Orthodox Jews celebrate the first two and last two of eight festival days.

Sukkot is also called the festival of booths, as the sukkah is a temporary booth in which families eat, drink, and sometimes even sleep during the holiday. The rituals and food commemorating Sukkot center around honoring God's protection of our ancestors. At the time, the huts or sheds they lived in had trellis-type roofs made of branches, just as we leave the roof open to let in light and allow us to see the stars. Today's sukkahs are built with roofs that are slatted or constructed with some type of latticework so they provide shelter but remain open at the same time. While we dine in the sukkah, we remember the hardships our ancestors suffered and praise them for their strength of body and will.

Temple Traditions

In the synagogue, the twenty-third chapter of the Book of Leviticus is read on Sukkot. On the Shabbat that falls during the week of Sukkot, the book of Ecclesiastes is read in the synagogue. And on the eighth day of the festival, a solemn day, synagogues hold services to honor those who have died in the past year and in this season in years past.

While Sukkot is about the year just past, this eighth day, called Shemini Atzeret, is about the year to come, and prayers are said for rain to aid the crops that will be planted in the future. The day after, the ninth day, is Simchat Torah, when the yearly cycle of reading the Torah ends and begins anew.

In ancient times, Sukkot was more important than any other holiday in the seasonal calendar. That is hard to understand today, when we are so secure about our sources of food that we scarcely think about how our people struggled in the past and may still struggle today in some parts of the world. As the Hebrew calendar is based on lunar movements, Sukkot is celebrated at the first full moon of the season, falling on the fifteenth of the month. It honors the success of the harvest, without which our people would not have survived to become our ancestors.

Food for the Holiday

Traditional Sukkot foods are rich in fruits and vegetables, especially vegetables that are stuffed. These include everything from zucchini, cabbage, vine leaves, and tomatoes to eggplant and peppers, both red and green. Many are filled with lean ground beef or veal and braised in a sweet-and-sour tomato or meat sauce.

Nourishing casseroles and thick stews are also traditional, and tzimmes, a slow-cooked stew made with vegetables and fruits, is a most popular dish. Preserved foods representing the harvest are also well loved. These include pickles, cucumber salads, and eggplant spreads. For dessert, filled pastries are the sweet of choice, especially strudels stuffed with apples, nuts, and dried fruits. The stuffing symbolizes a bountiful harvest and is considered extravagant and thus perfect for a holiday that celebrates opulent food.

Because Sukkot calls for dinner out every evening—out in the sukkah, that is—some hosts like to cook their food there as well as eat it. Grilled turkey breasts make an especially nice entrée and can be easily prepared on a small barbecue placed just outside the sukkah door. On the other hand, if you are planning to carry out platters of already cooked food to guests or family in the sukkah, don't plan to cook anything too fragile, like a soufflé, for example.

For your party, a variety of menus can be planned that symbolize the

Sukkah Fruit Hang-Ups

Materials Needed

Scissors
8 to 10 feet of thick string or cord
Pen
1 sheet of white paper
Red and yellow construction paper or felt
10 large paper clips

Directions

1   Cut the string or cord to the right length to go from one end of the sukkah to the other, leaving enough slack for a knot at each end. Tie it to the sukkah frame at both ends.
2. With the pen, draw an apple and a leaf, each about three inches across, on white paper.
3. Cut them out and trace them five times each on the red and yellow paper or felt.
4. Cut out the apples and leaves and write the name of one family member or guest on each one.
5. Attach alternating apples and leaves to the string with the paper clips.

abundant harvest and nourish and satisfy hungry guests. For a cold buffet with a lot of variety, you might try:

Cold Avocado Soup
Citron Poppy Quickbread
Poached Salmon With Dill Sauce
Herring in Cream Sauce
Barley and Orzo Pilaf
Pear Strudel
Lemon-Yogurt Cake

Or if you have room to serve a sit-down dinner in your sukkah and want to serve your guests a more traditional meal, consider this menu:

Harvest Vegetable Soup
Apple Beet Salad
Stuffed Cabbage in Tomato Sauce
Couscous With Shredded Carrots
Cranberry Nut Bread
Apple Walnut Strudel

When to Have Your Sukkot Party

The most festive dinners are served during the first and last days of Sukkot. If the Sabbath falls in the middle of the holiday week, this is also an ideal time to have a Sukkot feast. Choosing which time of day can depend on the type of food you want to serve or how you believe the weather will turn out.

In the early fall, the warmest part of the day is at noon or in the early

Citron Poppy Quickbread

Because quickbreads do not use yeast, they do not require a long time to rise before they are ready to bake. Consequently, they make wonderful mealtime accompaniments that can be added quickly to a meal, making them perfect for busy cooks of all kinds. This loaf can be baked in a traditional loaf pan or divided into muffin tins and served individually.

2 cups all-purpose flour
¼ cup honey
¼ teaspoon salt
½ teaspoon baking soda
1 teaspoon baking powder
1 large egg

¾ cup whole milk
½ cup butter
Juice of ½ lemon
1 teaspoon grated lemon rind
1 tablespoon poppyseeds

1. Preheat oven to 350° F.
2. Grease an 8½ × 4½-inch loaf pan.
3. Blend the flour, honey, salt, baking soda, and baking powder in a bowl.
4. Beat the egg in another bowl and add the milk, butter, lemon juice, lemon rind, and poppyseeds.
5. Add the flour mixture and stir together.
6. Scrape the batter into the loaf pan and bake for 35–40 minutes or until golden brown.
7. Allow to cool on rack for 10 minutes, then turn onto serving dish and slice.

Yield: 8–10 servings

Harvest Vegetable Soup

If there is one food that seems inherently soothing, it would have to be soup. Warm and tasty, the aroma alone is sure to make your sukkah feel like home. You can serve it from the center of the table in a big tureen or carry it out on trays in individual bowls or cups. Either way, a first-course soup will set the tone for a hearty, homey meal your guests will enjoy.

3 cups chicken or beef stock
2 medium potatoes, diced
¼ cup diced onions
½ cup diced carrots
½ cup corn kernels
½ cup lima beans

½ cup diced zucchini
1 large leek, diced
½ cup stewed tomatoes
Salt and pepper
¼ chopped parsley

1. Combine all ingredients except for salt, pepper, and parsley in a large saucepan and bring to a boil, then reduce heat and simmer for 10 minutes.
2. Add salt and pepper to taste.
3. Pour into a large serving tureen or individual bowls and sprinkle parsley on top.

Yield: 6 servings

Stuffed Cabbage in Tomato Sauce

Enjoying stuffed foods is one way to recognize abundance, and choosing cabbage leaves filled with a meat and rice combination fulfills the wish for a plentiful harvest. If you freeze the cabbage for 24 hours, then defrost at room temperature overnight (or for 30 minutes on microwave defrost), the leaves will peel off easily. Prepare the dish two or three days in advance to enhance the flavor.

1 large cabbage head	1 cup water
¼ cup vegetable oil	3 cans (28 ounces) tomatoes
½ cup diced onion	1 pound ground beef, veal,
½ cup brown sugar	or turkey
½ cup lemon juice	½ cup cooked rice, white or brown
1 teaspoon salt	1 egg
¼ teaspoon pepper	½ cup breadcrumbs

1. Remove 12–14 cabbage leaves by boiling the head in 4 quarts of water for 5–10 minutes or by freezing.
2. Heat the oil in a saucepan and brown the onions lightly.
3. Add the sugar, lemon juice, salt, pepper, water, and tomatoes and stir.
4. Mix together the meat, rice, egg, and breadcrumbs.
5. Place an inch-thick roll of the meat mixture at the base of a cabbage leaf.
6. Fold in the sides and carefully roll up.
7. Repeat steps 5 and 6 with all the other leaves until you have used up all the filling.
8. Add the stuffed leaves to the sauce and cook over low heat for 1½ hours, checking the pan every 30 minutes to make sure nothing is sticking on the bottom.

Yield: 6–8 servings as a main course, 10–12 as an appetizer

Apple Walnut Strudel

Making strudel dough takes practice and patience, but your family won't mind eating your mistakes the first few times you try it; even if it comes out lopsided, it will still taste great. Before you plan to serve it to guests, though, limber up with a few practice runs. Each time you do, fill it with something different—mixed dried fruit, poppyseeds, cherries, cheese, or shredded coconut.

2½ cups flour
½ teaspoon salt
2 tablespoons sugar
1 teaspoon baking powder
1 egg
½ cup oil
½ cup cold water

6 apples, peeled, pared, and diced
1 cup chopped walnuts
2 tablespoons grated lemon rind
¼ cup sugar
1 tablespoon cinnamon
½ cup raisins
½ pint heavy cream

1. Preheat oven to 375° F.
2. Sift the flour, salt, sugar, and baking powder into a bowl. Drop the egg, oil, and water into the center and stir together, then knead until smooth.
3. On a floured board, roll out the dough until it is thin.
4. Mix together the apples, nuts, lemon rind, sugar, cinnamon, and raisins.
5. Spread the filling mixture over the dough.
6. Roll up the dough like a jelly roll and brush with oil.
7. Sprinkle with sugar and cinnamon and bake on a greased cookie sheet for 45 minutes.
8. Beat the heavy cream.
9. Cut into 1-inch slices and serve with whipped cream while it is still warm.

Yield: about 30 slices, or 15 servings

afternoon, so brunch might be your best answer to balance comfort and convenience. This time of day enables you to serve your meal buffet style, which works very well within the limited confines of the sukkah, and also enables you to place an extra table outside to hold additional food, if needed.

If you like the middle of the day but prefer the greater formality of a luncheon, you might invite guests home to the sukkah after morning services on the first day of Sukkot. A celebration at this time will allow a natural carryover of good feeling from the gathering at the synagogue to your party.

On the other hand, dinner or a dessert party under the stars can be a distinct and memorable experience, as we rarely eat outdoors once the summer has passed, so you may choose an evening party for this reason. If you are interested in putting a little romance in the air, this is definitely the right time of day. Soft candlelight in the sukkah or burning torches lighting the way outside will add a glow to your party that is sure to rub off on your guests.

The seventh day of Sukkot is called Hoshanah Rabbah, a day celebrated with a special service in the synagogue. After the service, many families return home for a festive meal, and this might be the ideal time for your dinner party in the sukkah. At services, a procession marches seven times around the sanctuary, and members of the congregation carry the *lulav*, myrtle, and willow branches and wave them at all four corners of the synagogue and out into the sukkah. Special decorations of falling leaves grace the sukkah and symbolize the hope for renewed life with a good harvest next year.

Parallels With Thanksgiving

Because celebrating the holiday shows our gratitude for the bountiful harvest, it has often been compared with American Thanksgiving, and many say Sukkot serves as a model for the secular November holiday. Many historians believe the Pilgrims looked to the Bible for a way to give thanks to God for their bounty and copied the idea of a Sukkot festival. They were grateful for the food and protection given to them in the new land, the same way our ancestors felt during the time of their wandering through the wilderness.

Historical records show that the first Thanksgiving occurred in October and lasted for three days, not a far cry from a weeklong, early-fall Sukkot festival.

How to Make Your Party a Success

Whether you decide on a buffet, luncheon, or dinner party, be sure to invite your guests in an elegant manner. You might write the invitations by hand and string them onto the stems of mini-gourds, available for a short while at this time of year at garden stores, farm stands, and some supermarkets. Delicate invitations such as these are best if hand-delivered, but they can be sent in small boxes or padded mailers as well.

Another invitation idea is to create a collage of information about Sukkot: Write various facts about the holiday around the main message of the invitation concerning the time, place, and purpose of the party. Your guests will be happy to learn about the holiday ahead of time. And if the party is casual, with a grass floor under the table, for example, they will be happy to know about that, too.

You can set a beautiful table with terra cotta pots at each place filled with small vegetables, such as cherry tomatoes, baby carrots, and herbs. Lay the produce gently on packed straw, available at garden shops, and tie ribbons around the pots to make them festive. If you have a green thumb and some herbs left growing in the garden, you could dig them up and plant them in the pots. Chives, thyme, and oregano have pretty foliage and are hardy enough to still be green by Sukkot.

These pots can also double as place markers, with each guest's name written on the front, and as favors, too, as guests can take them home at the end of the party to help remember the good time they had.

Welcome Flag for the Sukkah

Materials Needed

Pencil
A white pillowcase
Colored markers
Water-based paints
A pole or broom handle
Stapler
Wire

Directions

1. With the pencil in large letters write on the pillowcase the words "*Baruchim Haba'im*" in Hebrew or English letters, as you prefer, or simply write "Welcome." You can write on one side or both sides of the pillowcase.
2. Draw fruits and vegetables and flowers around the words to decorate them. Go over all the words and pictures in colored markers and paints.
3. When the painting is dry, wrap one short end of the pillowcase around the pole and staple it on. Carefully attach the other end of the pole onto the roof of the sukkah with wire.
4. Hope for wind to make the flag wave when your guests arrive!

Beautiful Centerpieces

As the focal point of your table, you might make a cornucopia out of fresh fruit, flowers, and vegetables placed in a horn-shaped wicker basket, or use a traditional display of a *lulav* and *etrog* tied together with myrtle and willow branches on each side.

Another idea for a centerpiece is a miniature sukkah. There are four different ways to make them. First, you can build one out of breadsticks and peanut butter, using zucchini strips and grapes for decorations. Or you can bake one out of gingerbread and decorate it with gumdrops. Also, you can make a simple sukkah out of a shoebox with real branches for a roof. And finally, you can build a sukkah out of cardboard, using icing for glue and cookies for the roof and walls. (See sidebar for directions on how to make the cookie sukkah.)

Even though you will be eating outdoors, use a pressed white tablecloth and your best china and glassware to honor the holiday. They will look especially appealing in the atmosphere created by fruit and flower decorations, the open sky and the sounds and scents of nature. For an extra touch of the outdoors, gather leaves, both green and newly golden, and strew them on the table, making good use of a way to add color, texture and brightness to a simple white cloth.

Especially for Kids

It is always a good idea to plan some activities for children, who are likely to grow restless waiting for the next course to appear from a kitchen they are sure to notice is farther away than usual. Keep them busy stringing popcorn and cranberries into garlands to decorate the sukkah. To arrange this, thread several yarn needles with kite-flying string and prepare large bowls full of cranberries and freshly popped corn. They will do the rest.

Cookie Sukkah

Materials Needed

1 cardboard cookie or cracker box
Scissors
Vanilla icing
Plain square or rectangular cookies
Pretzel rods
2 or 3 kinds of small leaves

Directions

1. Lay the cardboard box on its side and cut off the top. Decide where your door and two windows should be and cut them out.
2. Cover the four sides of the sukkah with vanilla icing and attach cookies to the outside walls. Finish corners, windows, and doors by piping icing through a plain or star tip.
3. Put six pretzel rods over the top to create a slat roof. Decorate the roof with sprigs of greenery from the garden.
4. Use the cookie sukkah for a centerpiece, and eat it as soon as dinner is over.

Teenagers put in charge of this activity will be happy to have the chance to go back and forth from kitchen to sukkah popping corn and fetching yarn. If you find the fresh cranberries are too juicy, use the dried variety, which will not stain fingertips or clothing. Florists' wire can be used instead of yarn and a needle, and once the popcorn and cranberries are threaded onto it, the wires can be bent into circles or joined together to make stars.

Harder to work with but fun for agile fingers are pomegranate seeds, which make beautiful collages when glued to cardboard or odd-shaped scraps of wood as a base. Open the pomegranate and remove the seeds, let dry and attach to the base in creative designs with a sticky, edible paste made of flour and a few drops of water. Pomegranates have been used for centuries in Jewish art as symbols of the fertility of crops, animals, people, and the ideas of the Torah.

Another activity for children is to loop together paper chains in a variety of colors. Simply cut strips of paper and provide tape for the children to join them together. When the garlands are finished, use them to decorate the sukkah.

Rituals and Traditions

First and foremost in celebrating Sukkot is building and eating in the sukkah. With a roof made of leafy tree branches or wooden slats, the sukkah must protect you from the sun by day yet not prevent you from seeing the stars at night.

If you are handy and can build a sturdy frame yourself, you can design and build a sukkah that will prove to be a satisfying project. Designed to resemble a makeshift hut, the sukkah can be constructed out of any material. Metal, plastic piping, or wood can be used for the frame, and the walls can be built of canvas, burlap, wood, or tarpaulin. Remember that only three walls are needed; the fourth can be the exterior wall of your house. For the roof, you will need something that grows and has been cut. Leafy branches, evergreens, and bamboo poles work well.

If you plan to build a sturdy, albeit temporary, structure, you will need eight sheets of plywood to form an eight-foot square. Make your doorway four feet wide, and join the panels at the corners with two-by-two-inch poles and the same size lengths at the top edges of the panels. Cut windows into the walls and use one-by-one-inch slats for the roof, which you can later cover with evergreen boughs or branches.

Sukkah-building kits abound for the less skilled. Through Jewish bookstores and Judaica shops, you can order sukkahs with tubular frames, canvas walls, and bamboo poles for the roof covering. At the end of the festival, simply dismantle it (making sure to save the instructions for putting it back together) and store it in the garage till next year.

You can decorate the sukkah with bunches or garlands of flowers (both fresh and dried), tapestries, candlesticks, decanters, children's drawings, photographs—anything that makes you feel more at home. Work to make the sukkah beautiful, and it will reward you with a peaceful place to read, study, eat, entertain guests, daydream, and even sleep.

Hanging a medley of fruit and gourds from the roof gives the sukkah a friendly feel. Vines, wreaths, and berry chains make very nice decorations both inside and on the outer walls. Decorations can go from sparse to lavish, and anywhere in between.

For light in the late evenings, depend on holiday and Shabbat candles, camp lanterns, or votive candles of all sizes, shapes, and scents. Vanilla, floral, and pine aromas are especially nice in the sukkah. Depending on when the holiday falls, you might need citronella candles to keep the insect population at bay. Some people set up rows of candles outside the sukkah to light the way; others depend on ambient light from inside the house or from nearby street lamps.

Getting Children Involved

Children will have a good time making ornaments and origami designs to hang in the sukkah. A few days before the holiday week begins, provide a table supplied with scissors, tape, construction paper, colored cellophane, mylar, wrapping paper, glitter, and glue, and let them enjoy themselves. Lightweight mobiles can be created on ordinary coat hangers and suspended from hooks on the walls and ceilings.

Save calendar pictures from year to year, especially pictures of the Holy Land and its trees, fruits, and flowers, and hang them on the walls in makeshift frames made of construction paper, or taped onto sheets of aluminum foil for background shine. Hang a strip of posterboard stapled into a circle with holes for stringing objects punched at intervals. Decorate with the seven kinds of produce for which Israel is famous: dates, almonds, pomegranates, figs, olives, wheat, and barley. Or, if they are easier to find, use oranges, apples, peaches, pears, corn, beets, and carrots.

When all the decorations are done, you might put up a sign above the sukkah entrance saying *"Baruchim Haba'im,"* meaning "welcome." (If you want to use a flag to say welcome, see sidebar.)

The Ancestral Hut and Its Meaning

The sukkah is a symbol of protection and peace, striking a balance between exposure and shelter, precariousness and protection. It symbolizes the ephemeral quality of life, and also the upheavals and uprootedness of the Jewish people. A spiritual shelter, it makes people think about what is temporary and what is permanent, what protects you and what leaves you exposed.

In Israel, twenty-five hundred years ago, Sukkot was the only time farmers rested for any length of time. Leviticus commanded them to "dwell in booths" for seven days, perhaps the earliest recorded form of vacation known to humans. The farmers were finished harvesting their crops, and it was not yet time to plant for next year. Life in the sukkah, limited to one week, was a time of rest and rejuvenation, a time of peace and reflection in an otherwise unyielding and laborious agricultural cycle.

It is customary on Sukkot to invite more than just your friends, family, and neighbors into the sukkah; many people believe in calling out to the spirits of loved ones who have died in years past to come and join the celebration of Sukkot. Though it may sound strange, it is even customary to include ancestors one has never met.

This idea is particularly poignant if you or your close relatives have lost family members in the Holocaust and wish to reconnect with them by inviting them to be there in spirit. Living relatives who have never talked about these loved ones might be moved to describe lost parents or children if they feel their presence is welcome, and this can open up new levels of understanding of your heritage as well as offer relief to those who might not yet have come to terms with their loss.

The Four Species

At the synagogue, joyous congregants parade through the sanctuary and out to the sukkah each day of the holiday week, carrying the four species of plants that celebrate the bounty of the harvest. Many people believe the four species are meant to represent the four different types of people in the Jewish community, from spiritually strong and knowledgeable to uninformed yet kind. All four species are held together in one hand during the service, symbolizing the unity of the Jews, with people of all levels of strength and fortitude helping one another.

The four special plants are the *lulav*, a tall, green, date-bearing palm branch that was the national emblem of ancient Israel; the shiny myrtle leaf, tied to the right side of the *lulav*; the delicate willow tied to the left; and the *etrog* or citron, a large, lumpy ancient lemon, which is believed to have grown in the Garden of Eden.

On Sukkot, people wave the *lulav* and point the *etrog* in the four directions of the compass while chanting prayers to show their gratitude that God is everywhere—north, south, in heaven, and on earth.

It is important to honor the holiday by purchasing the best specimens of *etrog* and *lulav* available at your local Judaica shop or temple store. The myrtle and willow should be fresh, unwilted, and unbroken; the *etrog* yellow and firm; the *lulav* green and straight.

Into the Future

The *etrog*, an unusually sour fruit, has a very thick rind and sparse pulp, and as such is not as useful as its close cousin, the lemon. Yet at the end of Sukkot, many people make the *etrog* into marmalade and eat it like jam on a slice of bread.

To do so, soak the *etrog* in water for four days, changing the water daily. Then slice it very thin, leaving the skin on, and boil it for ten minutes. This will get rid of the naturally bitter taste. Slice and remove the seeds of six lemons, limes, or oranges (or a combination of these) and simmer with the *etrog* with one cup of water and three cups of sugar for about thirty minutes. When it is cool, serve it with toast. It should keep in the refrigerator for about a month.

Another way to use the *etrog* is to cut the skin in little cross-hatches, insert cloves in the openings and sprinkle it with cinnamon. This can then be used with your Havdalah spices at the end of Shabbat or wrapped in gauze and placed in a drawer or linen closet as a sachet.

Some people keep the *lulav* to use instead of a brush to gather together the last of the crumbs before cleaning their kitchen for Passover.

Enjoying the Sukkah

It is important to eat in the sukkah the first night of the holiday, even if it rains, because it creates a feeling of celebration that will last all week. If the weather is inclement, just say the blessing over the bread (see appendix A) and share a few small bites before running inside to shelter.

At sundown each evening, enter the sukkah, light two candles, and say the blessing (see appendix A), then spend some time reflecting on the day and its meaning.

There is an old custom of inviting guests into the sukkah every night, a custom inspired by Abraham, who is said to have invited many strangers and passersby to eat at his table. In modern times, of course, this is difficult to do, but every evening if you spend some time in the sukkah, consider the people whose paths crossed yours that day and see if there is someone you would like to invite tomorrow. It is required that we rejoice in the sukkah; perhaps our festivities will be even more joyous if we find a way to open our hearts and homes to one new friend each day of Sukkot.

4

Simchat Torah: Dancing With Joy

*The commandments are the lamp
and the Torah is the light.*

—Proverbs 6:23

An End and a Beginning

SIMCHAT TORAH, WHICH CELEBRATES the annual cycle of Torah reading, brings
to a graceful close the three-week holiday period that began with Rosh
Hashanah. Some say it is the easiest of the Jewish holidays to celebrate,
marked as it is by jubilant festivities. Literally, *simchat Torah* means
"rejoicing in the law," and that is exactly what we do.

On the eve of the holiday, the Torah is taken from the ark and carried
up and down the synagogue aisles, with singing and dancing congregants
following it in an exuberant parade. Children wave flags with apples

impaled on the flagstaffs and lit candles balancing where the cores used to be, and a general air of raucous fun prevails. Torah processions have been known to spill out of the synagogue onto the streets, carried along by the enthusiastic marching and clapping of revelers and picking up new enthusiasts as the parades wind through the community and observers get caught up in the merriment.

Many people feel this is a time of a great solidarity with Jews in other countries and cultures, a holiday on which we gather together to express our fervent, intense, shared love for the Torah and its teachings.

When the Holiday Takes Place

The day on which Simchat Torah officially occurs varies by geography and degree of observance. It is celebrated in Israel and by Reform Jews throughout the world on the eighth day of the Sukkot holiday, the twenty-second of Tishri, in late September or early October. Conservative and Orthodox Jews, however, celebrate it on the ninth day, the twenty-third of Tishri.

The reason for this discrepancy is that Simchat Torah follows hard on the heels of another, older holiday, Shemini Atzeret. Reform and Israeli Jews combine these two festivals into a one-day celebration, while Conservative and Orthodox Jews commemorate them with unique, day-long festivities for each.

Meeting the Challenge of Change

Simchat Torah is a great example of how Jewish festivals grow and evolve to meet people's changing needs. The holiday is not mentioned in the Bible, nor did it even exist in Talmudic times. It is a relatively recent creation built on the ancient and enduring tradition of publicly reading from a Torah scroll.

Shemini Atzeret, on the other hand, is a biblical festival that means, literally, "assembly of the eighth day." It is a day on which it is said that God looks over and judges the world's waters. We say a prayer for rain, asking for enough to water our crops but not so much that we cause flooding and famine. It has traditionally been a day of rest and meditation.

Like other holidays, this one was extended to two days in the Diaspora by rabbis who feared making an error in calculating the exact day of celebration, since they were so far away from Israel. The second day became Simchat Torah, the only holiday on which the Torah is read at night.

A New Tradition Is Born

Of course, it took centuries for Simchat Torah to develop into its current form. In ancient Palestine, Jews traditionally read the Torah on a three-year cycle. While this fit comfortably with their pace of life, it conflicted with the more widely accepted practice of the Jewish community in Babylonia to finish it in one year. By the eighth century, more and more Jews in Palestine wanted to switch to the one-year cycle, and after great debate the Babylonians won worldwide acceptance and the annual observance emerged.

Once the transition was complete, it became customary to celebrate the end of one annual cycle and the beginning of the next. By the eleventh century Simchat Torah had developed, along with its name, its time—the ninth day of Sukkot—and the festive ritual we celebrate today. Hence, a system of Jewish learning that had no end combined with a holiday that gave its people a chance to sing, dance, and publicly share their love for the law.

The holiday of Simchat Torah could easily have evolved into a dry salute to scholarship, but fortunately it did not. By the sixteenth century it was customary to take the scrolls from the ark and make seven circles around the synagogue with them, giving everyone who wanted it a chance to dance with the Torah.

Understanding the Scroll of Law

Nothing symbolizes Judaism better than the Torah, the handwritten double scroll made of parchment and written to exacting specifications. The Torah contains our history, our heritage, our laws, and our wisdom, and it is so sacred that when we pick it up, we hold it as though it were an infant, cradled in our arms with the top leaning on our shoulder.

The Torah contains the first five books of the Bible, also known as the Five Books of Moses, or the *chumash*, the Hebrew word for "five." It is also sometimes called the Pentateuch, the Greek word for "five books," or the Holy Scriptures. It is the most sacred object in the synagogue. Jews never call the Bible the Old Testament, because this would imply that we recognize a new testament beyond it.

The Torah is divided into fifty-four sections, called in Hebrew *parashot* or *sidrot*. One section is read each week, so that the reading is completed in one year. Sections of the Torah are read on all holidays and three times each week: on Shabbat, and on Monday and Thursday, the two ancient market days.

The Torah scroll is traditionally covered in velvet or some other luxurious fabric and adorned with silver breastplates and topped with bells or finely crafted crowns, showing deft, artistic workmanship.

The Torah itself is divided into three sections: The Five Books of Moses, from which the Torah portion is taken, the Prophets, and the Writings. The Five Books of Moses are Genesis, Exodus, Leviticus, Numbers, and Deuteronomy. On Shabbat and the festival days, the Torah portion is followed by a specific section read from the Prophets. This is called the Haftarah.

On Simchat Torah, the final verses of Deuteronomy are read, and we hear about the death of Moses, our teacher. These last words are solemn: "Be strong, be strong, and let us be of good courage." Then with hardly a pause we open a new scroll and turn once again to the fabled words that open the Book of Genesis: "In the beginning . . ." and thus starts a new year and the wonderful story of creation.

Reading Beyond the Torah

Because Simchat Torah is a holiday that celebrates a book, many Jews who become educated in Torah wish to go on to gain an understanding of the other Jewish volumes. Most prominent among these is the Talmud. This is a two-part collection of writings that is centered on interpretations of passages of Scripture and includes legend, law, and opinions on ethical concepts and their applications. After the Bible, it is considered the most important document dealing with the spiritual life of the Jewish people.

The first part of the Talmud is called the Mishnah and is a statement of the laws that govern Jewish life. This book, which is a compilation of oral interpretations and discussions of portions of the Bible, codifies Jewish oral tradition since the Torah. It is generally accepted to have been completed by the end of the second century C.E.

The second part, called the Gemara, contains discussions and commentaries about material in the Mishnah. This book was finished at the end of the fifth century.

The other basic book studied by Jewish scholars is the Midrash, which provides interpretations of Biblical literature that explain the Scriptures through stories, originally created to make the Bible understandable to the Jewish masses. Despite their instructional intent, they contain some of the most beloved stories of our culture and history—for example, the story of Lillith, Adam's first wife, who would not be subservient and was replaced by Eve.

Planning Your Holiday Party

Official celebrations of Simchat Torah begin at nightfall with readings in the synagogue, followed by Torah processions and plenty of singing and dancing. We are celebrating not a historical event but a cyclical event, the never-ending circle of Torah reading. The holiday honors our continuing commitment to studying the Torah and living as Jews, and as we end one cycle of readings and begin the next, we show our deep dedication to lifelong learning.

Many people enjoy serving a Simchat Torah dinner on the eve of the holiday, filling guests with good food and good cheer and preparing them for the readings and festivities that are to follow at services.

Simple invitations cut in the shape of a chef's hat with a Jewish star on it or drawn over a picture of a plaid potholder with little menorahs inside the boxes will evoke warm kitchens with pots bubbling on the stove and secret recipes handed down from mother to daughter through the generations. Or, if you prefer, a note in the shape of a Torah scroll will alert guests to the meaning of the holiday, and festive colors and a friendly typeface will let them know it will be a joyful event from start to finish.

To greet your guests when they arrive, say "*Moadim lesimcha,*" Hebrew for "happy holiday."

Dinner With a Theme

If you want to center your party around a specific time in Jewish history, consider honoring our heritage by drawing on the colorful history of the Twelve Tribes of Israel. This is a good choice for Simchat Torah, when flags are so important, because each tribe had a unique emblem that was used to design a banner flown across its camp. Translated into simple designs, these banners can make eye-catching decorations for your entryway, echoed in the placecards for your table. Later in the evening they could be stapled to dowels and used as flags to wave during the synagogue service and at the Torah procession.

According to Genesis, the Twelve Tribes were made up of the descendants of Jacob's twelve sons: Reuben, Simeon, Levi, Judah, Issachar, Zebulun, Joseph, Benjamin, Dan, Naphtali, Gad, and Asher. The Torah tells us that each tribe received a portion of land when the Israelites entered Canaan after the Exodus from Egypt, and that they thrived and multiplied there.

Each tribe enjoyed a distinct and separate identity for many generations, until the time Israel became a more consolidated nation. Although

Flags for the Torah Procession

Materials Needed

Glue-on fabric letters
Felt piece, about 9 × 12 inches
Glue
Yarn and a needle
Stapler
18-inch dowel
1 firm apple

Directions

1. Pick out the letters that spell one of these four sayings: "Rejoice in the Torah"; "Torah = Joy"; "Happy Simchat Torah"; "I Love My Torah."
2. Arrange the letters in the order you want them and glue them to the felt. If you have enough letters, you can glue them on both sides.
3. Use the yarn and needle to sew around the edges of the felt flag in large overhand stitches for a decorative look.
4. Staple the felt flag to the dowel, leaving about an inch of wood at the top.
5. Spear an apple on the end of the wood dowel.
6. If you have any felt left over, you can make another simpler flag by gluing a triangular shape to a chopstick, or a tiny shape to a toothpick. These will be pretty even without decorations.
7. Follow the Torah parade and wave your flag with pride!

Jacob fathered each of the tribes' leaders, several had different mothers. Leah, for example, was the mother of Simeon, Levi, Judah, Reuben, Issachar, and Zebulun, while Rachel mothered Joseph and Benjamin. Rachel's maid Zilpah was the mother of Gad and Asher, and Leah's maid Bilhah was the mother of Dan and Naphtali.

Depending on the size of your party, you might divide the table to honor the four mothers, assigning each one the correct number of tribes. Or if you plan to serve exactly twelve guests, each could represent one of Jacob's sons. In the case of thirteen guests, you could include a complete history of Jacob's children by adding Dina, his only daughter, and the youngest of the family.

Each tribe's unique banner was made up of an emblem and a color or set of colors not used by the others. Some or all of these might be replicated for your party.

The tribe of Benjamin was represented by a wolf on a multicolored cloth. Dan used a serpent on a deep blue background. Naphtali's symbol was a deer on a wine-colored banner. Asher depicted a woman and an olive tree on a pearly background. For Levi a mixed red, white, and black design with twelve squares for the twelve tribes served as a banner. The tribe of Judah was represented by a lion on a sky-blue background, and Issachar used a donkey on black. Zebulun's banner portrayed a ship on a white cloth, and Reuben used a mandrake on red. For Simeon, the city of Shechem was drawn on a green banner, and Gad's tribe was symbolized by a camp on a gray cloth. The property rights of Joseph were transferred to his children, Ephraim and Menashe, who used a bullock and a unicorn on a jet-black cloth.

For Dina, if you are including the last child of Jacob, it would be appropriate to consider a bird emblem on a white background.

If you have some artistic talent, try your hand at creating drawings for these banners yourself. If not, check with your library or look on the Internet at the many Jewish websites for images that you can turn into appropriate symbols. Get your children involved in the search—you can promise them a painless history lesson—or consider providing art materials and having your guests create banners of their own.

Flag for Your Car Antenna

Materials Needed

Pinking shears
A man's white handkerchief, or 9 × 12-inch piece of white fabric
Pencil
Puffy fabric paint
Glue
Buttons
Appliqués
A wood dowel, about 18 inches long
Colored yarn
3 wire twist ties

Directions

1. Decide if you want the flag to be rectangular or pennant shaped, then use pinking shears to cut the fabric into the shape and size you want.
2. In pencil, draw the design for your flag. It might be a Jewish star, two stone tablets, or a Torah.
3. Create a border around your picture with straight or squiggly lines.
4. Use puffy paint to color in your drawing.
5. Embellish by gluing on buttons and appliqués.
6. While the paint is drying, take the dowel and wrap yarn around it, keeping the strands close together to cover the wood in an attractive color or set of colors. You can alternate colors every inch or so, or twist two or three together for a tweedy look.
7. Glue the flag onto the dowel. When the glue is dry, attach the dowel to your car antenna with the twist ties.

Holiday Food for Simchat Torah

An early holiday supper is sure to create the atmosphere you want to bring to services. Some cooks fill their menu with all kinds of foods that have been baked, steamed, or cut into rounds to symbolize the hope for a round, full, satisfying year. For example, carrots are sliced into circles and made into a tasty, traditional dish called tzimmes. A round challah can grace the holiday table, with honey for dipping, and stewed cranberries might fill round side dishes with tartness and tang.

The holiday motif of roundness can be expanded to encompass the concepts of sweetness and fullness, and desserts such as stuffed pastries shaped into balls and pinched together at the top can finish off a satisfying meal.

As on Sukkot, Simchat Torah dishes are intended to reflect the bountiful harvest. Thus thick soups and stews incorporating freshly ripened vegetables of the season make good fare. Stuffed foods of all kinds, particularly specialties such as veal breast and filled poultry, are in order here.

A vegetarian buffet would do well to feature stuffed peppers, with green, red, and yellow varieties lined up alongside one another. Zucchini bread can be made with just a touch of sweetness to symbolize the abundance of the harvest.

On Simchat Torah Israeli bakers make a fruity candy called Turkish delight, and street vendors sell candy-coated apples. Honey cookies are devoured worldwide, as are individual cakes stuffed with nuts and fruits.

A complete menu for your holiday dinner might be built around the following dishes:

Barley-Bean Soup
Roast Turkey With Date and Almond Stuffing
Tzimmes With Biblical Fruits
Holiday Corn Pudding
Baked Stuffed Zucchini
Turkish Baklava
Hot Mulled Cider

A good selection of wines to accompany a roast turkey dinner enhanced by lots of seasonal fruits and vegetables could be selected from imported or domestic varieties of Sauvignon Blanc, Chardonnay, Beaujolais, or Reisling.

A Special Time for Children

Much of the merrymaking that makes up the heart of Simchat Torah takes place during services. For once the children do not have to sit quietly in their seats with their hands in their laps and absorb long sermons from the rabbi. Their hardest chore will be to resist the temptation to munch on the apples stuck on the tops of the sticks that hold their flags.

Flags to wave at Simchat Torah services can be made of construction paper, felt, cotton handkerchiefs, styrofoam, and even Israeli newspapers. Decorative materials include rick-rack, glitter, puffy paint, fabric letters, and yarn. Directions for how to make a variety of flags can be found in the sidebar.

Some congregations add to the delight of children by handing them gaily decorated paper bags filled with nuts, fruits, and candy to symbolize the sweetness of Torah as the children march up and down the aisles.

In this partylike atmosphere, when all solemn behavior tends to be forgotten and fun and frivolity are the reigning themes, children can sometimes find themselves caught up in Judaism in a way that carries over into their studies and makes their heritage seem more real and immediate. This can have a positive impact on their religious identity for many years to come.

It has become customary in many synagogues to call up all the children under the age of thirteen to the bimah for a special blessing. With the children huddled close together, two congregants are called up to spread a tallit, or prayer shawl, over their heads while the rabbi blesses them. In other temples, children just entering religious school are called to the bimah and blessed in a ceremony of consecration.

Everyone over the age of thirteen who wants an *aliyah* at Simchat Torah is entitled to one. Often the rabbi will call up people in groups,

Tzimmes With Biblical Fruits

The word *tzimmes* means "excitement" or "fuss" in Yiddish. It's not that this is a hard dish to make, it's just that if made well, it can cause quite a stir among your guests. In the best of times everyone will ask at once for the recipe; at the very least, you're sure to get compliments on the variety of flavors blended together in the long, slow cooking process.

4 large carrots	½ cup honey
4 ounces prunes	½ cup water
4 ounces apricots	½ cup orange juice
4 ounces figs	½ cup raisins
1 teaspoon cornstarch	

1. Preheat oven to 350° F.
2. Scrape the carrots and slice into circles.
3. Halve and pit the prunes, apricots, and figs.
4. Layer the carrots and fruits and in a greased 9 × 13-inch baking pan.
5. Mix the cornstarch, honey, water, orange juice, and raisins in a bowl.
6. Sprinkle the mixture over the carrots and fruits and bake for 1½ hours or until tender.

Yield: 6–8 servings

Holiday Corn Pudding

Corn goes well with just about every kind of meat or fowl, and its earthy and creamy texture makes it perfect to accompany a roast turkey dinner. You can use canned or fresh corn for this pudding. If you give fresh ears a quick dip in a pot of boiling water, the kernels will come off more easily. Cooking them also slightly intensifies the flavor.

6 ears fresh corn or 3 cups canned corn	¼ teaspoon salt
	¼ teaspoon basil
1 cup heavy cream	Pinch of pepper
½ teaspoon sugar	½ cup cornmeal
1 large egg	1 tablespoon butter

1. Preheat the oven to 350° F.
2. Butter a 9 × 13-inch glass baking dish.
3. Scrape the kernels into a bowl and add the heavy cream, sugar, egg, salt, basil, and pepper.
4. Mix well with a fork.
5. Add the cornmeal and stir well.
6. Spread the mixture into the baking dish and dot with butter.
7. Bake the pudding for 30–35 minutes. Serve hot.

Yield: 6 servings

Baked Stuffed Zucchini

This is a nourishing side dish you can make hours ahead of time and then warm in the oven or microwave. In addition to adding flavor and nutrition to a turkey dinner, it can serve as a hearty vegetarian main dish too. Make sure the zucchinis you select are firm to the touch and have clear, unspotted skins. The stuffing reminds us of our gratitude for the abundance of the harvest.

3 large zucchinis	2 teaspoons dill
3 tablespoons butter or margarine	¼ teaspoon salt
½ cup diced onions	¾ cup bread crumbs
2 cloves garlic, finely diced	2 eggs
3 teaspoons finely chopped parsley	

1. Preheat the oven to 400° F.
2. Halve the zucchinis lengthwise.
3. Cut out the pulp and chop it coarsely.
4. Heat 1 tablespoon of the butter or margarine in a skillet and brown the onions in it.
5. Mix together the chopped pulp, onions, garlic, parsley, dill, salt, and bread crumbs.
6. Whisk the eggs and mix into the pulp mixture.
7. Scoop the mixture into the zucchini shells.
8. Dot with butter.
9. Place the zucchinis in a large baking dish and bake about 30 minutes, or until tops are lightly browned.

Yield: 6 servings

Turkish Baklava

Baklava is a wonderful stuffed pastry that can keep for two weeks in the refrigerator and up to three months in the freezer. For the paper-thin layers that characterize this magical dessert, we recommend using commercially prepared filo dough; it is a tricky, sticky process to make your own. Use your energies instead to perfect the tasty Turkish filling and sugary syrup that make this dessert memorable.

12 ounces pistachio nuts, shelled
   and chopped
12 ounces walnut meats, chopped
1¼ cups sugar
½ teaspoon cinnamon

2 sticks butter
1 pound filo dough
1 cup water
½ cup honey
1 teaspoon lemon juice

1. Preheat the oven to 325° F.
2. Mix the nuts with ¼ cup sugar and the cinnamon.
3. Melt the butter.
4. Open the package of filo dough, making sure to keep the layers moist by covering the stack with damp paper towels.
5. Butter a 9 × 13-inch baking pan.
6. Put two layers of dough at the bottom of the pan, brush with butter, and spread a thin layer of the nut mixture over it.
7. Repeat step 6 until you have seven layers, ending with a layer of dough on top.
8. Brush with butter.
9. With a sharp knife, cut the pastry down to the bottom in two-inch squares or diagonals.
10. Bake for 60–75 minutes, or until golden brown.
11. While it is cooking, combine the remaining sugar, water, honey, and lemon juice in a saucepan, bring to a boil and reduce heat, then simmer for 20 minutes.
12. Remove pastry from the oven and pour the syrup over it. Let cool for a full 2–3 hours before serving.

Yield: 10–12 servings

sometimes according to a straightforward system (summoning rows one through eight, for example), sometimes in a zany way, by calling up all left-handed people, or all congregants who own cats. Because of these amusing customs, children often find Simchat Torah a favorite service to attend. As they get older, it is often one of the first services they offer to help plan.

Simchat Torah Traditions

Amid the noise, commotion, parading, rejoicing, clapping, singing, and dancing of the festival, Simchat Torah represents an unbroken stream that connects generations of Jews to the Torah, a shared history, and common beliefs.

It is considered a mitzvah to participate in the Torah procession, and carrying the scrolls during the parade around the temple is an option available to all congregants at a Simchat Torah celebration. Holding the scrolls and feeling their weight often provides a visceral sense of the laws contained within them and can open doors to a deeper understanding of the meaning of our heritage.

In addition, rabbis have devised creative Simchat Torah practices to help congregants grasp the concept of the enormousness of the Torah. One way is to have the entire congregation line the aisle of the synagogue and hold out their hands. The rabbi then puts one end of the Torah scroll in the hands of the first person and proceeds to unroll it all the way down the aisle. It is an awesome experience to see the double pages roll out one after another until the entirety of the law is open for us to see.

Another moving practice is to have the congregation bunch together in the center of the room and for the rabbi to roll the open Torah around the outside of the circle, literally wrapping the congregants in the scroll of the law.

Many temples honor the Israeli tradition of holding folk dancing after services. Even though congregants have gathered to march behind the

Torah and dance, often they are just getting warmed up by the time the service is over. For them, and for those who enjoy sitting in their seats and watching the Torah procession pass by, a special evening of folk dancing adds to a night of fun and high spirits.

There are some people who believe that as we dance we let the Torah enter our bodies first, then make its way up to our heads. They believe that by dancing with the Torah, and expressing our joy through the movement of our feet—our lowest part—we take the Torah deeply into our lives.

Celebrating With Gusto

Often synagogues set up tables with candy and pastries to provide fuel for marchers and those who want to continue dancing as the Torah procession goes around the sanctuary the seven prescribed times. Sometimes there is even a schnapps table, with spirits and cordials to enliven congregants. If you want to contribute to these treats, consider offering to bake a cake in the shape of a Torah.

Festivities end at evening services after snacks and desserts have been enjoyed by all, but begin again the next morning. This is when two honored congregants are called to the bimah to read the last words of Deuteronomy and the first words of Genesis. With the opening verses immediately following the final verses, it seems as if the reading of the Torah never ends. In a way this is true, for Simchat Torah shows that the teaching, study, and practice of Torah are continuous.

While the Torah has been read for over three thousand years, many people feel it always has something new to say to them. Every time they read it, it seems different, perhaps because they have grown and changed and become able to see new meaning in the words. This sense of intellectual liveliness has powered Jewish life throughout the ages, placing our cycle of Torah reading in an eternal circle of study.

In the 1960s, Jews all over the world began to use Simchat Torah as a

Centerpiece Torah Mobile

Materials Needed

Scissors
Plastic drinking straw
2-inch wide gauze bandaging
Tape
Pipecleaner
Blue and white felt pieces
Glue
Puffy fabric paints
Thin cord or string, about 10 feet long
Wooden embroidery hoop
Utility or key ring

Directions

1. Cut off two 2-inch-long pieces from the straw.
2. Cut a 15-inch-long piece of gauze.
3. Lay the gauze out unrolled and tape a section of the straw to each end.
4. Roll the straws inward until they touch.
5. Tape the two gauze rolls together.
6. Cut off two 3-inch-long pieces from the pipecleaner.
7. Put the pipecleaner sections into the straws and loop the ends at the tops and bottoms to make the Torah handles.
8. Cut a piece of felt as wide as the gauze rolls are high and long enough to wrap around the rolls.
9. Cut little fringes on the bottom for decoration.

(continued on next page)

10. Wrap the felt around the rolls and glue it in place at the back.

11. With the puffy paints, draw a squiggly line around the top of the felt and another one on the bottom. With the other colors, draw a vine with flowers or a Star of David.

12. Repeat steps 1 through 11 until you have made three blue Torahs and three white ones.

13. Cut six 10-inch lengths of string, and loop one end of each through one set of Torah handles, then tie the other end onto the embroidery hoop, spaced evenly apart.

14. Cut four 12-inch lengths of string, and tie them to the embroidery hoop, evenly spaced around. Tie the tops together through the utility ring.

15. Hang the mobile from a chandelier over the dining room table as a mobile centerpiece, or give as a gift to a family with a new baby, to be hung as a mobile over the crib, out of the infant's reach, of course.

way to show solidarity with Soviet Jews who were forbidden to practice their religion. Many Soviet Jews insisted on amassing in force on this holiday to show the strength of their beliefs, streaming out onto Red Square, carrying flags with Jewish stars, and proclaiming their right to study Torah. In countries thousands of miles from the former Soviet Union, Jews still hold rallies dedicated to religious freedom for repressed Jews everywhere, and in synagogues dancers often dedicate one of the seven circles to them. Jewish spirituality is enhanced by these joyous outbursts, and the Israeli custom of dancing in the streets with the Torah has truly been spread all over the world.

The holiday is often a good time to begin attending weekly services or holding study sessions at home. Because the early parts of Genesis are the most familiar sections of the Bible, it is easiest to feel connected to the first few readings of the year. To make a lasting commitment to honor the holiday, consider attempting to read the Torah portion each week. Many people have been pleasantly surprised at how words written thousands of years ago can offer useful guidance in today's vastly different world.

PART II

Sweetness and Abundance

5

Hanukkah: Holiday of Lights

There was oil enough for the needs of a single day.
A miracle was wrought and it burned eight days.

—Talmud B, Shabbat 21b

A Holiday of Opposites

THE SIZZLE OF LATKES frying in the kitchen, the glow of the Hanukkah candles in the window, the sounds of children playing with dreidels—it's no wonder we look forward to this festive time all year. For in it we celebrate a fierce military victory, but we do so with jolly songs, gifts, family parties, games, and lights. Originally a minor holiday, it has now become a major celebration.

The holiday commemorates Judah Maccabee and the small band of heroic Jews who defeated an army of Syrian Greeks in 165 B.C.E. to regain their religious freedom. We celebrate for eight days, from the twenty-fifth of Kislev to the third day of Tevet in the Jewish calendar, in December in the secular year. The holiday always falls near the winter solstice, when the days are short and the warmth and light from the Hanukkah candles are most welcome.

In medieval Venice, Jews carried their Hanukkah menorahs on gondolas and made it a festive practice to visit Jewish homes, which were marked with outside lights, on the first night of the holiday. Today we put our menorahs in our windows to fulfill the mandate that we make known the miracle of Hanukkah.

In Israel the holiday primarily celebrates the military victory of the underdog Jews over a tyrannical superpower, and it has taken on an athletic theme in the form of the Maccabee Games, in which Jews from all over the world compete, just like in the Olympics.

While the Israelis have rediscovered Hanukkah as a holiday of national liberation, in America we celebrate not so much a victory as a miracle—the miracle of the oil and the achievement of religious freedom. Focusing primarily on the spiritual dimension of the holiday rather than the military aspect, we mark the event with family celebrations, special foods, and gifts.

The Origins of Hanukkah

Unlike most Jewish holidays, Hanukkah is not mentioned in the Bible. The historical events on which the holiday is based are recorded in a collection of books called the Apocrypha, which means "hidden writings" in Greek.

Most scholars say the story of the Maccabees is true but the miracle of the oil is most likely folklore, set down many years after the event in the Gemara, one of two sets of commentaries on the Bible that make up the Talmud.

Yet even if it is not true, and based on nothing more than Talmudic legend, our celebration of the miracle of the oil represents two things that are basic to our belief system: that Jews will prevail against all odds even if small in number, and that the light of Judaism burns brightly even in the darkest days.

The two Books of the Maccabees in the Apocrypha tell us that after three years of fighting, the Jews marched into Jerusalem and captured the sacred city. But what they found was that the Holy Temple had been defiled and desecrated, made into a shrine to Zeus with pigs sacrificed on the altar.

They set to work cleaning up the mess. After destroying the statues of the Greek gods that had been built in the Temple, the Maccabees washed the floors and scrubbed the walls and rebuilt the altar, but when they went to rekindle the eternal light, they found only one small vial of purified oil. Not knowing what else to do, they lit the lamp and set out to press and purify new oil.

It took eight days to complete the preparations, and to their amazement the oil that was sufficient to last only one night had lasted eight. In celebration, people lit lights in front of their homes and marked their victory with an eight-day festival called the Feast of Lights. This celebration has developed into our modern-day holiday of Hanukkah, which means, literally, "dedication."

Lighting the Menorah

Light is the preeminent theme of Hanukkah, so appropriate for the time of the winter solstice when the light is dim but about to increase. The central ritual is the lighting of the menorah, the Hebrew word for "candelabrum," which specifically means the eight-branched candle holder often called the hannukiyah.

In all, forty-four candles are burned during the eight days of the festival. Lit at nightfall, the candles should be tall enough to burn for at least half an hour. Hanukkah candles are small, but when they stand together they can light even the deepest darkness.

It is traditional on Hanukkah not to do any work by the light of the candles. The Talmud says the light is there to proclaim the miracle and should not be used for any other purpose. It is an old custom to place the menorah where it can be seen from outside the house.

The menorah originated as a religious symbol in biblical times, and today a menorah stands before the Knesset building in Israel. When our ancestors created the first hannukiyah, they didn't want to imitate the seven-branched menorah that stood in the Holy Temple in Jerusalem, so they made it with nine branches, including the shammash, the helper candle, by which all the wicks were lit.

Today the original seven-branched Temple menorah is pictured on the official emblem of the State of Israel and is also drawn in relief on the Arch of Titus in Rome. It is described in Exodus as being seven feet high and made of a solid slab of gold.

Modern Alternatives

The menorah as we know it was not used at Hanukkah until the Middle Ages. Before then it was considered sacrilegious to copy the menorah in the Temple. Instead, people used individual lamps, lining up one additional lamp each night until there were nine.

Today some people still use individual lights instead of a menorah. Some float flower-shaped candles in a bowl of water; others use tea lights in a dish of marbles. Still others line up groups of halved potatoes with a candle in each one.

You can make a free-standing oil lamp by filling a small bottle or bowl with salad oil and using a pipe cleaner or mop string for a wick. Judaica stores sell floating wicks for those who want the ready-made variety.

Most standard menorahs are made of metal, but variations exist in all kinds of materials, most often clay and wood. The only rule is that the shammash stand above, below, or slightly separate from the other candles, and that the flames of the candles not touch. Most common are menorahs shaped like trees, which are thought to combine earthly strength with heavenly light. In many families, tradition holds that every member have his or her own menorah to light in its entirety.

The Ritual and Its History

Candlelighting is a special ritual unto itself. On the first night, one candle is placed at the far right of the menorah and one in the place of the shammash. First you light the shammash, then the other candle. On the second night, put in two candles in addition to the shammash (placing them from right to left), then lighting them from left to right with the shammash, and so on each night until there are eight.

This is how we do it today, but for years arguments raged among the rabbis about the correct way to light the candles. Sammai, a first-century rabbi, wanted to light eight candles on the first night and go down to one on the last in order to symbolize the decreasing amount of oil. But Hillel, another first-century rabbi, and the one who reputedly won most disputes, argued that adding a candle each night represented the spread of faith and light and the continuation of the legacy of Hanukkah.

The Courage of the Maccabees

How Hanukkah came to be a holiday is best understood in its historical context, beginning with Alexander the Great, who ruled Palestine over 2,400 years ago with an open hand, allowing the Jews religious and cultural freedom in exchange for taxes.

While today we see religion as a personal choice, in those times it was part of the total economic and political structure of a country, and new rulers enforced new religious practices to ensure support of their government. In 164 B.C.E., the Alexandrian empire was breaking up, and Antiochus, a Syrian-Greek, came to power in the region. Unlike his predecessors, he prohibited the observance of Jewish law and customs, not specifically out of anti-Semitism, but to further unify his domain.

The Jews were harshly suppressed, often with brutal violence. Many assimilated with the Greeks and took Greek names, adopting their language and dress, but others banded together to fight the deadly threat to their way of life. One such family was the Hasmoneans, led by Mattathias and his five sons.

In the small town of Modin, Mattathias killed a group of Greek officials who tried to force the Jews to slaughter pigs on their altar, then fled to the hills and called on everyone who supported them to orchestrate a revolt, one that would become the first great war for religious freedom.

Mattathias died in the first year of the struggle, but his son Judah, a brilliant military strategist, took over. Judah was called Ha-makkabi, after the Hebrew word for "hammer," because his blow was so deadly. His guerilla band of farmers, shepherds, and grape growers were called the Maccabees. With only sticks and farm tools for weapons, Judah led them to victory over the well-trained Syrian army which, although equipped with swords, javelins, and even elephants, could not prevail over the wily tactics of the Maccabees.

Miracle of the Oil

It took two more years of battle until the Maccabees forced Antiochus to end the persecution of the Jews, but when they did so they reclaimed and rededicated the Temple in Jerusalem. It was the twenty-fifth of Kislev, and they proclaimed it the Feast of Dedication. Scholars believe their hope was that by having an eight-day festival, they would successfully compete with the pagan midwinter firelighting Saturnalia that was so popular at the time. It took twenty-five more years for political and religious freedom to finally be won, and at that time Simon, the last surviving son of Mattathias, was named high priest.

The miracle of the oil is not mentioned in either of the Books of the Maccabees, which celebrate the rededication of the Temple for eight days as a second Sukkot. The miracle story was first written about briefly in 100 C.E. by the Jewish historian Josephus, who speaks of a Festival of Lights, then again in 200 C.E., when the Talmudic rabbis wrote the Gemara, the second part of the Talmud. There they tell how the Maccabees, after cleaning and rededicating the Temple, relit the *ner tamid*, the eternal light. They attributed the eight days of Hanukkah to the miracle of the little bottle of oil, and gave instructions on how to light the menorah. Many historians believe this was an attempt to interpret the ongoing practice of firelighting in acceptable religious terms.

The miracle of the oil has become a worldwide metaphor for the miracle of Jewish survival. It is important to remember that at the time the story was written, the Temple had already been destroyed by the Romans and the Jews dispersed all over the world, an event that took place just two hundred years after the victory we celebrate at Hanukkah.

No matter what their original meaning, though, the Hanukkah lights always spread joy and hope. When we light them today we celebrate three miracles: that the little jar of oil lasted eight days, that the Maccabees won over the powerful forces of tyranny, and that the Jews have survived thousands of years of oppression in many different countries.

Hanukkah in Israel

Hanukkah is a national holiday in the State of Israel, and huge menorahs are placed on the tops of public buildings and in all the synagogues. The Israelis of today are sometimes called modern Maccabees, a group of fighters whose courage made possible the miracle of the Jewish state.

A special ceremony is held on the first night of Hanukkah, beginning in Modin, the hometown of the Maccabees, which is north of Jerusalem and about halfway to Jaffa. First the Israeli flag is raised, and then the people of the town light a bonfire. Torches are lit from the bonfire and carried by runners for several miles to another group of runners, who wait with unlit torches in their hands. When the fire arrives, they light their torches and run the next few miles to yet another group.

Finally the torch runners reach Jerusalem, where the fire is given to the president of Israel, who lights the candles on a giant menorah in the public square. From there the torch runners go to Mount Zion to illuminate a memorial service for those who died in the Holocaust. The runners then spread out, in relay fashion, and carry the light through the whole country, lighting candles in all the cities in Israel and connecting them all to Modin, where the revolt of the Maccabees and the story of Hanukkah began.

Sharing Hanukkah With Family and Friends

There are five traditions that are common to all Hanukkah festivities each year: we celebrate for eight days, we light candles in a menorah, we eat latkes or *sufganiyot* (jelly doughnuts) that have been fried in oil, we give small gifts, and we play the dreidel game.

There is no prescribed festive meal, as on Purim, but you can host one anyway. Many people do, bringing the various traditions together on one memorable holiday evening.

Because the holiday goes on for eight days, there is always a weekend on which to have your party. Some people choose the Saturday night or Sunday afternoon; others select the last night of Hanukkah, when all the candles are lit and the glow is the warmest and brightest. Some choose the sixth day, Rosh Hodesh, which is the new moon and the beginning of the month of Tevet, and this could make the right celebration day for you, too.

How to Host Your Celebration

If you are planning a formal celebration with written invitations, cutouts of dreidels or candles are a natural. If you want to do something a little fancier, you can buy plastic dreidels with removable tops and put a note inside each one explaining the details about the party.

For a centerpiece you can decorate a large box to look like a dreidel and fill it with small gifts wrapped in blue and white paper, taping mesh bags of Hanukkah gelt, real money, or chocolate coins to the top.

You can purchase or make all the gifts yourself, or ask guests to bring gifts to exchange from a grab bag. If you plan to put the gifts in the centerpiece box, restrict your guests' contributions to a specified size, and have them wrap the presents with ribbons attached to make it easier for children to pull them out.

If all your guests bring menorahs from home and light them together, you can set up a beautiful ceremony. Make sure you have enough candles, and buy them in a variety of colors, sizes, and textures, making a point to include those made in Israel. Then place the menorahs around the dining room table with each one at the appropriate guest's place, say the appropriate blessings (see appendix A) and light the shammashes together, then light the other candles in the correct order.

Many people then sing the classic Hanukkah song, "Ma'oz Tsur," also known as "Rock of Ages," a favorite holiday song composed in the thirteenth century. The most common version sung today was borrowed from German Protestant church music of the fifteenth century. If you copy song sheets ahead of time, you can give them out to your guests so they can all join in. In addition, some families read the beautiful thirtieth Psalm, called "A Song of David," and also "A Song of Dedication of the Temple."

Party Activities

Many kinds of Hanukkah crafts can enhance your party and involve children and adults working together in small, friendly groups. If you have a place in your house where guests can make a mess, they will certainly enjoy making a small menorah out of clay or commercial or homemade play dough.

A Menorah of Your Own

Materials Needed

A strip of wood or plastic, about 12 × 2 × 1 inches
Tempera paint
Craft glue
10 metal hardware nuts that candles will fit into snugly
9 Hanukkah candles

Directions

1. Paint the piece of wood one color or many, according to what looks best to you. You can stripe it, dot it, paint on little stars, or just make it one solid color.
2. With craft glue, paste on eight nuts evenly spaced for the candles, then glue two nuts together with one on top of the other and paste that down a little distance from the others to serve as the shammash.
3. Fit candles into the nuts and place in the window, ready to light on the first night of Hanukkah.

One easy way to do this is to roll two pieces of clay or dough about eight inches long and one inch in diameter. Place one on top of the other, curving them into a half-moon shape so they stay put. Then shape eight small figures and seat them on the clay "bench." Figures four and five should have their arms around each other's shoulders, and on those arms place a ninth seated figure, the shammash.

With a Hanukkah candle, make a hole about half an inch deep in the heads of all nine figures. Let the clay harden and then paint the new menorah.

If your guests would enjoy hearing a Hanukkah story while they are doing a craft project or just waiting for dessert, you will not find a more delightful tale than Isaac Bashevis Singer's "Zlateh the Goat," from his collection *Zlateh the Goat and Other Stories*. For a wonderful poetic treat, read aloud from Emma Lazarus's poem, "The Banner of the Jews," which extols the courage of the Maccabees in their fight for Jewish survival.

Love, Laughter, and Latkes

Traditional foods served on Hanukkah are related to the miracle of the oil and are generally fried in some type of vegetable oil. In Eastern Europe, where oil was scarce, *schmaltz*, or chicken fat was often substituted.

At Hanukkah parties today, the candlelighting is followed by a festive meal, which often features beef brisket (pot roast) as its main course, probably because it goes so well with potato latkes.

Latke is the Yiddish word for "pancake." The traditional potato latke originated at a time when the common foods were potatoes and bread; our ancestors came up with a way to cook the potatoes in oil to serve something different to celebrate the holiday and commemorate the cleansing and rededication of the temple.

Latkes can be made with white potatoes or sweet potatoes and come in many fry-and-try varieties: For example, you can add onions, apples, zucchini, carrots, parsnips, leeks, or beets. They can be served for breakfast, lunch, dinner, brunch, or as canapés at a cocktail party. You can eat them with white or brown sugar, pumpkin pie spices, apple sauce, sour cream, or just plain.

Potatoes were discovered in South America in the sixteenth century and brought to Western Europe from the New World. Before that, our ancestors ate cheese pancakes in honor of Judith, the brave woman who saved the lives of the Jews in the village of Bethulia in Palestine by feeding a dinner of cheese to a Syrian general named Holofernes.

As told in the Book of Judith, a volume in the Apocrypha written at about the same time as the Books of the Maccabees, Holofernes had made a plan to kill all the Jews in the village. Judith heard about it and went to his tent in secret with her picnic basket, ostensibly to offer him information and a good meal. She fed him so much cheese that he became thirsty. Knowing this would happen, she had brought plenty of wine, and gave him glass after glass until he grew drowsy and then fell asleep by her side.

While he slept, she cut off his head and, tucking it neatly in her empty picnic basket, left the tent. She displayed the head on a stake at the village gates. The sight so unnerved the Syrian soldiers that they fled from Bethulia in terror, never to be seen again.

For many years our ancestors ate cheesecakes in her honor, and today the potato latkes we eat can be served along with the story of her courage and cunning. Some people turn their Hanukkah celebration into a wine-and-cheese party in honor of her bravery.

Fine Food and Wine

Latke lore abounds among Jewish cooks in all lands and cultures. For the best latkes, many experienced latke-lovers like to use a heavy cast-iron skillet, which offers a very consistent frying temperature, but others swear by an electric frying pan. Most recommend using Idaho or russet potatoes, because they contain less moisture than boiling potatoes and will make your latkes crisper.

You can use any kind of oil to fry them in: corn, peanut, olive, canola, safflower, or any combination of these. If you are making a big batch, make sure to change the oil after every twenty-five or so latkes to keep it fresh. You will know the temperature of the oil is high enough when it starts to shimmer, but don't let it get so hot that it smokes. If the temperature is very high, the latkes will absorb very little fat.

You have many choices in making latkes, and the best thing to do is try the ones that sound appealing to you and see which ones work best in your kitchen. To mix up the batter, you can use matzo meal or flour as a thickener and either sauté the onions or leave them raw. You can use salt in the potato mixture or sprinkle it on the latke after it is cooked, and use either coarse or fine potato and onion shreds. You can also serve them fresh or freeze them.

But no matter how you prepare them, after they have been cooked, try draining them on brown paper bags from the grocery store. They stay crisper this way than if you use paper towels. Keep them uncovered in a 300-degree oven until ready to serve.

Another special treat for the holiday is edible Hanukkah gelt, special foods made to look like coins. You can experiment with zucchini rounds either fried, battered, or boiled, or melt chocolate drops into round forms and wrap in silver or gold foil when they have cooled.

In Israel, the most popular Hanukkah dessert is *sufganiyot*, a confection named after a spongy dough mentioned in the Talmud. *Sufganiyot* is the Hebrew word for jelly doughnuts. These filled treats are sold at bakeries and markets all over the country, but they are not hard to make in your own kitchen once you have had a few tries.

For a festive menu fit to commemorate a joyous holiday, try:

Yogurt and Barley Soup
Brisket à la Modin
Honeyed Parsnips
Potato Latkes With Pink Applesauce
Tomato and Cucumber Salad
Israeli Jelly Doughnuts

The best wines to serve to complement a dinner centered around a beef brisket entrée are red zinfandel, Cabernet Sauvignon, and an aromatic Pinot Noir.

Brisket à la Modin

This brisket is named for the town in which the Maccabees' revolt began, and it is a no-fail recipe for a tender, flavorful entrée. Brisket has become a favored Hanukkah dish not only because it brings out the special qualities of latkes, but also because it warms the body and creates a comfortable feeling of fullness. The brisket in this recipe needs nearly 4 hours of baking time, but it can be made ahead and reheated, which actually enhances the flavor.

1 brisket, first cut, about 3–4 pounds	2 carrots, sliced into circles
¼ teaspoon salt	3 stalks celery, chopped into chunks
⅛ teaspoon pepper	Two 8-ounce cans tomato sauce
½ teaspoon paprika	1 teaspoon thyme or rosemary

1. Preheat oven to 450° F.
2. Rub the meat on all sides with salt, pepper, and paprika.
3. Place the meat in a baking dish with the fat side up.
4. Place the vegetables around the meat and pour the two cans of tomato sauce over it.
5. Sprinkle the thyme or rosemary over the sauce.
6. Cover the baking dish tightly with aluminum foil.
7. Place a sheet of foil on the oven shelf to catch any drippings during the roasting process.
8. Put baking dish in oven and bake for 15 minutes at 450° F.
9. Reduce the heat to 325° F and bake 3½ hours or until tender.
10. Remove from oven and let stand about 15 minutes before carving, then slice the brisket diagonally against the grain.

Yield: 8–10 servings

Classic Potato Latkes

Legends abound about the secret of making outstanding latkes, but the truth is far simpler than the stories: use fresh potatoes, fry them as soon as they are grated to prevent them from turning brown, don't overuse the oil, and drain the pancakes well. It is important to remember that different oils impart specific flavors to the potatoes. Let your own good taste be your guide!

8 medium russet or Idaho potatoes	2 teaspoons salt
2 onions	½ teaspoon baking powder
3 tablespoons oil	2 cups applesauce
2 large eggs	8 ounces sour cream
½ cup matzo meal or ¼ cup flour	

1. Wash the potatoes thoroughly and peel them (or leave the skins on for a slightly earthier flavor), then grate them by hand on the coarsest side of the grater or in a food processor with a medium-blade grater.
2. Put the grated potatoes in a sieve and let sit for 5–10 minutes until the water starts to separate out, then squeeze out as much liquid as you can.
3. Turn the potatoes into a large bowl.
4. Peel and dice the onions, heat 1 tablespoon of the oil in a skillet, and lightly sauté the onions in the oil.
5. Beat the eggs.
6. Add the onions to the potato mixture, along with the eggs, the matzo meal, salt, and baking powder. Mix well.
7. Heat the skillet and cover the bottom with the remaining oil, then drop table-spoons of batter into it.
8. Flatten the batter with a spatula or cake knife.
9. Turn when edges start to brown.
10. When done, drain on paper towels or brown paper grocery bags.
11. Serve with applesauce and sour cream, and enhance the flavor with the glow of the Hanukkah candles.

Yield: about 18 latkes

Pink Applesauce

Nowhere is the simple earthy goodness of apples quite as satisfying as when it is served with warm, crisp potato latkes, and nothing says Hanukkah quite so clearly. Some cooks prefer Golden Delicious, others use only Granny Smiths or Russets. You can experiment with single types or mix and match for a pleasing variety of flavors and textures.

7 to 8 medium apples	½ teaspoon vanilla
½ cup water	¼ cup honey
2 tablespoons lemon juice	1 teaspoon red food coloring
2 tablespoons orange juice	

1. Peel, core, and slice the apples and place them in a saucepan.
2. Add the water, lemon juice, orange juice, and vanilla.
3. Cover and bring to a boil. Cook over low heat until soft, about 25 minutes, adding more water if needed.
4. Mix in the honey.
5. Stir in the food coloring, which will turn the applesauce an appetizing pink.
6. To make the texture finer when cooking is done, put the mixture in a food processor and purée, or serve as is.

Yield: 1 quart, or 6–8 servings

Israeli Jelly Doughnuts

These fancy jelly doughnuts, called *sufganiyot* in Israel, are a special treat served at Hanukkah to honor the miracle of the oil. They can be complicated to make, but even novice cooks will master the technique after a couple of tries if someone at home volunteers to eat up the mistakes! Try a variety of jams and jellies for the filling.

2 packages active dry yeast	½ cup butter
3½ cups flour	2 large eggs
¼ cup granulated sugar	1 large jar raspberry jam
½ cup warm water	Oil for frying
½ cup warm milk	Powdered sugar
½ teaspoon salt	

1. Dissolve the yeast in warm water.
2. In a large bowl, mix together half the flour, the sugar, yeast, water, milk, and salt.
3. Stir in the butter and add the eggs.
4. With an electric beater, mix the batter until it is smooth.
5. Add the remaining flour and knead by hand.
6. Cover the bowl with a dish towel and let the dough rise in a warm place for about an hour, until doubled in bulk.
7. Knead the dough for a minute or two on a lightly floured surface.
8. Let it rest for about 10 minutes, then roll it out to ½-inch thickness on a floured surface.
9. Use a cookie cutter or the top of a jar with a 2-inch diameter to cut out circles.
10. Place a tablespoon of jam on every other circle and cover with another circle of dough, making sure to pinch the sides together all the way around.
11. Cover with a dish towel and let rise for about one hour, until doubled in size.
12. Pour about 2 inches of oil into a heavy skillet and heat it until it shimmers.
13. Gently place a few of the doughnuts into the oil and fry them, turning once, about 1–2 minutes per side.
14. When done, remove from skillet and drain on paper towel, then sprinkle generously with powdered sugar.

Yield: about 18 doughnuts

The Dreidel Game

Brightening the winter nights as much as the lights from the menorah are the games played during the Hanukkah festivities. Because you can't work by the light of the candles, adults as well as children play traditional games like chess, cards, riddle and puzzle games, and dominoes. But of all of them, the most beloved is dreidel, a game of chance based on an old German betting game called Trendle.

The dreidel game has been part of Hanukkah celebrations since the Middle Ages and is played with a spinning top that is inscribed on each of its four sides with one of the Hebrew letters *nun, gimmel, hay,* or *shin.* The letters stand for Yiddish words that direct the play: *nun* for *nichts,* or nothing; *gimmel* for *ganz,* or all; *hay* for *halb,* or half; *shin* for *shtell,* or put in.

Children take turns using their Hanukkah gelt—or nuts, raisins, pennies, or marbles—to place bets on which side of the spinning dreidel will face up when it falls. If it is *nun,* it means nothing happens; *gimmel* means the player gets the whole pot; *hay* means the player gets half the pot; and *shin* means the player puts in the entire bet. During Hanukkah, the rabbis permit games of chance that are not allowed at any other time of year, just as on Purim it is considered acceptable to drink alcohol, when it is discouraged the rest of the year.

The letters on the four sides are believed to be an anagram for a Hebrew saying: *Nes gadol hayah sham,* meaning "A great miracle happened there." Since the rebirth of the State of Israel, Hebrew dreidels, called *sivivon,* have seen the letter shin replaced with the letter *pay,* with the sentence reading, *Nes gadol hayah po,* meaning "A great miracle happened here."

Many people like alluding to the holiday this way, feeling it invests an ordinary game with Jewish values. Other games can be made more Hanukkah-friendly by adding Jewish themes; for example, chess can be played with one team being the Maccabees, the other the Syrians, or in

Simple Paper Dreidel

Materials Needed

Scissors
Cardboard egg carton
Markers
A short sharpened pencil, about 4 inches long

Directions

1. Cut out the cup for one egg, trimming neatly around the edges.
2. Using the markers, write the four Hebrew letters, *nun, gimmel, hay,* and *shin* around the sides of the cup.
3. With the point of the pencil, push down through the center of the cup. Let the point protrude about ½ inch.
4. Grasp the pencil and spin the top.
5. To make several dreidels, so you can play several games at once, repeat steps 1 through 4. Each egg carton will make twelve dreidels, of course!

Scrabble ten extra points can be awarded for every word that relates to Judaism.

Those who want their children to play dreidel without gambling can have them compete to see who can spin the dreidel longest, who can spin it upside-down, whose spinning dreidel can knock down someone else's, or who can spin the most at once of a handful of dreidels.

There is an old legend about the dreidel that tells how at the time of the Maccabees, when Jews were not allowed to study Torah, groups of people who knew portions of it by heart would meet to teach one another. They always brought along dreidels and put them on the table. If they heard soldiers approaching, they would quickly spin the dreidels so they would not be caught studying.

Gifts on Hanukkah

The modern tradition of exchanging gifts on Hanukkah grew out of the old practice of giving Hanukkah gelt. Gifts are largely an American invention of the twentieth century, most likely begun because of the holiday's tendency to coincide with Christmas. The giving of Hanukkah gelt, however, goes back to the time of the Maccabees, who celebrated their newly regained independence as a nation by minting coins.

When the Maccabees returned in triumph to Jerusalem, they achieved more than religious freedom; they gained political autonomy, too. At the time, only a free people had the right to strike their own coins, and the act symbolized in a very concrete way the freedom they had won. To honor the full meaning of the holiday, our ancestors began giving coins to schoolteachers and the poor on Hanukkah, and eventually the practice carried over to their children.

Today, some families give their children small gifts every night for the eight nights of Hanukkah. Truly, though, gifts are not an important part of the holiday. Hanukkah emphasizes enduring religious and ethical values, and its most important message is the translation of its name: "dedication."

Simchat Torah

Simchat Torah, literally "rejoicing with the Torah," marks the end of the annual cycle of the reading of the Torah, and the beginning of its reading too. The Torah scroll is rewound, and the last verses of Deuteronomy and the first ones in Genesis are read.

It is traditional at services to carry the Torah around the sanctuary and dance with it, passing it from one congregant to another to share the excitement of holding the sacred scrolls of Jewish teaching in one's arms. Often children lead the procession, waving flags and singing joyful songs. (PHOTO COURTESY OF THE AUTHOR)

Hanukkah

On Hanukkah we light the menorah, a candelabrum with eight branches and a shamash, the worker candle used to light the others. Every night of the eight-day holiday we add one more candle, until the menorah is ablaze with light, commemorating the oil that lasted eight days when it was meant to last only one.

Along with eating potato latkes, one of the most popular activities of the Hanukkah holiday is playing the dreidel game, a game of chance played since the Middle Ages. Because you can't work by the light of the candles, adults as well as children enjoy playing games each night.

Hanukkah is celebrated at the darkest time of winter. Candles are lit to warm the spirit, honor the miracle of the oil, and celebrate the victory of the Maccabees, the small band of farmers who crushed the army of Syrians that defiled their temple and tried to force them to give up Judaism.

Purim

One thing that makes Purim fun is dressing up and being someone else. Both children and adults get into the spirit of the holiday by donning costumes and pretending to be Esther (like this little girl), Mordechai, Vashti, King Ahasuerus, even Haman. Some act out parts in Purim spiels; others take part in festive costume parties and parades.

The story of Purim comes to life in the kitchen through the baking of hamantaschen, the comic cookie-rendering of the three-cornered hat of the villainous Haman. The sweet treats are traditionally filled with jam, dates, raisins, fruit, or poppyseeds.

Your Own Hanukkah Gift Paper

Materials Needed

    Scissors
    Sponges
    Tempera paints
    Plastic or ceramic bowls
    Pitcher of cold water
    Several large sheets of white paper, 11 × 17-inch sheets from a stationery store, or rolls of butcher paper or newsprint

Directions

1. Cut the sponges into the shapes of Jewish symbols, such as the Star of David, a menorah, the Torah, and the Tablets of the Law.
2. Pour about ¼ inch of paint into a bowl and add 3 tablespoons of cold water. Mix well.
3. Lay out the paper, dip the sponge into the thinned paint and dab it on the paper, either in regular or random patterns. Use a different sponge for another color or another shape.
4. Let the paper dry, cut it to match the size of the gift you want to wrap, and fold the paper neatly around the box.
5. Secure with tape and decorate with a pretty bow.

Just as the Maccabees fought to keep Judaism alive, the holiday tells us that our mission is to strengthen our dedication to Judaism and our people.

If you plan to give your children gifts, you might consider asking that they donate one old toy to charity for each new one received. Another way to keep the spiritual dimension alive is to suggest that some of the Hanukkah gelt be given as *tzedakah*. In addition, one Hanukkah gift for each child might be something of Jewish significance: a book of Jewish history, a personal menorah, or a mezuzzah for the doorway of the child's room.

6

Tu b'Shevat: The New Year of Trees

*As the days of a tree, so shall be
the days of my people.*

—Isaiah 65:22

Warmth in the Heart of Winter

JUST WHEN WE THINK we can't stand one more snowy day—usually by late January or early February each year—a festive holiday comes around to take us out of doors, reconnect us with the intricate beauty of nature, and show us the miracle of rebirth.

In Israel at this time of year, the month of Shevat, most of the winter rains have already fallen, and the almond trees are beginning to show their first pink and white blooms. Deep within the buds, the fruits of the trees are starting to form. It is the beginning of spring in the Holy Land, time to celebrate the reawakening of the land from the grip of winter and the blossoming of meadows, orchards, and vineyards.

The holiday of Tu b'Shevat is sometimes called the New Year of Trees or the Holiday of Fruits. It falls under a full moon on the fifteenth day of Shevat, the month of hope. Tu b'Shevat derives its name from the number fifteen. Every letter in Hebrew has a numerical value, and *tet* is nine and *vav* is six, adding up to fifteen. *Tu* is spelled in Hebrew with the letters *tet* and *vav*. Thus we have the name Tu b'Shevat, to signify the holiday that is celebrated on the fifteenth of Shevat.

A Wine and Fruit Celebration

Because it is a holiday without many prescribed observances, those who celebrate Tu b'Shevat do so by honoring the customs that have grown up around it. The holiday is agricultural in origin, and is celebrated today by the eating of fruits and nuts grown in Israel. Some of the ancients considered it a nature festival, combining the elements of tree worship and the celebration of the midwinter full moon. It is one of the few Jewish holidays that is not connected to a historical event. Instead of honoring the past, it celebrates our hope for the future: to make the world a better place by creating more greenery and good health.

Since the time the Holy Temple in Jerusalem was destroyed and Jews went into exile all over the world, we have sought ways to reconnect with Israel through the cycle of seasons. On Tu b'Shevat this takes the form of a seder, in which alternating samplings of wine and fruit are interspersed with selected readings.

On the eve of Tu b'Shevat, it is customary to gather friends and family for a sit-down dinner, a friendly lunch, or a casual sit-on-the-floor event. You can lead the service yourself or pass around sheets of blessings, stories, and poems or a makeshift Haggadah, asking your guests to take turns reading. In this way the holiday is much like Passover, but in another way it resembles Rosh Hashanah. Just as we hope our names will be inscribed in the Book of Life at the New Year, our ancestors believed that on Tu b'Shevat God decides how bountiful the fruits on each tree will be in the coming year.

The Roots of the Holiday

Tu b'Shevat is not mentioned in the Torah, but scholars believe it marked the beginning of spring in Palestine. On that day, two things happened: Tithe payments were due to the Temple in Jerusalem, and trees were planted.

At the time of the Second Temple, one-tenth of every farmer's income was given in tithes to support both the priests and the poor. This included a one-tenth payment on fruit. The payment had to come from this year's fruit crop; thus there had to be a way to define a tax year and create an orderly line between the end of the fruit crop of the previous year and the beginning of the new one. Tu b'Shevat was devised to demarcate that line. Each year on Tu b'Shevat, each tree got one year older; hence it became the birthday of trees.

After the destruction of the Temple and the beginning of the Diaspora, Jewish leaders felt it necessary to find a way to maintain the significance of the holiday, since farmers could no longer bring tithes to the Temple. Thus they instructed the people to eat a variety of fruits and nuts from Palestine, in hopes of creating a physical association with the land and a spiritual connection with Israel.

This became the basis for the Tu b'Shevat seder. On the evening before the holiday, Jews would gather together for a fifteen-course meal, each course presenting one fruit or nut dish from the Holy Land. Between courses they would read from an anthology called Peri Etz Hadar, or Fruit of the Goodly Tree, a compilation of passages on trees that was drawn from the Bible, the Talmud, and the mysterious Zohar.

A Modern Tu b'Shevat

One hundred years ago, when Jews began returning to Israel to resettle the land, what they found was mostly swamp and desert, with few trees. Since then, millions of saplings have been planted to reclaim the land and make it fertile. Many were planted on Tu b'Shevat or paid for by donations to the Jewish National Fund from Jews throughout the world in honor of the holiday.

These activities have given the holiday new meaning. Today many people call it the Jewish Arbor Day or the Jewish Earth Day and think of it primarily as a way to rebuild the land of Israel. It is also a time to direct our attention to the earth and how we treat nature.

Tu b'Shevat is one of four new years' celebrations in the Jewish tradition, and each makes us focus on a different aspect of our lives. The first day of Nisan, which falls in March or early April, is the new year for kings, and is a day when they are supposed to take stock of their policies and evaluate how they are ruling. The first day of Elul, generally in August, is the new year for tithing and is ancient Israel's tax day. The first day of Tishri, in September or early October, is Rosh Hashanah, when we think deeply about our lives and our relationships. And the fifteenth day of Shevat, in late January or early February, is the birthday of trees, when we take stock of our relationship with the environment.

Spring in Israel

At Tu b'Shevat, as warmth comes softly and slowly back to the Holy Land, life is reasserting itself under the ground in the roots of the trees and within our sight on their branches. The land is shaking off winter and nurturing the roots of trees, our symbols of strength and beauty, birth and life.

In Israel, trees are particularly important because they are closely related to the conquest of the desert, the draining of the marshes, and the enrichment of the soil. They symbolize the restoration of the land and the creation of the ecological web of seeds, ground water, insects, and small animals that make possible crops of all kinds. By planting trees, the Holy Land is in our thoughts and hearts, even if it is not under our feet.

For some, celebrating trees is an acknowledgment of God's presence in all of nature, as the day on which the holiday falls is the time in Israel when the sap begins to rise and the new fruit begins its cycle of nourishment and growth.

In the Jewish tradition, honoring trees celebrates the continuity of life. A Talmudic scholar once said that if you are holding a sapling and the arrival of the Messiah is announced, you should first plant the tree and then go and greet him. This is because no matter how deep our longing for the Messiah may be, trees are real and need to be nurtured and tended even before our dreams and our yearnings.

Jews have always considered trees, and fruit trees in particular, a kindness from God; they give us food, graceful branches, healthful shade, beautiful fragrance, and life-giving oxygen. Jewish scholars have written about the spiritual marriage between the tenacious strength of the Jewish people and the timeless beauty of the tree. While people need trees, trees need strong roots in the ground, and all of us need to be rooted in the strength, beauty, and wisdom of the Jewish tradition.

Understanding the Value of Trees

In the Bible, we are told that the Tree of Life stands in the middle of the Garden of Eden and that Adam and Eve were banished because they ate from the Tree of Knowledge. Our tradition tells us that that tree and the Tree of Life remain standing in Paradise, though they are guarded by angels so that humans can never reenter and gain immortality. Instead, the Torah itself is seen as the Tree of Life, a growing and abundant source of spiritual sustenance to our people. And as we are told in the Proverbs, it offers "length of days for those who hold to it."

Trees have always been a special symbol for Jews, embodying the great value our tradition puts on all plant and animal life and the reverence and respect Judaism holds for the natural world. The Bible commands Jewish soldiers who conquer a city not to destroy the trees. From that statement in Deuteronomy, rabbis created a wide range of restrictions against waste or defilement of nature. Scholars say that if you chop down a fruit-bearing tree, its cry goes forth from one end of the world to the other.

How to Celebrate the Holiday

Tu b'Shevat is an official national holiday in Israel, complete with elaborate parades, singing, merrymaking, and festivals surrounding the planting of trees.

In ancient times, marriage trees were planted on Tu b'Shevat. It was customary for parents to plant special seedlings on that day for babies born during the previous year. They planted cypress trees for girls and cedars for boys. When the children grew up and got married, branches from the trees were cut off and used to build the *chupah*, the marriage canopy.

For Jews throughout the world today, Tu b'Shevat means a day of honoring trees in a variety of ways. Some people follow the old custom of giving ninety-one cents to charities of their choosing. In Jewish numerology, ninety-one is the numerical equivalent for the Hebrew word *ilan*, meaning tree. An excellent choice would be the Jewish National Fund, an organization established in 1901 as the land-purchasing agency of the Zionist movement, which has dedicated itself to restoring the land. In 1949, on the first Tu b'Shevat after the creation of the Jewish State, thousands gathered to plant the Forest of the Martyrs, a huge grove that will one day contain six million trees, one for each Jew killed in the Holocaust.

From the quote in Deuteronomy about war and the protection of trees, Jews have created an ethic of protecting the whole of nature, issuing a "Do Not Destroy" warning to the world. On this holiday, many use the day to commemorate our protection of the natural world and to renew our vow to do so. As trees and other plants are struggling to come

A Parsley Planter

Materials Needed

Empty cereal or cracker box
Scissors
2 sheets of construction paper
Tape
Aluminum foil
Potting soil
One package of parsley seeds
40-inch length of ribbon

Directions

1. Lay the box on its side and cut off the top, leaving a wide opening.
2. Cover the outside of the box with construction paper, turning the edges under neatly and taping them down.
3. Line the inside of the box neatly with aluminum foil.
4. Fill the box with potting soil or dirt from the garden. Dampen it with a small amount of water.
5. Plant the parsley seeds about ¼ inch down into the soil.
6. Sprinkle gently with water.
7. Tie the ribbon around the box for decoration and knot firmly, then tie a bow.
8. Place the box in a sunny spot and water every other day. Your parsley should sprout in a week and be fully grown in time for Passover. Snip off the individual parsley plants and use them to dip in salt water at your seder.

back to life after the long icy winter, the holiday offers us the perfect time to commit ourselves to nurturing the environment.

Ancient Jews put a ring of raisins and other sweet fruits around trees and prayed for an abundant fruit season and the birth of many children. Children today could plant a sapling in their own backyard or sprout beans or alfalfa in a dish. In Hebrew school, many children purchase leaf stickers and paste them on a picture of a tree. When the branches are filled, the money is sent to Israel in the child's name and a tree is planted.

More Tu b'Shevat Commemorations

Many people take Tu b'Shevat as a day to review their recycling habits and look for ways to improve them, reconsidering our connection to the earth and our obligation to take care of it. In this way, the Jewish tradition of *tikkun olam*, repairing the world, can be thought of in an ecological as well as a spiritual sense.

Some synagogues arrange for their Hebrew school children to plant trees specifically in memory of loved ones. This not only helps the environment but can also be a healing act to help children cope with the loss of a dear friend or relative. This can be done at home, too, in the yard or even in a window box or planter on a terrace. A small plaque can be attached to the sapling so the person will be honored for years to come.

This is a good time of year to begin to cultivate miniature fruit trees indoors. You can grow these small orange or fig trees with a minimum of care, as long as you keep them warm through the icy winter months. Fig trees can be cultivated indoors in large pots and taken out into the sun in the spring, after all danger of frost is past. They look beautiful on a patio or lining the front walk when the weather is fine and can winter in a heated garage or even a basement if artificial lights are used. If you have never tasted a freshly picked fig, try one at your local garden center this summer.

Next year at Sukkot, consider saving your *etrog* in the freezer. About a week before Tu b'Shevat, thaw it out, cut out the seed, and put it in a damp paper towel. It will sprout in four to five days, and then you can plant it. This way you link the two holidays and perhaps will be able to cultivate an *etrog* tree that will serve you well for future Sukkot festivities.

Another way to honor Tu b'Shevat is to plan a recycling project, especially one using paper, which, of course, comes from trees. Bring neighbors together to take unwanted cartons and packing materials to a recycling plant, arrange for the local scout troop to visit when the plant is operating, or set up boxes for coworkers to collect white paper refuse for recycling.

The Story of the Seder

The word *seder* means "order," and, just as on Passover, there is a definite order of service for a Tu b'Shevat celebration. The seder became popular in the sixteenth century in Israel, when a group of Jewish mystics first took some of the symbols associated with the Passover seder and adapted them to this holiday. For example, in the Tu b'Shevat seder, we say blessings over four cups of wine, with the wine changing each time from white to pink to rose to red, representing the changing seasons. We eat fifteen varieties of fruits and nuts—fifteen for the name of the holiday— particularly figs, pomegranates, dates, and olives. Between the courses, we read poems, prayers, stories, and biblical passages relating to trees and fruits.

But beyond these general guidelines lies a lot of room for creativity. Because this is a relatively minor holiday, new rituals and customs are being established every year. The fact that you can bring your own ideas into the seder makes this an especially rewarding holiday to celebrate.

Planning Your Celebration

You can invite family and friends to your own special brand of Tu b'Shevat seder, held on the eve of the holiday or on the day itself, either at

Candy Garden

Materials Needed

Chocolate wafer cookies
Large bowl
Chocolate and butterscotch or vanilla puddings
Plastic drinking straws
Almonds or hazelnuts
Gummy worms
Chocolate covered raisins
Thin pretzel sticks

Directions

1. Make "soil" by crushing the cookies and swirling them together in the bowl with chocolate pudding and butterscotch or vanilla pudding, using the straws as utensils.
2. Plant almonds or hazelnut "seeds" in the middle of the soil.
3. Add some worms.
4. Around the edges of the bowl, plant the chocolate covered raisins.
5. Build little fences around the planted areas with pretzel sticks.
6. Talk about the holiday and the wonderful trees that are planted in Israel every year on Tu b'Shevat. Explain about reclaiming the land from swamps and deserts and how every saplings starts with a seed.
7. Eat the candy garden—"seeds," worms, soil, and all!

lunchtime, in the early afternoon, or at night. You can serve a meal and hold a seder, or just hold the seder. It's your choice.

For invitations, you might send a handwritten note and staple a seed packet to it. Easily mailed in a lightly padded mailer, or with a piece of cardboard inserted in the envelope, the invitation will let your guests know they are in for a spring festival in the middle of winter.

Set the table with green paper plates and multicolored napkins with fruit or flower patterns. Use potted plants for a centerpiece, one small one for each guest to take home, or two or three larger ones grouped in the center.

Another centerpiece idea is to make a small tree out of branches by tying on tiny lady apples, little seckel pears, and strawberries with silver and gold strings. If you can hot-glue some silky leaves near the fruit stems and stand the branch in a container filled with sand, you will have a lovely focus for your table.

For a sit-down dinner, place four cups of wine at each place with three small dishes containing pieces of the fruits to be used in the seder. You might want to use a plain white paper tablecloth and write the order of service on it instead of creating formal Haggadahs.

For a casual afternoon seder, one without a meal, make trays of cut-up fruit so people can pass them around the table and take small pieces for each course. On another tray, set out small paper cups of wine to pass around also.

Music for your party could be folk songs such as "Sung by the Pomegranate Tree," by Hillel and Aviva, or the orchestral piece created by Aaron Copland called "In the Beginning." If you like the rich sound of cantorial music, try "Cantorial Masterpieces" sung by Maurice Gauchoff.

How to Lead the Seder

To begin, introduce the holiday to your guests, explaining its purpose and telling why the seder is held. Some rabbis like to say the purpose of the ritual is to increase the flow of God's blessings into the world, and that by eating the fruits we help bring fruit into our world from the divine Tree of Life. Then you might read this passage from Genesis 1:11: "And God said, let the earth put forth grass, herb-yielding seed, and fruit trees bearing fruit after its own kind, wherein is the seed thereof on the earth."

Now raise the first cup of wine, which is white to symbolize winter, and say the traditional blessing over the wine. (All blessings are included in appendix A.) Drink the wine, and have your guests do so, too, then hold up the plate of first fruits, and explain that they represent the simple physical being, a body covering a soul, and also the protection given to us by the earth. They are all fruits with a shell—carob, walnuts, coconuts, almonds, pomegranates, grapefruit, and pineapple—hard on the outside and soft on the inside. The plate, prepared in advance, should contain any five of these.

Now recite the blessing for fruit and distribute the fruit among your guests. This format, with these blessings, is repeated four times, with different wine and fruits each time. Some people also add the Shehecheyanu (see appendix A) each time a new fruit is tasted.

Now hold up the second cup of wine, which is mostly white, with a little red mixed in, or a golden sherry or light Concord wine, to symbolize the sap rising in the tree. Explain why it is pink in color, and then pass around samples of the second category of fruits. These are fruits that have an inedible pit, representing a higher level of spirituality, where the heart is inaccessible or protected. They include dates, apricots, olives, plums, and peaches.

The third cup of wine symbolizes the change of the seasons and is deep pink for the blossoms that are just beginning to sprout on branches. You can use a rosé or a white wine with a little more red mixed into it. The fruits for this third part are soft throughout and completely edible, including figs, grapes, raisins, pears, apples, and cranberries, symbolizing a purer form of spirituality, one that is totally accessible to us.

For the fourth and final part of the seder, drink a cup of red wine to symbolize the concept of fire and the idea that the spark of God resides in all living things. The fourth fruit has a tough skin on the outside but sweet fruit inside. You might use bananas, mangos, avocados, or the desert pear, known as the *sabra*, for which native Israelis are named. These represent our study of Torah and how we are continually nourished by its fruits.

Especially for Children

If kids are part of the group, prepare cups of juice for them to take the place of the wine. A way to do this is to serve apple for the first part, orange for the second, followed by cranberry and then grape. This gives children something different for each course, just like the grown-ups, and also takes them from light to dark to darker as the seder progresses.

Kids love finger food and will enjoy the cut-up pieces of fruit throughout the seder. For an extra treat, you might want to serve carob ice cream for dessert. This is easily made from a chocolate ice cream recipe, substituting carob for cocoa in equal amounts. For a quick carob ice cream treat, soften a cup of vanilla ice cream and stir in one tablespoon of carob.

Readings for the Haggadah

In addition to saying the blessings for the wine and fruit at the beginning of each of the four parts of the seder, extra readings interspersed throughout the seder add richness and texture to the event.

If you want to use biblical passages, consider reading from Deuteronomy 8:7–10 for the first cup of wine, as this passage talks of a land of fig trees, pomegranates, and olives. For the second cup, Deuteronomy 28:3–6 is a good choice, with passages about the fruit of the land. The third cup calls for Genesis 2:7, which tells of God's creation of human beings, and for the fourth consider Exodus 3:2, in which an angel appears as a flame of fire.

In addition, Ezekiel 17 tells about the spreading vines in the Holy Land, symbolizing the people of Israel. Leviticus 26:3–13 talks about the divine promise of agricultural abundance for those who keep the commandments, and Psalms 65:10–14 describe the blooming of trees in spring.

You could also borrow books from the library on the folklore of plants and fruits and integrate some scientific readings into the seder. Or find a recording of Judy Collins singing "Turn, Turn, Turn," written from Ecclesiastes 3:1–8, with the famous first line, "For everything there is a season."

Joyce Kilmer's poem "Trees" is most appropriate and easily found in many anthologies, as is e. e. cummings's, "i thank God for most this amazing day." For more poetry, see the works of modern Hebrew poets like Saul Tchernichowsky. In addition, check with the National Jewish Fund to obtain a copy of their Planter's Prayer, available in a beautiful English translation.

If you want to create a formal Haggadah for your guests to follow, collect the prayers and readings and draw some pictures to liven up the pages, or borrow artwork from seed catalogs or gardening books. You might even use an encyclopedia and create a question-and-answer game about trees and fruits.

What to Serve for Tu b'Shevat

At Passover, the foods on the table serve as symbols and teaching tools, and the real eating comes after the reading is done, while on Tu b'Shevat, the symbols and the food are one and the same. In addition to the fruit and wine, however, you will probably want to serve a holiday dinner. Usually that is done after the seder is over, but you could serve a formal lunch and then hold the seder later in the afternoon.

It is customary to serve food containing fruit, nuts, wheat, or barley to commemorate the holiday. Your guests will enjoy a challah made with nuts and raisins, and also fruitcake for dessert. Pastries similar to those served on Purim are traditional for Tu b'Shevat, with baked dough pockets filled with fruit. If you made jam on Sukkot from the *etrogs* you used for the celebration, you can serve it at this holiday meal.

Here is a sample menu for a formal lunch or dinner party:

Orange-Almond Muffins
Dried Fruit Noodle Casserole
Lemon Chicken Schnitzel
Stewed Cinnamon Fruits With Port Wine
Poached Prunes With Pecans
Fancy Fig Squares

If you want an uncomplicated party, serve food that is easy to eat on your lap and doesn't require cutting with a knife. Try this menu:

Avocado Salsa
Black Bean Chili
Tuna Wraps
Tabbouleh
Apricot Strudel
Prunes Stuffed With Almonds

A favorite snack for Tu b'Shevat, called *schnecken*, is made of dried fruit and nut morsels that you can munch while you are waiting for the seder to begin, offer as finger food when guests first arrive, or serve as an extra dessert.

Orange-Almond Muffins

What better way to enjoy the fruits and nuts of Tu b'Shevat than by combining two popular varieties in a warm, fluffy muffin? Shavings from the fragrant orange peel are sure to give these popular muffins a special appeal, while the slivered almonds provide crunch and texture. You can make the batter the day before, refrigerate overnight, and bake just before guests arrive.

2 cups flour	½ cup sugar
½ teaspoon salt	½ stick butter
1 tablespoon baking powder	1 teaspoon vanilla
2 extra-large eggs	Peel of 1 small navel orange
1 cup whole milk	½ cup slivered or sliced almonds

1. Preheat oven to 400° F.
2. Grease a standard 12-muffin pan or a 48 mini-muffin pan, or line either with paper baking cups.
3. Whisk four, salt, and baking powder together in a large bowl.
4. In a separate bowl, mix the eggs, milk, sugar, butter, and vanilla.
5. Grate in about 1 teaspoon of orange peel and add slivered almonds. Stir well.
6. Combine ingredients of both bowls into the larger one.
7. Spoon the batter into the muffin cups.
8. Bake 12–15 minutes.
9. Cool on a rack and serve immediately.

Yield: 12 regular-size or 48 miniature muffins

Lemon Chicken Schnitzel

This quick and easy main course combines two foods that are very popular in Israel: chicken and lemons. As a reminder of the wonderful citrus crop grown there today, lemons provide a tasty and zesty flavoring to this traditional chicken cutlet dish.

3 pounds chicken cutlets, thinly sliced	¼ cup bread crumbs
1 large egg	¼ cup matzoh meal
1 teaspoon water	3 tablespoons margarine
	1 large lemon

1. Trim the cutlets, removing any fat.
2. Beat the egg, adding a teaspoon of water to thin it.
3. Mix together the bread crumbs and matzoh meal.
4. Melt the margarine in a frying pan.
5. Slice the lemon.
6. Dip each chicken cutlet in the egg, then dredge through the bread crumb mixture.
7. Heat the margarine in the skillet, add the cutlets, and sauté for one minute on high flame.
8. Turn the cutlets over, cook for one minute on high flame, then reduce to medium flame.
9. Scatter lemon slices over cutlets and push down slightly on lemons with a fork to release some of the juice.
10. Cook on low heat, covered, 8–10 minutes.

Yield: 6–8 servings

Fancy Fig Squares

Tasty figs are a well-loved dried fruit for a Tu b'Shevat celebration because they are mentioned in the Bible on many occasions and are grown widely in modern Israel. Their sweetness and chewiness make them ideal for dessert squares, layered between hearty crusts. They can be prepared well ahead of your party and frozen without losing any of their flavor.

8 ounces chopped figs	2 cups flour
½ cup apple juice	½ cup slivered almonds
2 tablespoons sugar	1 cup brown sugar
1 teaspoon vanilla	½ cup softened butter

1. Preheat oven to 350° F.
2. Mix together figs, apple juice, sugar, and vanilla in a saucepan and cook over low heat, stirring continuously until blended into a paste.
3. Prepare the crust by mixing together the flour, almonds, and brown sugar in a bowl, then stirring in the butter.
4. Press half the dough into an 8 × 12-inch glass cooking dish and spread the fig mixture over it.
5. Using the other half of the dough, add another layer on top, first pressing flat small sections of dough and placing them on top of the figs.
6. Bake for 30 minutes.
7. When cool, cut into squares and serve with hazelnut coffee and whipped cream.

Yield: 4–6 servings

Tabbouleh

This is a special salad made throughout the Middle East and savored all around the world. It makes a great stuffing for pita bread, but it can be enjoyed as a side dish with meats, casseroles, and vegetable entrées. Its unique flavor comes from the cracked wheat or bulgur mixed in with the dressing and allowed to sit overnight.

1 cup cracked or bulgur wheat
3 teaspoons salt
2 cups boiling water
8 black olives
1 tomato
1 cucumber

⅓ cup lemon juice
½ cup olive oil
1 cup chopped parsley
½ cup chopped mint sprigs
½ teaspoon ground allspice

1. Mix the cracked wheat, 1 teaspoon salt, and the boiling water together in a bowl. Leave for 30 minutes, or long enough for the water to be absorbed. Drain in a sieve if any water remains.
2. Dice the olives, tomato, and cucumber and add to the cracked wheat.
3. Blend together the remaining ingredients and pour over the wheat and vegetables.
4. Mix well and refrigerate overnight.
5. Serve either chilled or at room temperature.

Yield: 4–5 servings

Leafy Picture Frames

Materials Needed

Ruler
Two sheets of cardboard, about 9 × 12 inches each
Scissors
Hole puncher
Yarn
White glue
Leaves and pine needles from the garden

Directions

1. With the ruler, measure a 2-inch border around the edges of one piece of cardboard. Cut out the rectangular shape in the middle.
2. Punch two holes in the top of the solid sheet of cardboard.
3. Thread the yarn through the holes, loop it, and tie the ends. This will be your frame hanger.
4. Now place the piece of cardboard with the rectangular opening on top of the other one and glue them together on three sides. Make sure to leave the fourth side open to insert a picture.
5. Gather the leaves and pine needles you found outdoors and arrange them around the frame. When you like how they look, glue them down.
6. Insert your favorite photo, a picture from a magazine, or a drawing of your own into the frame.
7. Close up the open side with a dab of glue and give the frame to a friend or relative as a gift. You can also handwrite a message instead of a picture and use the frame as a fancy greeting card.

Activities for Your Seder

To make the seder more fun for kids and to provide a little entertainment for the adults, too, consider reading aloud a short, colorful book by Dr. Seuss called *The Lorax*, a story that celebrates trees and the preservation of nature. In this cleverly illustrated book, a fuzzy little man stands on the stump of a tree that has been chopped down and pleads with the creature holding the ax to stop destroying the earth. The book is witty and entertaining, with wonderfully twisted language, and fits beautifully with the values espoused on Tu b'Shevat.

After the seder, you can give each child a green bean and a small plastic cup. Send the kids out into the garden with a spoon to dig up a handful of soil, or arrange to have a messy area in the basement where they can fill their cups from a bag of potting soil. Allow them to mix in water and then plant the green bean, putting it about one-half inch under the soil.

Provide markers for children to write their names on the bottoms of the cups, and let them take their cups home. In three days the beans will sprout, and in four weeks if the plants have been in the sun, small vines will develop.

Other plants that grow nicely from seeds are grapefruits, lemons, and oranges. These seeds need to be sprouted before planting. To do so, cover them with water and let them soak for two days, then plant about one-quarter inch down in the dirt. These plants sprout in one to two months.

To grow a sweet potato vine, fill a glass three-quarters full and put the tapered end of the potato in water, using toothpicks to hold it up. Add water daily. Roots will grow down and leaves will sprout in a few weeks. At this point, plant in a pot with soil and watch it grow. You can cultivate an avocado pit the same way. Even the top of a pineapple plant can be placed in a container of water to sprout, then transferred to a pot of soil when the root growth is apparent.

After the seder, when only the pits and seeds remain, distribute them among the children so they can take them home, grow them into plants, and remember the values of Tu b'Shevat.

7

Purim: The Book of Esther

*Observe these days for feasting and gladness, and as a time
for sending gifts to one another and to the poor.*

—Esther 9:22

Celebrating With Panache

OF ALL THE HOLIDAYS of the Jewish year, the one that lends itself most joy-
fully to a party is Purim. Purim is a time to feel good, make fun of yourself, dress up, and be someone else.

Though it is one of the most beloved holidays of the Jewish year, it is
not strictly a religious one. Purim is considered a minor holiday, compared
with the serious pilgrimage festivals of Shavuot, Sukkot, and Passover, and
of course the reflective and meditative tone of the High Holy Days. You do
not light candles on Purim or say kiddush. You are allowed to work, and
there are no holiday restrictions.

Like Hanukkah, Purim is a holiday of deliverance. Hanukkah commemorates a time when our enemies tried to destroy Jewish spiritual life;
Purim, a time when they tried to destroy us physically. In both cases we

triumphed and were delivered from our fate. Many cooks serve similar dishes on Purim and Hanukkah, in an attempt to connect miracle with miracle.

Some historians challenge the authenticity of the story of Mordechai and Esther and claim that neither the events nor characters were real. But despite the scholarly debate, we have embraced this holiday and taken it into our hearts, so we celebrate it with exuberance. The holiday is unique in its joy and sense of the absurd, yet it has its serious side, too, as it celebrates the underlying values of faith, sharing, charity, and sheer joy in Judaism.

With the approach of Purim, troubles are left behind and festivities play an important role. We celebrate the victory of Mordechai and Esther over Haman with two annual recountings of the story in the synagogue (one the evening prior to the holiday and one on the day of Purim) plus a *seudat* Purim—a special meal—in the late afternoon of Purim.

Special Purim Foods

The traditional Purim celebration ranks second only to the Passover seder in importance as a special meal, and because it offers the promise of a good time, it is a perfect occasion to invite guests to your home.

Typical foods at the Purim feast are hamantaschen, kreplach, chickpeas, and beans. Many people also serve turkey. Since the country of Hodu—India—is mentioned in the Megillah, some Jews eat turkey, which is called the "hodu bird." Also, the turkey is considered a stupid animal—it has been known to drown if left out in the rain because it doesn't know enough to close its mouth—and it is eaten on Purim because it is a reminder of Ahasuerus, who was considered historically to be a very stupid king.

Many Purim dishes involve a filling, alluding to the numerous secrets and intrigues of the court of Ahasuerus that unfold in the Purim story. Most common are sweet fillings, which are thought in the folklore that surrounds the holiday to send out wishes for a "good lot" or a sweet future.

It is also traditional to begin the feast with a large braided challah, symbolizing the thick rope on which Haman was hung.

Chickpeas, fava beans, and baklava are served to commemorate the belief that Esther ate only vegetable dishes made of nuts, seeds, and legumes while living in the palace, since she was unable to obtain kosher food.

And, of course, the traditional hamantaschen, the preeminent Purim pastry, a triangular sweet filled with nuts, poppy seeds, prunes, or apricots, always take their place of honor at the Purim table. Recipes for hamantaschen come in two varieties, one made of cookie dough, the other of yeast dough. By eating Haman's three-cornered hat, we symbolically erase him from existence—and enjoy the experience along the way.

It's Not Purim Without a Spoof

After dinner, it is traditional for guests to put on Purim skits and parodies of the Torah and Talmud, sometimes even making fun of the rabbis themselves. These spoofs are called Purim spiels, and they enable us to poke good-natured fun at everyone—especially ourselves.

Purim is, after all, a day when everything is topsy-turvy, and a Mardi Gras spirit is allowed, even encouraged, to run wild. Many people, adults and children alike, dress up in costumes for the holiday. The tradition of wearing costumes on Purim originated in Italy at the end of the fifteenth century, following the great success of the masked entertainers of the Commedia dell'Arte. Purim skits emerged about a century later in Europe. Today, many scholars believe that at Purim people dress up to show that understanding God is a difficult task and things are often not what they seem to be.

The celebratory meal at Purim centers on the family table, but unlike a normal Jewish family dinner party, your co-host or your guests can present a spoof kiddush, mixing up common phrases into a string of nonsense words. For children, and some newcomers to observing Jewish traditions, this often comes as a needed relief, since the Hebrew words can sound strange and mixed up even when correct, until enough time has passed that one instinctively grasps some of the cadence and rhythm of the language.

In Israel people enjoy live media broadcasts and family farces of all types, and even sometimes publish family newsletters filled with news of absurd events. Costumed merrymakers enjoy the lavish floats, the dressed-up marchers, the loud music and joyous dancing in Tel Aviv at the famous Adloyada carnival and parade.

The Four Central Rituals

There are four major Purim activities from which the traditions and customs surrounding this holiday flow.

The first is the reading of the Megillah, also known as the Scroll of Esther or the Book of Esther, in the synagogue. During the reading, Haman is hissed and booed, groggers are shaken, and unlike at any other time, there is a carnival atmosphere to the entire service. Even the rabbi and cantor sometimes get involved in the fun, occasionally switching places and playing one another's roles, often as poorly and imperfectly as possible.

Next is sending *mishloach manot* baskets to friends and neighbors, particularly the elderly or shut-ins. These baskets are generally gifts of food, including hamantaschen, fruit, nuts, and a variety of juices.

We also give gifts to the poor at Purim, usually in the form of monetary donations to an organized charity. People who regularly give *tzedakah* often give an extra donation at Purim.

After services, we enjoy a festive meal in the afternoon, complete with entertaining costumes, creative Purim spiels, and parodies of the readings from the Talmud in which verses are strung together to make no sense at all.

The story of Purim celebrates Esther's faith and determination in the face of danger and says in no uncertain terms that Jews must always struggle against enemies who seek to destroy us. It is a sobering message

Purim Masks

Materials Needed

1 cup flour
1/3 cup water
1/4 cup salt
Shower cap
Vaseline
Plastic knife

Portable hair dryer
Two 10-inch lengths
    of string
Tempera paint
Glue
Feathers

Directions

1. Mix together flour, water, and salt into a dough ball.
2. Find someone who is willing to serve as a model for you. Have the model put on the shower cap and put Vaseline over his or her entire face. Make sure it goes over the chin and up to the hairline.
3. Roll out the dough into a 1/4-inch-thick rectangle.
4. Have the model lie down and drape the dough over his or her face.
5. Pat the dough in place around the model's features, and with a plastic knife cut away excess dough around the edges. Make sure to make sufficient air holes for breathing.
6. With a hair dryer, blow warm air over the dough until it begins to feel firm, usually about 20 minutes.
7. Remove gently, make one small hole on each side just above the ear to attach strings and let dry overnight, or bake at 350°F for one hour.
8. Put strings in the holes and tie firmly, then paint the mask, making colorful designs and gluing feathers around the top edged and at the eyebrows for accents.
9. Wear the mask to your Purim celebration!

delivered in a frivolous form when acted out in a Purim spiel, but a serious story when read from the Megillah.

In the Megillah, it is significant that it is not God who rescues the Jews, but Esther. This act of heroism encourages all of us to take our fate into our own hands and seek to bring forth our innermost courage and determination.

We celebrate Purim with cookies and costumes, gift baskets and a festive meal, the reading of the Megillah, and some wine. But under the surface, there is a serious message. It is a holiday of letting go, feeling joy, and placing emphasis on the physical delights that surround us. Yet, in the midst of the raucous good cheer, we are reminded of our obligation to do good deeds and stand up to tyranny, and that everything in life can be lost in a moment.

The Book of Esther

The Book of Esther, or Megillah, is read in the synagogue on the evening and the day of Purim. Most historians consider it to be an allegorical story and do not believe it really happened. It is not part of the five books of Moses, our Torah, but is in the part of the Bible called the Writings.

The scroll is handwritten on parchment and sometimes illustrated. When it is read it is unrolled and folded back on itself like a letter, because letters were sent to all the Jews by Mordechai and Esther.

The Megillah tells us to celebrate our being saved "with days of feasting and gladness" and instructs us to "send portions to one another;" thus our tradition of bringing friends and neighbors *shalach manot* baskets.

It also encourages us to give gifts to the poor, thus encompassing the two main customs of most Jewish holidays—to enjoy a feast and give *tzedakah*.

During the reading of the Megillah, whenever Haman's name is mentioned, we are obliged to boo, hiss, stamp our feet, twirl groggers, bang cymbals, or blow horns to drown out the evil name. Noise is, of course, an age-old device for driving away evil spirits, called on in this case in an attempt to erase an enemy from our midst.

Hadassah and the Story of Purim

Hadassah, the Women's Zionist Organization, was founded in Israel on Purim in 1912 by Henrietta Szold. Hadassah is the Hebrew equivalent of Esther, and the worldwide welfare organization was named in honor of the heroine of the Purim story. Today Hadassah is synonymous with good deeds and vastly improved health care in Israel. Hundreds of chapters exist throughout the world, and Jewish women everywhere collect money and work to further its goals.

When to Have Your Celebration

Most Purim parties take place in the late afternoon of Purim following services, in honor of the banquets that are mentioned in the Book of Esther, or on the closest Sunday following the holiday.

You will enjoy planning a party to continue the festivities begun in temple with a Mardi Gras–like masquerade affair, dinner and a Purim spiel, and crafts, songs, and possibly even a costume parade. You can plan a festive meal for an early dinner on Purim afternoon or a buffet on Sunday. Either way, you will enjoy sharing the color and excitement of the holiday with your guests, both adults and children.

Because of the creative aspects of Purim, many congregations have happily found that it is the holiday that most easily engages teenagers, and opportunities to run carnivals, create costumes, and write and direct Purim spiels often bring out the post bar and bat mitzvah crowd. Sometimes they rediscover the reasons they liked going to temple as children and decide to stay on, renewing their commitment to Jewish life and bringing a deeper spirituality with them when they return.

Homemade Groggers

GROGGER #1

Materials Needed

Aluminum soda can
Half a dozen pennies
About 3 square inches
of aluminum foil

Rubber band
Gold spray paint
Red and purple markers
Stickers

Directions

1. Remove the top and contents from a soda can.
2. Drop in several pennies.
3. Cover the top with aluminum foil, securing the edges with a rubber band.
4. Decorate the can with spray paint and draw Jewish stars on it with markers.
5. Apply stickers to add color.

GROGGER #2

Materials Needed

2 same-size paper cups
$^1/_4$ cup uncooked rice or beans

Stapler

Directions

1. Add $^1/_2$ inch of rice or beans to one cup.
2. Invert the other cup over the first one and staple around the edges so the lips meet, making sure to secure firmly all around.

(continued on next page)

Grogger #3

Materials Needed

Plastic soda or water bottle
A handful of marbles, pebbles, beads, or bells
Colorful stickers
About 20 inches of ribbon

Directions

1. Empty the bottle but keep the cap.
2. Fill one-quarter full with marbles, pebbles, beads, bells, or a combination of these.
3. Recap the bottle.
4. Decorate with stickers.
5. Tie the ribbon around the neck of the bottle in a pretty bow.

In each case, shake your grogger whenever Haman's name is mentioned. The noise you make will be sure to drown out the sound, which is just what your grogger is made for.

What's for Dinner?

You can serve your guests a delicious meal without spending all day in the kitchen if you plan ahead. The challah can be made one week ahead and frozen, then warmed slowly in the oven, and you can toss the salad in the morning if you keep it refrigerated with a damp paper towel covering the bowl. Prepare the chicken mixture a day ahead and marinate overnight.

Try this menu for your Purim celebration:

Braided Rope Challah
Melon Balls in Strawberry Sauce
Mushroom and Barley Soup
Old-Fashioned Orange Chicken Breasts
Chickpea and Avocado Salad
Heavenly Hamantaschen
Cherry-Peach Punch

Time for Wine

On Purim, moderate amounts of alcohol are encouraged, although in the Jewish tradition liquor is disapproved of during the rest of the year. This is because Purim is a holiday of letting go, a time to be loud and raucous as we revel in our good fortune.

Wine plays a major role in the story of the holiday—Haman drank too much at Esther's banquet, and Vashti, the first queen, was killed because the king was drunk.

Yet according to the ancient Babylonian scholar Rava, we are mandated to consume enough liquor on the night of Purim to render us unable to distinguish Mordechai from Haman.

If you would like to honor this dictum, even to only a small degree, you could provide a fruity punch at your party laced with liquor. Or, to give your guests a choice, you might serve both a spiked version and a plain one. Some hosts like to float scoops of pineapple and orange sherbet in a large bowl of champagne for a mild and enjoyable champagne punch. Also, you might consider serving a dessert with alcohol in it, such as fruitcake with rum flavoring.

If you prefer wine, some good suggestions for the Purim dinner menu are Chardonnay, Sauvignon Blanc, or Beaujolais. Offering a variety of

Old-Fashioned Orange Chicken Breasts

A favorite main course for celebrations of all kinds, orange chicken is especially well suited for Purim because it combines the traditional tastes of brown sugar and soy sauce with the spicy flavors of ginger and white wine. For a variation, you can sprinkle slivered almonds on top just before serving. Serve with a side salad and rice.

3 large oranges	2 tablespoons soy sauce
1 teaspoon ginger	¼ teaspoon salt
2 tablespoons cornstarch	Pinch of pepper
½ cup white wine	2 tablespoons olive oil
1 tablespoon brown sugar	2 pounds chicken breasts

1. Section the oranges.
2. Combine the ginger, cornstarch, wine, sugar, soy sauce, salt, and pepper in a measuring cup.
3. Stir in the orange sections.
4. Heat the oil in a skillet.
5. Cut the chicken into small strips and sauté in the oil.
6. Pour the liquid mixture over the chicken and simmer, covered, for 5 minutes.

Yield: 6 servings

Chickpea and Avocado Salad

Because Israel is known for its abundance of vegetables and fruits, many traditional main dishes contain no meat at all. This salad can be served by itself or as a side dish with one of the chicken or lamb dishes that appear frequently at celebrations. You should make the salad just before your guests arrive for maximum freshness and crunch, but you can prepare the dressing days in advance and keep it refrigerated.

1 orange	Seeds of half a pomegranate
1 cup chickpeas	¼ cup apple vinegar
2 figs	½ cup olive oil
1 avocado	1 clove garlic, mashed
1 hard-boiled egg	Salt to taste
1 head iceberg lettuce	½ teaspoon sugar
1 endive	1 teaspoon mustard
1 bunch watercress	

1. Peel and slice the orange into circles.
2. Rinse the chickpeas.
3. Chop the figs into small bits.
4. Peel and dice the avocado and the egg.
5. Separate and wash the leaves of the lettuce, endive, and watercress.
6. In a decorative glass layer together the orange slices, chickpeas, figs, avocado, egg, and the greens, sprinkling in pomegranate seeds for color.
7. To make the dressing, mix together the vinegar, olive oil, garlic, salt, sugar, and mustard.
8. Pour the mixture over the salad. Do not toss; just let the dressing seep slowly through the mixture of fruits and vegetables.

Yield: 6 servings

Heavenly Hamantaschen

Haman's three-cornered hat has served as the inspiration for these delectable treats in Jewish kitchens throughout the world. We enjoy them not only because they taste so good, but because by eating them we are consuming Haman and his evil ways. There are many traditional fillings for hamantaschen, including prunes, poppy seeds, dates, raisins, chocolate, jam, and every fruit imaginable. Some kids even like them filled with peanut butter and a touch of jelly.

4 cups sifted flour	1 cup white sugar or honey
2 teaspoons baking powder	¼ cup milk
¼ teaspoon salt	1 jar raspberry preserves
4 eggs	1 jar apricot preserves
½ half cup butter	

1. Preheat oven to 350°F.
2. Sift the flour, baking powder, and salt together in a large bowl.
3. Beat the eggs and mix them with the butter, sugar, and milk.
4. Pat the dough into a ball and divide it into four equal parts.
5. With a rolling pin, roll out one part onto a floured pastry board or counter top, about ¼-inch thick.
6. Cut out cookie with a round cookie cutter or a drinking glass about 3 inches in diameter.
7. Put either raspberry or apricot filling in each circle.
8. Pinch the edges together to make a triangle.
9. Place on a greased cookie sheet and bake for 30 minutes.
10. Repeat steps 5 through 9 until all the dough is used.

Yield: about 4 dozen hamantaschen

these, both chilled and at room temperature, will enhance your holiday meal and please your guests.

Planning Party Invitations

Most dinner parties and buffets you will hold in your home will be small enough for a telephone invitation, but if you are inviting more than fifteen guests, or simply enjoy the formality, you might find it easier to send written invitations. A note composed on the computer in several unmatching fonts, especially if it can be produced on a color printer, can be very festive. Ask your children to help design it. They will enjoy a task that lets them do exactly the opposite of what they are required to do at school.

Check specialty stationery stores for card stock with a Jewish theme. You can usually find it if you ask to see bar and bat mitzvah stationery. For an extra touch, send the invitation with a grogger attached in a padded envelope or Jiffy bag. The kind designed to mail videos will be just the right size to protect the noisemaker. Tell guests to bring the grogger with them to the party.

Decorating the Table

The holiday atmosphere of Purim invites lots of color. Decorate with masks, feathers, sequins, streamers, Mylar confetti, and beaded necklaces. Lots of glitz can enhance a party of this type, and it can be fun to bring out colorful trinkets you may have saved from bar and bat mitzvahs you have attended in the past.

For a centerpiece, fill fancy champagne flutes with colored marbles, top them with feathers and group them together in the center of the table.

You might also ask the children of your guests to make small puppet figures of Esther, Haman, Mordechai, Vashti, and Ahasuerus out of ice cream sticks or papier mâché. When the figures arrive, stand them up in a small vase lined with florists' pebbles at the bottom. One grouping in the middle of the table or several small ones around the table can be festive and attractive and reinforce the theme of the holiday. It is also a nice way to get your guests involved in the festivities.

Mood Music

While a wide variety of Israeli folk songs are always welcome at holiday parties, you can also buy a tape of specific Purim songs performed by the Kiddush Cups, a children's chorus, at most Judaica stores.

For a more formal musical selection, look for the recently composed "Aliyot" symphony, performed by the St. Louis Orchestra. Or if you want to stimulate singing at your table, consider the rousing Klezmer music of Yale Strom. Most come with the words included. With some foresight, you can reproduce these ahead of time to distribute at the party. Put one under each dinner plate, and when the main course is finished and the plates are removed, someone is sure to suggest playing the music and singing along.

Dressing Up for the Holiday

Costumes are an integral part of the holiday atmosphere at a Purim celebration. Anything goes, including face painting and funny hats. You never know what your guests will pull out of the recesses of their closet before coming to your house.

Encourage both children and adults to dress up. Make sure you tell them this in your invitation. Costumes can be found at rummage sales or in your attic—or someone else's. Even old Halloween costumes can be useful, especially if you mix and match parts of several costumes or themes.

Of course, most children will want to dress up as Esther, Mordechai, Haman, Ahasuerus, or Vashti, but it is also perfectly acceptable to dress up as a clown, troll, queen, circus performer, king, ballerina, bride, any sort of animal, colorful flower, or cartoon or movie character.

Songs to Sing Together

After dinner or between courses, you can hand out song sheets of music you do not have on tape and lead a sing-a-long for your guests. If someone can accompany on the piano or the guitar, it will richly enhance the experience. Favorite Purim songs include "In Shu, Shu, Shushan," the traditonal folk song "A Wicked Man," "Yom Tov Purim" or "We Have a Day," and "Ani Purim," in Hebrew.

Ask the holiday coordinator at your temple or your child's Hebrew School teacher for song sheets and additional suggestions, or check the nearest Judaica store for songbooks you can purchase. They are sure to be a good investment for future parties, as well.

Favorite Activities for Purim

Because of the color and fun associated with Purim, the festive event lends itself easily to craft projects, and activities abound to teach children about the values of the holiday while creating objects that will make celebrating more fun. Chief among these are groggers, the noisemakers used by children and adults alike during the reading of the Megillah. There are numerous types of noisemakers children can make out of beans and paper cups, soda bottles and marbles, and balloons waiting to be popped (see sidebar).

While kids are waiting for dinner, you can set up a station where they can fill hamantaschen, the favorite Purim pastry (see sidebar for recipe). Prepare the dough in advance, supply variously sized plastic cups as cookie cutters, have fillings ready, and assign an adult guest to supervise the baking.

Children of all ages know that being someone else is half the fun of Purim, and nothing works as well as a mask to make this happen. Masks can be made of fabric, paper, cast plaster, or even clay or play dough (see sidebar).

If children are interested in putting on a Purim spiel with puppets, they can make them out of plaster and empty water bottles (see sidebar).

Papier Mâché Puppet Heads

Materials Needed

Large mixing bowl	Cardboard tube from paper
1 cup water	towel roll
1 cup flour	Plastic bottle
Paper towels	Water-based paints
Old newspapers	Glue
Masking tape	Fabric scraps

Directions

1. In the bowl, mix together the water and flour to form a thick paste.
2. Tear 20 pieces of paper towel into long strips. Set aside until needed.
3. Take two sheets of newspaper and form into a ball, taping around it to get it into the right shape.
4. Cut a 2-inch piece off the tube, fit it over the neck of the bottle, and tape it on.
5. With masking tape, attach the newspaper ball onto the top of the tube.
6. Decide if your puppet will be Esther, Mordechai, or Haman, and use pieces of newspaper to add long hair and a crown, a beard, or a three-cornered hat.
7. Take the paper towel strips and coat them with the flour paste, then wrap around bottle, neck and newspaper ball head. Continue to cover with strips until all three pieces look like one.
8. Use extra paper towel to mold features, such as the crown, the beard, or the three-cornered hat.
9. Set aside overnight in a warm place to dry.
10. In the morning, paint the puppet, outlining the face with appropriate colors, and when it is dry, glue on scraps of fabric to form features.
11. Repeat steps 3 through 10 until you have enough puppets for your Purim spiel. Then make them sing, dance, argue, and enjoy the show!

Another option is to simply dress up one's favorite dolls or action figures to turn them into Purim characters. Everything your child needs can be found around the house.

For example, Queen Esther needs a long white gown, which you can easily make from tissues, with a pipe cleaner tied around her waist as a belt, and both she and King Ahasuerus need crowns, which you can make from aluminum foil. Use cotton balls to make a beard for Mordechai, and dress Haman all in black, with a triangular hat made of cardboard.

How to Make Shalach Manot Baskets

Purim is the last festival before Passover, and we are all supposed to use up all the flour in the house; thus the tradition of making and giving away baked pastries of all kinds in *shalach manot* or *mishloah manot* baskets came into being.

Mishloah manot literally means "sending of portions." Following this tradition has often had the happy result of bringing neighbors together and making friends out of strangers. In other words, taking part in the Great Annual Jewish Cookie Exchange.

Traditionally these baskets contain at least one pastry and one fruit, each packed with a specific blessing. Often children are used as messengers, enlivening their relationships with friends and neighbors and bringing nourishment and good cheer to older people in the community.

To make the baskets, you can decorate gift bags, paper plates, food boxes, or even Chinese food containers with stickers, pom-poms, googly eyes, crayons, streamers, glitter, stars, and handwritten messages. Fill them with hamantaschen, nuts, dried fruits, miniature bottles of wine, grape and apple juice, pennies, and many varieties of small candy.

And remember that if you are making them for friends and neighbors, make one for your own family, too. It's easy to overlook the people nearest you, but they are the ones who are likely to be most surprised and pleased by your generosity.

Purim Spiels

Clever, satirical after-dinner plays can be written by adults or children who get into the spirit of Purim, but if your guests would like a ready-made play to act out, check your local public library to find the correct version for the age of your children. You can usually find them in family treasuries or tales of Jewish celebrations in the holiday section.

You will enjoy reading through published spiels and deciding how to put them on. Switching roles in the middle of the spiel is permissible, of course, since this is a holiday of confusion and fun. You might use them as a resource at first and try writing your own next time, once you have a full grasp of the story and the characters that made it happen.

Other After-Dinner Activities

It can be a lot of fun to stage a mock debate over the relative virtues of hamantaschen vs. latkes, for example, or even the value of chairs vs. sofas.

Your guests can form teams and argue the religious significance of the circle vs. the triangle, the political importance of frying in oil, the medicinal and other properties of prune filling, and any other angle their fertile minds come up with. Another possible debate topic is the relative merits of wine vs. water. Which is healthier? Which is better for mental acuity? Which produces the most creative thought?

If you go the debate route, you might want to modify your menu for Purim dinner and consider serving both hamantaschen and latkes, wine and water, prune and chocolate filling. Get all your guests involved in talking and eating. After all, what could be more festive—and more Jewish?

8

Passover: The Road to Freedom

*Remember this day on which you went free from Egypt, the house
of bondage, how God freed you from it with a mighty hand.*

—Exodus 13:3

The Birth of the Jewish People

PASSOVER CELEBRATES BEGINNINGS. It is a holiday with its own rules, rituals,
and food, centered around the warm and inviting feast during which we
reenact the Exodus from Egypt by telling the story of how we came to be
a free and independent people. It is the oldest continually celebrated religious ceremony in the world, and is observed by more Jews than is any
other holiday.

The holiday is agricultural as well as historical in origin. In ancient
Israel barley was harvested in early spring. Passover is also called Hag
ha-Matzot, "the feast of unleavened bread," and Hag ha-Aviv, "the holiday
of spring." It begins at sundown on the fourteenth day of the month of
Nisan, falling in March or early April in the civil calendar.

In Israel and among Reform and Reconstructionist Jews, Passover is celebrated for seven days, with the first and last as full-festival, no-work days. For traditional Jews outside Israel, the holiday is eight days long.

Why the difference of a day? More than twenty-five hundred years ago, Jews were informed about the holiday's start by an elaborate network of mountaintop bonfires, and in order to protect against errors an extra day was added. Many people dropped the extra day when reliable calendars were developed in the fourth century C.E.

Passover begins on the night of the first full moon of spring and commemorates the midnight escape of six hundred thousand men, women, and children from slavery and their transformation into a distinct Israelite nation. This crucial event marks the beginning of our sacred history.

Experiencing the Holiday

Perhaps more than any other holiday in the festival year, Passover exerts a strong pull on the Jewish soul. The seder begins by putting us back into slavery and ends by calling upon us to imagine what the world will be like when all people are free. More than a meal or a family reunion, it is at once a stage and an altar. On it we relive the experience of physical and spiritual oppression and our liberation from bondage.

The Haggadah asserts that all people in every generation must regard themselves as having been personally freed from Egypt. It is not enough to think that our ancestors were freed after two hundred years of slavery; it is required that each of us make the journey ourselves. This journey starts, and ends, at the seder table.

To help us along, the seder provides rich symbolism in its foods, wines, and table settings, and the ceremonial stories, songs, prayers, psalms, and poems in the Haggadah make the experience deep and multidimensional. We eat what the Israelites ate just before they left Egypt: lamb, unleavened bread, bitter herbs. And we follow the format of the great talk-feasts of the Greeks of the first century C.E., who held banquets with philosophical discussions as part of the meal. The seder has remained virtually unchanged since the first century.

For centuries the ancient Jews celebrated Passover with a pilgrimage to the Temple in Jerusalem, the first of three annual pilgrimage festivals of the year. When the Temple was destroyed in 70 C.E. and the Jewish community was exiled, the rabbis created the ritual meal we call the seder, following the injunction in Deuteronomy that says it is the duty of parents to tell the story of the Exodus to their children. Their goal was to preserve historical memory and the symbolism of ancient traditions. Later generations set down the order of the seder in the Haggadah.

No one knows who wrote the Haggadah, though the first one appeared as an appendage to a prayer book. It became its own book in the thirteenth century, and the first one was printed in Spain in 1482. New editions appear almost every year, and today over three thousand different Haggadahs have been published worldwide.

The Story of Passover

Every year at Passover we contemplate the importance of freedom by telling the story of how the Israelites became a nation. With its emotional nature and universal symbols, the story has become representative of the enslavement of any people. With its fire and drama, it is at bottom a simple story of faith.

It is about 1200 B.C.E., and Moses, a shepherd, has been chosen by God to go to Pharaoh and demand that he free the Israelites. Despite Moses' pleading, Pharaoh says no. To force the tyrannical king to his will, God sends down ten plagues, each one worse than the one before. The river turns to blood, frogs descend on the land, locusts eat everything that is growing—but still Pharaoh will not give the Israelites their freedom. Finally God creates the tenth plague, the worst of all, in which the firstborn son in each Egyptian family will be killed.

He tells Moses to instruct the Israelites to roast a lamb and smear some of its blood on their doorposts so the angel of death will pass over them. When Pharaoh's son dies, Pharaoh's grief knows no bounds, and he tells Moses to take the Israelites away with him. Overjoyed, Moses gathers his people, and they leave in haste, not taking the time to let their bread dough rise, but taking it with them as it is.

When the Israelites reach the banks of the Red Sea, however, they hear the sound of chariots and horses behind them. Caught between the army and the sea, they fear their lives will end, but God parts the waters and Moses leads them through to safety. When the Egyptians enter the sea in pursuit, God drowns them, horses and all.

Thus begins the Israelites' forty years of wandering in the desert, time in which to throw off the shackles of slavery, band together, and become a nation of free and liberated people.

Freedom and Peace

Passover is the preeminent Jewish home holiday, and the experience of joyous, communal observance of its elaborate rituals is one of the reasons Jewish home life is so beautiful. The holiday's themes are freedom, Jewish continuity, and our belief in the potential for a just and peaceful world.

Because the message of Passover stresses the ethic that liberty is a basic right of all people and that the dignity of every human being is sacred, the festival has grown beyond its original meaning as a Jewish event to become a worldwide symbol of liberation for people of all nations, creeds, and colors.

It is not a coincidence that Passover occurs in the spring. Both spring and liberation summon rebirth and hope. And the journey from winter to spring echoes the Israelites' march from slavery to liberation.

Passover also marks the beginning of the covenental relationship between Israel and God. At the seder we learn that God fulfilled the promise to bring us out of Egypt and, having redeemed us, promises to make us his people.

In the Synagogue

Services for Passover are traditionally held on the evenings of the holiday before sundown, and the poetic biblical book known as the Song of Songs is read. Morning services are held on the first and last two days.

On the first day of the holiday, a special prayer is chanted for *tal,* or dew, to fall on the Holy Land in the coming months. Passover falls toward the end of the rainy season in Israel, and spring and summer are a crucial time for the crops. All over the world, on the first day of Passover, Jews pray that there will be dew in the dry summer months when no rain falls.

A Matzoh Medley

While several symbolic foods are prescribed for the Passover seder, the liturgy is especially clear about which foods are not permitted at all. No bread or food with any trace of leavening or fermentation is allowed to be consumed during the weeklong Passover holiday. This includes barley, oats, rice, rye, and wheat, except in the form of matzoh, which must be specially prepared for the holiday.

More than any other food, this flat bumpy bread, similar to a cracker or wafer, has come to symbolize Passover. Matzoh is made exclusively from flour and water. To be considered kosher for Passover, however, the matzoh must be made from a dough whose leavening process is interrupted by baking it so quickly that it stops the dough from rising. The rabbinical limit on the amount of time from kneading the dough to removal from the oven is eighteen minutes.

In Talmudic times, matzohs were made with artistic designs, including such elaborate figures as fish and doves. Until the nineteenth century, however, matzohs were round and baked by hand. The first matzoh-baking machine was invented in Austria in 1857, and because it could not be tooled to create the customary circular cakes, matzoh became rectangular in shape.

To make matzoh, mix Passover flour with cold water until you can knead it into a dough. Roll the dough flat with a rolling pin and perforate it with a sterilized comb to remove the air bubbles. Then bake it at 500°F for eighteen minutes.

Matzoh is mentioned in the Torah in both Exodus and Deuteronomy as a food prepared quickly for unexpected guests. In Deuteronomy it is referred to as the bread of affliction, alluding to the food our ancestors ate in Egypt when they were slaves and making it a symbol of oppression.

Matzoh is eaten at Passover to remember the Jews' great haste in leaving Egypt and their inability to wait for the bread to rise. The Haggadah tells us that when Moses called them to leave, they put wooden boards across their shoulders to hold the newly kneaded dough, which was baked by the hot sun into the flat, crisp bread we know as matzoh.

In the nineteenth century, matzoh consumption was considered so significant in the lives of Jews that the Jewish population of major American cities was estimated by determining the matzoh production for the year and allotting five pounds per person.

Other Food Traditions

Many people begin the Passover meal by dipping hard-boiled eggs in salt water. Eggs possess a great deal of symbolism, both in Jewish tradition and in the secular world. They are universally recognized as a religious symbol of rebirth and hope, and to Jews they offer a sign of mourning for the destruction of the Holy Temple in Jerusalem. As a sign of the season, they also represent the meaning of new life and the coming of spring.

In addition, eggs become harder when they are cooked longer, unlike most foods, which become softer. Thus they represent the stubborn resistance of the Jews to those to try to destroy us.

Chicken soup is an almost universal staple of the Passover seder, most often served with *knaidlach,* or matzoh balls, and served after the traditional fish appetizer. For the soup, use a pullet—an older, plumper

Matzoh Cover

Materials Needed

    4 men's white handkerchiefs or 4 white cloth napkins about
       12 × 12 inches
    Ribbons, rosettes, fabric decals
    Sewing needle and thread
    Colored felt-tip markers
    Embroidery needle and colored yarn

Directions

1. Select one of the four squares to be the top layer of the matzoh cover. Lay out your design, using the available ribbons, rosettes, and fabric decals from the sewing store.
2. Sew the elements of the design in place. Fill in details with colored markers.
3. Make three separate pouches, each made of two layers of cloth, by using the embroidery needle and yarn to stitch around three sides of each set, using a decorative overhand stitch.
4. Attach the top, decorated pouch to the middle one with a small stitch through the middle of the bottom layer of one and the top layer of the other. Attach the bottom pouch the same way.
5. Insert three matzohs into their slots and place on the matzoh plate at the head of the seder table.

chicken—to make a better soup. To dress up the broth, consider adding julienned vegetables.

Four cups of wine are required at the Passover seder, symbolizing the four times God promises to redeem the Israelites in the Exodus story. For those whose tastes run to nonalcoholic drinks, and for children, of course, grape juice can be substituted. Because of the likelihood of staining the pristine white Passover tablecloth, place a coaster or small dish under each wine goblet when you set the table.

Until a few years ago, only sweet Concord grape or blackberry wines were available for Passover. Today, however, an array of kosher wines, many from Israel, can be used at your seder. Kosher wines from California include Baron Herzog, Gad Eden, and Weinstock. Herzog Selections import kosher wines directly from Israel, and Yarden and Carmel are the main Israeli exporters.

Look for these varieties to offer your guests. And keep in mind that they do not all have to drink the same wine. If some prefer the traditional sweet Concord grape and others a full-bodied red, it is not difficult today to accommodate them. Be sure to order your wine in advance to make sure you have enough to serve four cups to each guest.

For a main entrée, it is customary to serve roast lamb in honor of the last meal the Israelites ate before they fled from Egypt and to commemorate the paschal lamb offered as a sacrifice in ancient times. Also popular as main dishes are veal, baked chicken, and roast turkey.

For dessert, rich chocolate flourless tortes and sweet macaroons are popular, along with an English-style trifle made with layers of sponge cake, berries, and cream.

Here is a hearty, tasty, traditional menu for your Passover seder meal:

Fancy Gefilte Fishlets
Herbed Chicken Soup With Matzoh Balls
Stuffed Breast of Veal
Asparagus Soufflé
Roasted New Potatoes
Viennese Chocolate Torte

Fancy Gefilte Fishlets

Jewish cooks have always appreciated the value of fish, especially the fresh-water variety, and it is traditional on Passover to serve a first course of salmon, carp, whitefish, pike, hake, haddock, cod or some combination of these. Making gefilte fish has become both an art and a craft. These fishlets can be prepared ahead of time and frozen either before or after cooking.

2 onions	1 pound carp
2 teaspoons salt	2 eggs
1 teaspoon white pepper	2 tablespoons matzoh meal
Fish bones and skin	½ teaspoon sugar
1 pound pike	2 carrots
1 pound whitefish	Beet horseradish

1. Cut one of the onions into chunks and add to 2 quarts boiling water.
2. Sprinkle in the salt and pepper.
3. Wash any fish bones and skin you have been able to obtain and add them to the boiling water.
4. Purée the fish and the other onion together in the food processor.
5. Add the eggs, ½ cup cold water, the matzoh meal, and sugar to the fish purée.
6. Mix well, then shape into little balls about the size of a golf ball. If they are too soggy, add more matzoh meal; too dry, add more water.
7. Drop the balls into the boiling fish stock.
8. Slice and add the carrots.
9. Cover and simmer for 1½ hours.
10. When ready, remove the fish with a slotted spoon and place in bowl.
11. Discard the bones and skin and cover the fishlets with the fish stock. Place in refrigerator, where the stock will gel nicely.
12. Serve three or four fishlets on a plate with spoonful of beet horseradish.

Yield: 8 servings

Herbed Chicken Soup

Nothing says Jewish cookery more clearly than chicken soup, and this variety is based on an old classic with just a touch of modern magic. Cooks of old used to rely on chicken feet for what they called the "strength" of a soup, but this ingredient is hard to come by these days. Today the secret of a flavorful soup is twofold: lots of bones and a plump, slightly older hen, called a pullet, available in the poultry case at most supermarkets and at specialty butchers.

1 pullet, about 3 pounds	1 onion
6 cups water	1 clove garlic
1 teaspoon salt	5 carrots
8 peppercorns	2 stalks celery
2 beef bones	3 parsnips
¼ cup chopped parsley	1 turnip
2 tablespoons chopped dill	2 tablespoons oil
1 leek	

1. Rinse the pullet and place in 6 cups of water in a large stockpot.
2. Add the salt, peppercorns, beef bones, parsley, and dill to the pot.
3. Slice the vegetables into small strips and sauté in 2 tablespoons oil for 2–3 minutes.
4. Add the vegetables to the stock and bring to a boil, then simmer for 2 hours.
5. When done, lift out the chicken and bones and strain the soup, saving the vegetables.
6. Refrigerate the chicken and vegetables for another meal and serve the soup with matzoh balls.

Yield: 4–6 servings

Traditional Matzoh Balls

At Passover, matzoh balls are the classic replacement for noodles in chicken soup, but these are so light and fluffy you may want to serve them at holidays all year round. Modern varieties can be poached in the microwave, but you might sacrifice flavor and texture for speed. Try this old-fashioned way of cooking them directly in boiling water or chicken stock.

3 eggs
1½ teaspoons salt
Pinch of pepper
4 tablespoons oil

¼ cup water
1½ cups matzoh meal
1 teaspoon baking powder

1. Whisk the eggs until frothy, then add the salt, pepper, oil, and water.
2. Stir in the matzoh meal and baking powder. Let sit for 30 minutes in the refrigerator until the mixture firms up.
3. Set 3 quarts of water to boil.
4. Form the mixture into little balls, about 1 inch in diameter, and drop into the pot of water.
5. Cover and cook on low heat for 30–35 minutes.
6. When done, spoon gently into warm chicken soup.

Yield: 8–10 servings

Viennese Chocolate Torte

Selecting a dessert to top off a Passover meal can be challenging, since nearly all cakes and pastries depend on flour as a base. This torte, however, is intense and flavorful because of its rich endowment with the essentials of great baking: chocolate, butter, and eggs.

¼ pound sweet butter (1 stick)	1 jigger rye
6 ounces unsweetened chocolate	2 teaspoons instant coffee
6 egg yolks	12 skinned almonds or coffee beans
5 egg whites	(optional)
¾ cup sugar	

1. Preheat the oven to 350°F.
2. Melt the butter and chocolate in a double boiler or in the microwave.
3. Separate the eggs, reserving one egg white.
4. With an electric beater, whip the egg yolks and gradually add the sugar, beating at least 10 minutes until all the sugar is dissolved and the mixture loses its grainy quality.
5. Add the butter, chocolate, rye, and coffee to the egg yolk mixture.
6. In another bowl, beat the egg whites until fluffy, then add to the yolk and chocolate mixture and stir gently.
7. Pour ⅓ of the mixture into a bowl, cover, and refrigerate.
8. Pour the other ⅔ of the mixture into a 9-inch springform pan and bake 40 minutes.
9. When the cake is ready, let cool and then remove the springform sides.
10. Spread the refrigerated batter over the top and sides as icing.
11. Decorate with skinned almonds or coffee beans if desired.
12. Refrigerate until ready to serve.

Yield: 6–8 servings

Rules and Customs

The customs of the holiday have remained virtually unchanged since they were established in the Middle Ages. The three most important rituals of the Passover celebration are ridding the house of all leavened food, taking part in a seder, and eating matzoh.

Getting rid of *chametz*, or any item containing prohibited food, entails a major cleaning task best shared among all members of the family. Traditionally every inch of the house is cleaned: sofa cushions are overturned in the search for old Cheerios, rugs are vacuumed to eliminate cracker crumbs, wood floors are scrubbed, and tiny scraps of old pizza crusts ferreted out from corners.

Every appliance in the kitchen is carefully washed, along with floors and walls; pots, pans, flatware, dishes, and glasses are all put away and replaced with special Passover ware. Then, the night before the seder, the family dims the lamps and lights a candle to conduct a search for leaven.

Parents with a sense of humor might plant mini-bagels in strategic spots in the den, the hallway, or the children's rooms. A special kit containing a large feather and a paper bag allow the kids to sweep the *chametz* away to be burned outside the next morning. Just make sure you remember where you hid all the bagels!

Some scholars believe the removal of *chametz* is more than a way of preparing the house for Passover; they look at it as a metaphor for an inner process of freeing ourselves from impurity, the negative parts of ourselves. Philo, a Greek-Jewish philosopher in the first century C.E. described *chametz* as arrogance, comparing it with leavened bread, which is all "puffed up." Pharaoh's struggle against the will of God showed such excessive pride, and Philo believed that at Passover we search for the pieces of Pharaoh's arrogance that lie within each of us.

In some traditional households, the oldest son fasts on the day before Passover to commemorate being spared during the plague of the first-born at the time of the Exodus. No one is allowed to eat matzoh on the day before the holiday begins, ostensibly to make it all the more sweet when it is permitted the next day.

Just for Children

Children have a natural role in the celebration of Passover, and because of their involvement year after year it is often the first holiday they feel confident about celebrating when they have grown up and created a home of their own.

To involve children ahead of time, consider asking them to prepare a skit to enact a story or a section from the Haggadah. For many children, this can be a welcome entree into the holiday action in a very hands-on way that is easy for them to understand. They can write a short play or narrative, create costumes, assign roles, run rehearsals—all activities that promote Jewish knowledge at the same time that they bring children into the celebration. Children can be painlessly enlisted to design and color place cards for the seder table, make matzoh covers, embellish pillow coverings for those who want to recline at the seder, and decorate kiddush cups for the guests. In the kitchen, a simple task would be to prepare the salt water in little bowls to put at the place of each diner.

At the service itself, it is the youngest child who asks the Four Questions, but before the seder older children can act as tutors to help the youngster get the words and the melody right. In addition, it is up to the children to find the *afikomen,* the half of the middle piece of matzoh without which the service cannot be ended. *Afikomen* literally means "dessert," and hunting for the "dessert" matzoh and devising ways to exact a price for its return has been known to occupy children for much of the seder.

It is also a child's role to open the door for Elijah, the prophet for whom we pour a glass of wine in hopes he will visit us as a herald to the arrival of the Messiah. Children can share this task by each pouring an inch of wine in his cup and taking turns opening the door. And who says it has to be opened only once?

How to Enhance the Holiday

Because it is important at the seder to have matching Haggadahs for all the guests so they can follow the service easily, it is often a big investment to purchase the books. Read them over carefully before you buy. Over the years it can be most satisfying to create a Haggadah collection, adding new ones when you travel, when you come across one in an antique store, or when you are browsing in a Judaica shop.

Haggadahs come in many shapes, sizes, and styles, including special ones for vegetarians, for feminists, for secular humanists, and for children. There are Haggadahs that honor the Holocaust victims, and that commemorate the creation of the State of Israel. Originally Haggadahs were not illustrated, as the Torah is not, but today they contain richly diverse drawings, etchings, and photographs.

You might also add specific readings to your standard Haggadah, clipping poems, prayers, and commentary from Anne Frank or Elie Wiesel, for example, and photocopying the sheet as an addition to each Haggadah.

Because of the emphasis on learning during the seder, an appropriate way to involve guests is to ask them to bring a question about Passover. Anyone at the table with the answer should feel free to give it, and when dissenting responses are presented a lively discussion is sure to take place.

Another good way to get your guests involved is to pass around the seder plate and have everyone make their own at their place. They can take a bit of parsley, a spoonful of *haroset,* a few tablespoons of salt water, a dab of horseradish. Then, with all the ceremonial foods in place right before them, the rituals will have more meaning and immediacy.

It is traditional to give *tzedakah* before the start of the Passover holiday. This came about as a way of providing the poor with enough money to buy matzoh and other foods for the celebration. A few days before Passover begins is the right time to make a donation to your temple fund for this purpose.

It is an old Passover custom to open your seder to a guest who is far from home. If you are aware of any visiting colleagues at work or travelers in your community, consider bringing them home for seder.

If you are invited to a seder as a guest, nice gift ideas to honor Passover include a kiddush cup, a seder plate, a matzoh cover, or a special dish for salt water.

A Cup for Elijah

Materials Needed

    Pencil and paper
    Colored felt-tip markers
    Clear plastic wineglass
    1 can of clear spray lacquer
    About 18 inches of ribbon
    Cellophane tape

Directions

1. Using the pencil, sketch a few designs on paper to see what shapes and patterns you like best—geometrics, animals, plants, and flowers, Jewish symbols—and which colors go with which.
2. When you are satisfied with your designs, use your markers to outline them on the glass and then color them in. You can color the base a solid color, cover it with designs, or leave it clear.
3. When the markers are dry, spray the glass with clear lacquer to make the designs permanent. Let dry.
4. Tape the ribbon to the top of the stem and wrap around it down to the bottom. Tape the remaining ribbon into a bow.
5. Fill with wine and set in the center of the seder table to await Elijah.

Preparing for Your Seder

The seder is a nostalgic event, a mix of ancient symbols and stories, a melding of food, ritual, and symbolism. It is also a warm family gathering in which hope is the honored guest.

You will be most comfortable at the seder if you have carefully reviewed the Haggadah before your guests arrive. Make sure you have time to select a Haggadah that reflects your own personal views of the holiday. If you have time, go to a Jewish bookstore and look over the many kinds before you buy the ones you will be using. Whichever Haggadah you use, however, the order of the seder is basically the same. Many hosts believe that Haggadahs graced with songs, illustrations, and lively commentary make for the most successful seders.

The word *seder* means "order," and *haggadah* means "recital" or "telling." In telling the story of our ancestors' exodus from Egypt, we focus the ceremonial meal on the message that freedom is attainable despite severe persecution, and that Jews will survive oppression.

If your guests are taking part in the seder, make sure to give them plenty of time to prepare. The best seders tend to be participatory events, so get them their part at least a week in advance. Make sure you know who can read Hebrew and who wants to do their part in English.

Plan well in advance who will ask the Four Questions and whether it will be one child or more. There is enough material for eight children if you read both the English and Hebrew. And decide whether you want the questions to be recited or chanted.

Passover melodies and songs sung during the ceremony add a touch of liveliness. Even if your Haggadah says otherwise, you don't have to leave them all for the end. Many of the best known Jewish songs are Passover songs: "Dayenu," for example, which tells of the miracles God performed, and "Chad Gad Ya," which is about a little goat. In addition, many people sing appropriate folk songs such as "Blowin' in the Wind" and "Go Down, Moses."

The Symbols of Passover

Preparing the table for the seder is a big job, one that requires thought, planning, elbow grease, and time. Plan to set your table with the best of everything: a pressed white cloth, polished silver candlesticks, spotless goblets, your Passover cutlery, and dishes.

Place a Haggadah and a wine glass at each place setting, along with a personal bowl of salt water for dipping. This prevents drippy parsley from being passed around the table. While it is most common to set the table completely before the service begins, some hosts have found that rolling up flatware in napkins and leaving them on the sideboard atop stacked plates keeps everything fresh and new for dinner. When the first part of the service is over, simply remove the wine glasses and bring in the napkins, flatware, and plates.

How the table looks is important for more than aesthetic reasons: Everything on the table has meaning and significance, from the matzoh to the bowls of salt water to the seder plate, the focus of attention and the true centerpiece. You do not need a special plate—any large platter will do—but you will find that a decorated plate with specially divided areas adds dignity and beauty to the table.

Ceremonial Foods and Their Roles at the Seder

Set up your seder plate following the directions at the beginning of your Haggadah, and make sure the five ceremonial foods are placed in the right spots on the plate. The five foods are a roasted lamb bone, a roasted egg, bitter herbs (usually horseradish), a green vegetable (usually parsley), and *haroset,* a mixture of chopped apples, nuts, and wine.

Each of these foods has a Hebrew name and a significant role in the service. The roasted lamb bone is known as *zeroah,* and it symbolizes the ancient Temple sacrifice of the paschal lamb. The egg, or *betzah,* is a reminder of spring and rebirth. The bitter herbs, *maror,* recall the misery

Passover Candle-Holder Boxes

Materials Needed

4 matzohs
Can of lacquer or polyurethane
Paintbrush
Glue gun with clear glue sticks
Aluminum foil
2 tall white candles
2 hardware-store candle bases

Directions

1. Break 1 matzoh carefully so you have 2 equal pieces that each measure approximately 4 × 4 inches. Break another matzoh so you have 2 more pieces.
2. Coat the matzohs with lacquer or polyurethane, using either a brush or sprayer.
3. With the hot glue gun, run a row of glue down the side of one edge of the matzoh and quickly attach another piece to it at right angles to form a corner wall. Let the glue gun rest on the aluminum foil when not in use.
4. Run a strip of glue and press on a third wall at right angles, then add a fourth side to close up the box.
5. Repeat steps 1 through 4 to make the matching candle-holder box.
6. Place the matzoh boxes at their places on the table, put the candles in their bases, and insert into the matzoh boxes.

of slavery. *Karpas,* the green vegetable, is a symbol of spring and renewal. And everyone's favorite, *haroset,* represents the brick mortar used by the Hebrew slaves.

If you are a vegetarian, many rabbis suggest using a roasted beet instead of the lamb shank. If you cannot obtain a lamb bone, it is permissible to use a chicken or turkey neck. In either case, roast it in the oven, then scorch it over a gas burner flame or a candle. To roast the egg, first hard-boil it, then brown one side of the shell by holding it between tongs over the gas burner or a candle flame.

You will also need either a bowl of salt water alongside the seder plate or individual bowls at each guest's place. The salt water represents the tears shed by our ancestors when they were slaves.

Next to the seder plate is the matzoh dish, with three matzohs covered in cloth. Additional matzoh to eat during the seder is on a plate by its side. Next to it is a wineglass for Elijah, the prophet whose spirit always attends the Passover seder. There is a Talmudic legend that says he will come back to earth and begin the golden age, the Messianic Era, when peace and freedom will exist everywhere on earth. Most people fill the glass before the seder starts, but others pass it around the table and ask each guest to add a few drops, representing the belief that we all have to act to bring the Messiah to us.

Making Your Seder a Success

Deciding whom to invite and when can be a confusing experience when it comes to seder planning. Most people have a seder on the first night, and many either give a second one on the next night or attend one as a guest. Often, though, seders are given on the last two nights also, and in recent years some synagogues have sponsored seders that serve other populations than our home celebrations. In any case, there is no restriction on the number of seders you may give or attend.

It has become customary for people to invite immediate family on the first night, extended family on the second, and close friends on the third.

However, many people either mix these groups on various nights or combine them all at one seder. All variations are correct, and the decision should revolve around how you believe your seder will work best.

To enhance the atmosphere, consider placing a bouquet of fresh spring flowers—particularly tulips or daffodils—on your seder table or on the nearby sideboard. As a variation from the stark white tablecloth, you might want to use a pale yellow one to reflect the warm spring sun. Fanciful frogs might grace your table, representing the second plague sent to the Egyptians and adding a touch of humor to the event. Toy stores and garden shops will have a variety of these for you to choose from.

To enhance your table even further, you could use hard-boiled eggs as place cards. The shells make beautiful drawing boards for showy markers and puffy paints. Write your guests' names on the eggs, then have them crack them open and eat them with salt water for a first course steeped in symbolism.

Tradition dictates that guests recline during the meal. This is because free people have the luxury of reclining if they so wish, while slaves are forced to stand during a meal. In practice, many people skip this custom, though they might still enjoy special pillows at their chairs to remind them of the joy that comes with their liberation.

It has become a custom to add a fourth matzoh to the three covered ones on the matzoh plate. This is called the matzoh of hope, and it is dedicated to Jews throughout the world who, like those in the former Soviet Union, were not permitted to practice their religion openly. This can be explained as part of the seder service. Some people even place an empty chair and an extra place setting at the table for those who are denied the right to live as Jews in their own country.

The Passover seder is more than a customary gathering, more than a ritual meal, more than the telling of a heartfelt story of freedom. Taken together, all these elements form an experience much greater than the sum of its parts, an experience that gathers greater depth and meaning each time it is lived.

Part III

Warmth and Renewal

9

Yom Ha'atzmaut: Israel's Independence Day

Sing with gladness, offer praises and say, "God has saved our people, the remnant of Israel, gathered them from the ends of the earth."

—Jeremiah 31:7

A Celebration of Hope

YOM HA'ATZMAUT IS A DIFFERENT KIND of holiday from all the others in the festival year. A recent addition to the Jewish calendar, it is more a patriotic event than a religious one. Yet it commemorates a day that brings overwhelming joy to the hearts of Jews throughout the world.

This joyous holiday celebrates Israel's Independence Day, the anniversary of the establishment of the Jewish State on May 14, 1948. After centuries of exile, Jews from more than seventy countries returned home to begin life anew in the newly formed State of Israel. Yom Ha'atzmaut, literally "Day of the Independence," is celebrated every year on the fifth day of the month of Iyar, on or around May 14, the day on which the country declared its own sovereignty and ended more than two thousand years of foreign domination. Because of its enormous political, cultural, and historical significance, Yom Ha'atzmaut reaches back into our history and far ahead into our future at the same time. It is a day for great rejoicing, and a day to honor everything Israeli.

The Third Jewish Commonwealth

The annual celebration of Yom Ha'atzmaut recognizes that a new chapter has begun in the life of the Jewish people, and Jews throughout the world celebrate our miraculous return to our homeland, 1,878 years after the Romans destroyed the second temple in Jerusalem. Although it is technically only a minor festival within the seasonal cycle, it is celebrated with jubilant dancing in the street, fireworks and festivals, parades and picnics in Israel and throughout the world wherever Jewish people live. It is as festive as the Fourth of July and equally significant; perhaps even more so to some, as many people who celebrate this holiday are old enough to remember a time when the State of Israel—and all it signifies—did not exist.

Holiday Traditions in Israel

Picnics, street performances, and parades with colorful floats and pageantry enliven the holiday for those celebrating out of doors. Noisy fun is the order of the day. Groups entertain on platforms set up in the city squares, and fireworks color the night, as singing and dancing take place everywhere.

Bible Quiz

You can create your own Bible competition to rival the international contest held every year in Tel Aviv on Yom Ha'atzmaut. Between dinner and dessert, while spirits are high and your guests are feeling relaxed, break out your homemade game and find out who knows what about whom and why. It's a fun way to entertain your friends and family and honor the origins of the holiday.

Directions

1. In advance of your party, make up questions to match the level of knowledge of your guests. For children, look for simple information in your kids' Hebrew school books and put together straighforward questions about people, places, and events. For adults, use the Bible to find specific passages, read them aloud, and see who can guess where they came from and who they are about.
2. A good number of questions for a between-courses quiz is eleven, provided they are not based on overly long Bible passages. If you are finished with dinner, you might want to extend the game to seventeen. You can use eighteen (chai, for good luck) as long as you have one extra question up your sleeve to break a potential tie.
3. Divide your guests into teams, with no more than four players on a team. This is the ideal number to discuss each question and decide on what the team leader should answer. Knowledgeable groups will appreciate the use of a simple egg timer to limit their discussion time. If all your guests are newcomers to Bible study, you might want to give them as much time as they want.
4. For a variation, you might play one round in straight question-and-answer mode and the second in *Jeopardy!* style, giving the answer and expecting contestants to supply the question.
5. Give a handful of sesame candy to the winning team as both a reward for their knowledge and a symbol that Jewish learning is sweet. If you are feeling generous, give a handful of sesame candy to the losing team, too.

Along with the parades featuring military hardware, such as tanks of all sizes, helicopters and fighter planes streak the sky, and Israeli air force jets entertain kids of all ages with their daring aerial feats and devil-may-care parachute tricks. At Hebrew University in Tel Aviv, government officials award prestigious cultural prizes on Yom Ha'atzmaut, and a giant Bible quiz is televised, testing the knowledge of children from all over the world who travel to Israel to take part in the contest. For Israeli students, the Bible is more than a religious book, of course; it is a history of their country.

On this holiday, people greet one another on the street with the words *Moadim le-simchah,* or in English, "Have a happy festival."

In Israel it is customary to walk a short distance to a place you have never walked to before. This custom grew up to help newcomers get to know their country a few steps at a time. At outdoor street festivals, Israeli poetry is read and Jewish music is performed by Klezmer bands and individual singer/songwriters on guitars.

Embassies and consulates throughout Israel hold receptions for the diplomatic community and others who wish the country well. On college campuses students often sponsor open houses with art shows, dances, and Jewish film festivals. Flag-waving, family barbecues, and a great deal of exuberant singing and dancing are commonly seen in parks and town squares.

At parades, children enjoy hitting each other over the head with plastic hammers that make a squeaking sound, and birthday cakes in honor of the anniversary of Israel's independence are enjoyed in schools, community centers, and synagogues.

How to Join the Celebration

In the United States, the day is filled with concerts of Jewish music, Jewish film festivals, and colorful Israeli fairs. A few weeks in advance, check listings in your local paper or Jewish weekly to find out what might be happening in your area. Many local Jewish community centers feature a family-friendly outdoor activity day. In New York City every year at this time, marchers in the Israel Day Parade delight audiences lining Fifth Avenue and inspire patriotic feelings for the Jewish State. Newcomers sometimes find themselves experiencing a strong sense of identification with the land of Israel, often enhanced by the show of Jewish affection and awe at the parade.

To help you enjoy the holiday, you might want to check local bookstores to see if they are sponsoring a reading of Israeli poets. If they are, go and bring your friends. If they are not, you might suggest one, offering to help research poetry by artists ranging from Yehuda ha-Levi to Hayyim Nahman Bialik to the modern Israeli poets.

Find out if there is any public Jewish entertainment planned in your area. If not, consider sponsoring an event by renting Israeli films or hiring Israeli entertainers, selling tickets, and donating the money to the Jewish National Fund. Call your local Israeli consulate to help locate performers, or look in the Jewish Yellow Pages to find dance teachers who could come and teach you and your family and friends Israeli folk dances.

Some people give *tzedakah* to a worthy cause or to the Jewish National Fund in honor of the day. Multiples of one, ten, or even one hundred dollars for each year of Israel's independence can be offered, helping to affirm the unity of the Jewish people.

To commemorate this day you might buy an Israeli bond to give as a gift or even to keep for yourself. Some families enjoy collecting Israeli stamps and showing them to children on this holiday, often sharing personal stories about their Jewish heritage or visits to Israel in the process.

An Independence Day Party

Israel Independence Day is a very musical, singing holiday, where people march together, hands joined and voices raised in unity. To replicate some of the natural energy of this happy occasion, you can have a lot of fun

Israeli Decoupage Boxes

Materials Needed

Tissue paper in varied colors
Small covered box; wood is best, but plastic or sturdy cardboard will do
Craft glue
Dampened sponge
Decorative Israeli stamps, available at Israeli consulate office in your city
    or through your temple or a local stamp dealer
Paintbrush
Clear lacquer
Scrap of velvet, about 6 inches square

Directions

1. Tear or cut the tissue paper into small pieces, about an inch square.
2. Remove cover from box.
3. Dab small amounts of glue on top and sides.
4. Glue on bits of tissue paper, overlapping the edges of different colors and placing them on the cover at irregular angles for texture.
5. Neatly turn the tissue paper up under the sides of the cover for a smooth edge.
6. Repeat steps 3 through 5 for the box itself, making a neat edge on the rim.
7. Depending on the size of the box, use the sponge to dampen one to four Israeli stamps and attach them to the top of the cover for decoration.
8. When the glue is completely dry, paint the box and the cover with clear lacquer. You may apply two or three coats if you like for a deep shine.
9. Place the velvet in the box as a soft lining.
10. When the glue is dry, put the cover on the box and use as a keepsake or a gift box for jewelry or candy. It makes an especially nice box for a bar or bat mitzvah or Hanukkah present.

hosting a theme dinner with traditional Israeli food and music. The right time to do this is on the eve of Yom Ha'atzmaut. In Israel, at 7 P.M. sirens blare, the national blue-and-white flag is hoisted, and celebrations begin with a bonfire lit at the tomb of Theodor Herzl, the founder of Zionism. This is the time to begin your party.

You might consider a campfire party and plan a cookout—some Israelis roast whole sheep at barbecues in the town square. Or you might think of the occasion as a birthday party and serve a cake for dessert made in the shape of the Star of David, using tiny Israeli flags from a Jewish bookstore instead of candles. As a centerpiece, consider using a menorah, the seven-branch variety, which is one of the most recognizable of Jewish symbols.

If you decide to have an outdoor festival, use blue and white tablecloths and napkins and sprinkle Israeli flags among the hors d'oeuvres. For invitations, you can make an Israeli flag with a piece of white construction paper. Just tape on two blue lines, one on top and one on the bottom, and put a Jewish star in the middle, drawn in blue.

You can make this same design on a rectangular white cake, using blueberries to outline the star and the lines, and serve it after a formal meal or at a dessert-only party.

Music for Your Celebration

If you want to create a dramatic entrance when you bring in your Star of David cake, give out songsheets containing the words to "Hatikvah," the national anthem of Israel, to your guests and have them sing as you enter. *Hatikvah* literally means "the hope." The song was written by poet Naphtali Herz Imber in 1878. The tune, which is based on a Romanian folk song, is familiar to Jews all over the world. It is traditional for everyone to stand when it is sung.

The words to "Hatikvah" are moving and soulful even in English: "As long as a Jewish heart beats, and as long as Jewish eyes look eastward, then our two-thousand-year hope to be a free nation in Zion is not dead."

If you want to do any Israeli folk dances at your party, an easy dance that most people know from their childhood is the hora. Move the furniture out of the center of the room, join hands, form a circle, and sing "Havah Nagila" together while you dance. Even guests who think they do not know the words will find themselves singing along, recalling all the weddings and bar or bat mitzvahs at which they sang and danced to this song.

Before the party, check your local library for CDs or tapes of Israeli folk music to play in the background. Traditionalists will like *Modzitser Melave Malke Melodies* on Neginah Recordings or *Theodor Bikel Sings Yiddish Songs* (Elektra), or you might try *Martha Schlamme Sings Jewish Folk Songs* (Vanguard) or *Sharona Aron Sings Israeli Songs* (Angel) for a more modern interpretation. There's also the *Anthology of Jewish Song* by Sylvia Schwartz (Classic) and *Sing, Israel,* by Moshe Nathanson (Metro).

Plans for Dinner

To honor the Jewish homeland, it is customary to serve traditional Middle Eastern dishes on Israel Independence Day. People in Israel are always on the run, starting work early and having a late lunch, and the way they manage to fill their nutritional needs is to snack on falafel, a dish made of deep-fried balls of mashed chickpeas. Even if you have never made it before, you will definitely want to serve this entrée on Israel Independence Day. Falafel, the primary street food in Israel, has gained international status by showing up on vendors' carts everywhere from London to Los Angeles. This very popular food will guarantee an Israeli flavor at your celebration.

Falafel is most often accompanied by sour pickles or turnips, with sliced lettuce and hot sauce, all stuffed into a pocket of pita bread, the Middle Eastern equivalent of our sandwich. Pita is flat and opens like an envelope, ready for filling. The sauce that most often accompanies it is called *tahini.* Flavored with ground sesame seeds, it is poured lavishly on top of the pita sandwich.

Pita bread is fun to make because it becomes hollow during baking. A staple in all Middle Eastern countries, it puffs up into bread balloons when it cooks, then collapses but maintains its open space inside.

Another favorite Israeli dish for your party is *shashlik,* the Russian name for skewered and grilled meat, what Americans call shish kebabs. In Israel, *kebab* refers to skewered ground meat; shashlik means skewered cubes of meat, either lamb, beef, or sometimes chicken.

Here is a menu to follow for your festive Yom Ha'atzmaut meal:

Marinated Shashlik on Sticks
Pita Bread Pockets
Fancy Falafel
Tahini Sauce
Haifa Hummus
Sliced Spiced Eggplant
Sesame Dessert Bars

Before the Festivities

In Israel, the day before Yom Ha'atzmaut is called Yom Ha'zikaron, or Remembrance Day, named in memory of the thousands who died defending the Jewish State. People visit cemeteries and light candles, and late in the day, when special sirens sound, everyone stops what they are doing and observes a few moments of silence in honor of the dead. Traffic comes to a complete halt while the country's heroes and heroines are remembered.

At nightfall, twelve torches are lit on Mount Herzl in Jerusalem, one for each of the twelve tribes of ancient Israel, to signify that Remembrance Day has ended and Independence Day is beginning. A gun salute honors modern Israel's existence, with one round fired for each year since 1948, the year the country declared its independence. Bonfires light the hills surrounding the cities, and exuberant dancing and singing usher in the time of celebration.

Marinated Shashlik on Sticks

This dish was brought to Israel from Russia and gained immediate popularity. It is similar to many Middle Eastern specialties and so contains that wonderful quality of being familiar yet exotic at the same time. For peak flavor and tenderness, marinate the meat for 4–6 hours or overnight, if possible.

½ cup red wine vinegar
¼ cup olive oil
1 tablespoon brown sugar
2 teaspoons ginger
2 garlic cloves, peeled and diced

½ teaspoon black pepper
1 tablespoon chopped parsley
2 pounds cubed lamb, beef,
   or chicken

1. Combine the vinegar, oil, sugar, ginger, garlic, pepper, and parsley in a ceramic bowl and mix well.
2. Stir in 2 pounds of lamb, beef, or chicken trimmed and cubed into 1-inch pieces.
3. Toss together until all the pieces are well coated.
4. Cover and marinate in the refrigerator for 4–6 hours.
5. Using wooden or metal sticks, skewer 5–6 pieces of meat on each.
6. Grill on a barbecue for 10 minutes, turning once.
7. Serve with rice, pita bread, or a hearty salad.

Yield: 6 servings

Pita Bread Pockets

Pita bread, popular throughout the Middle East, is also called Armenian or Syrian bread and has a natural pocket in the center. Round and flat, it is adaptable to many kinds of filling. It can be cut in half to make two envelopes or sliced into strips and dipped in hummus or tahini. If there are any leftovers, store them in a plastic bag to prevent drying.

3 packages dry yeast   1 teaspoon salt
1 cup water, lukewarm   ½ teaspoon sugar
4 cups sifted flour

1. Dissolve the yeast in lukewarm water and place in a warm spot for 5 minutes.
2. Blend together the flour, salt, and sugar and add to yeast mixture.
3. Knead the dough mixture well on a floured work area and then place in a lightly oiled bowl, covered with a damp cloth.
4. Place in a warm area for about 1 hour to let it rise.
5. When the dough has doubled in size, punch it down onto a floured area and divide into 6 parts.
6. Shape each part into balls and let them sit for 30 minutes, covered with a damp towel.
7. Preheat the oven to 500°F.
8. With a rolling pin, make each ball flat and shape into a circle about ¼ inch thick.
9. Place two at a time on a non-stick baking dish.
10. Bake 5–7 minutes.
11. Remove from oven while bread is puffed up. It will collapse when it cools, leaving a pocket.
12. Serve with falafel or shredded vegetables.

Yield: 6 loaves

Fancy Falafel

More than any other food, falafel has come to symbolize Israeli cuisine to Jews around the world. It is available in every city and small town in Israel, most often from street vendors, and families cook it frequently as a side or main dish. You can save preparation time by using canned chickpeas, although many cooks claim that only fresh ingredients will do. Try it both ways and decide for yourself. This recipe makes about two dozen patties.

2 cups chickpeas (see note)

1 large onion, diced

2 eggs, lightly beaten

2 tablespoons parsley leaves, finely chopped

1 tablespoon lemon juice

1 teaspoon salt

2 cloves garlic

¼ teaspoon ground coriander

¼ teaspoon ground cumin

Dash tabasco

⅔ cup breadcrumbs

Oil for cooking

Note: If chickpeas are fresh, soak in water overnight, then drain; if canned, drain completely.

1. Mash the chickpeas and combine with the diced onion.
2. Add the egg, parsley, lemon juice, and spices and mix well in a blender. Pour in a bowl.
3. Add the breadcrumbs and stir, mixing the ingredients well.
4. Form the mixture into balls a little smaller than golf balls and flatten slightly.
5. Heat a small amount of oil in a frying pan and fry patties for 5 minutes until golden brown.
6. Remove with a slotted spoon and let drain on paper towels.
7. Serve with pita bread, sliced tomatoes, cucumbers, and tahini; a sauce made with ground sesame seeds.

Yield: about 2 dozen patties

Sliced Spiced Eggplant

Eggplant is abundant in Israel and has become a local favorite in casseroles, as a side dish, and in a variety of baked entrées. This recipe makes a flavorful companion to marinated shashlik or chicken strips on skewers.

1 large, firm eggplant	½ cup breadcrumbs
3 cloves garlic, peeled and minced	2 tablespoons butter, melted

1. Preheat the oven to 350°F.
2. Skin the eggplant and slice into six round pieces of about equal thickness.
3. Combine garlic, breadcrumbs, and butter.
4. Cover a baking sheet with aluminum foil and space the eggplant rounds on it.
5. Spread the breadcrumb mixture evenly over the tops of the eggplant rounds.
6. Bake for 40 minutes or until tender. Serve hot.

Yield: 6 servings

The day of sadness and mourning that precedes the excitement and fun of Yom Ha'atzmaut is in keeping with the Jewish philosophy to not forget sorrowful times as we celebrate the good ones.

A Life-Changing Celebration

If you want to do something you will never forget to honor Independence Day, consider making a pilgrimage to Israel with your family. Plan to stay at least two weeks, if at all possible, to see the historic sites, soak up the culture, and connect with your heritage. The best time to go is early spring or late fall. The weather is warm and dry then, much like the normal climate in Los Angeles. It rains only in the winter, and summers are uncomfortably hot, making sightseeing difficult.

Six thousand miles from New York City, Israel is about the size of Massachusetts and is home to about five million people. Four million are Jews, nine hundred thousand are Muslim Arabs, and one hundred thousand are Christians.

On your trip you can visit the Red Sea the Israelites crossed, the wall of the Great Temple of Jerusalem, the spas of Eilat, the cities of Tel Aviv, Haifa, and Jerusalem, and as many points in between as you can. Many people take organized tours, but renting a car and traveling on your own is not difficult. English is widely understood and spoken.

Perhaps the best thing about a trip to Israel is meeting the Israelis. People who were born in Israel are called *sabras,* after the fruit of a cactus bush. The fruit is prickly on the outside and soft and juicy on the inside. Most native Israelis agree this is a good description of themselves.

In the Synagogue

Some temples hold services on the eve of Yom Ha'atzmaut, others in the morning of the day, still others not at all. There are special Torah and Haftarah portions assigned to Independence Day, and it has been designated as a permanent annual festival in the religious calendar. But since it is still a new holiday, it lacks the ritualistic feeling that helps make the other festive days so satisfying.

The Reform prayer book has a service written especially for the day, and the Conservative movement has written a special prayer in its honor. In all cases, Psalms 98 and 100 are recited during the service, and Psalm 126 is sung to the tune of "Hatikvah." Evening services are generally preceded by a festive meal, eaten either indoors or out, with singing, lighting of candles, and the blessing over the wine.

An Independence Day Craft

If you are planning an outdoor barbecue or cold picnic for your celebration, what nicer way to help children look forward to the event than to make a picnic cloth (see sidebar) on which to spread out the food? This picnic cloth features the Star of David, a design that harks back to the time of King David, who used it to decorate his shield when he went out to battle. Because he survived so many assaults, the Star was believed to possess magical powers. Both Jews and non-Jews used the design for hundreds of years, but it was only in the mid-nineteenth century that it began to appear as a synagogue decoration.

At the end of the nineteenth century, when Theodor Herzl's movement for a Jewish State was beginning to coalesce, the World Zionist Organization adopted the design and created a flag with the Star of David in the center and the blue and white stripes of the prayer shawl, the *tallit,* on the top and bottom. This design was adopted as the Zionist flag, and when Israel became a state, the new government selected it as the official flag of Israel.

How Zionism Was Born

Theodore Herzl was a young writer in Vienna who published a tract in 1895 called "The Jewish State," which drew widespread attention from

Independence Day Picnic Cloth

Materials Needed

1 white sheet, preferably twin size
Sharpened pencil
Ruler or yardstick
Several indelible blue markers, with different size tips

Directions

1. Open up the sheet on a flat, hard surface, preferably a wood or tile floor with no carpeting.
2. In pencil, draw a huge Star of David in the center of the sheet. Use a ruler or yardstick to make the sides perfectly straight, or draw freehand if you like the more casual look.
3. When you like the shape and size, color it in with a thick-tipped blue marker. Decorate with thin-tip markers by adding rows of dots, vine designs, or, if you are an accomplished artist, mini-menorahs or lions of Judah.
4. In pencil, draw two horizontal lines at the top of the sheet, about three inches apart, and the same at the bottom. When they look straight, use a blue marker to go over them. Use a yardstick for these lines.
5. With a thin blue marker, fill the space between the lines with appropriate messages: "Happy Independence Day," "Go Israel," your name, the names of all your guests, the date, the menu for the picnic, the weather, the names of entertainers, the kinds of games you will be playing—anything that will help you remember the day.
6. Use the cloth at your picnic. Bring along a blue marker and let friends sign their names.
7. After the picnic, wash the cloth, fold neatly and save for next year. Each year, add the date and some more specific information about your activities between the lines.

both Jews and non-Jews alike. In 1897 he called a meeting of Jews from all over the world to try to recreate the Jewish homeland. Thus, the World Zionist Organization was born, created with the goal of building a Jewish state. The ancient name for Israel was Zion, and the new movement was named Zionism.

For nearly two thousand years, since the Romans drove the Jewish people out of Israel with the destruction of the Second Temple, our ancestors were without a country of their own. The idea of a rebirth of the state of Israel, the political manifestation of Zionist belief, became a symbol of hope to Jews throughout the world.

A Bit of History

After World War II, the European Jews who had survived the Holocaust tried to enter Palestine, then administered under the British mandate, but due to opposition from neighboring Arab countries, the British government wouldn't lift its strict immigration quota. Finally, in 1947, Britain went before the United Nations General Assembly and dumped the problem in the organization's lap. The U.N. voted 33–13 for a plan to partition Palestine into a Jewish state and an Arab state. The Zionists accepted the plan, but the Arabs did not. In the spring of 1948, the British pulled out. On May 14, 1948, members of the new government, led by Prime Minister David Ben-Gurion, gathered in a small museum in Tel Aviv to issue its Proclamation of Independence. The severe restrictions on the immigration of Jews to their homeland were declared null and void. But first they sang "Hatikvah," the Jewish national anthem.

The next day, armies from five Arab countries attacked the new state and war ensued. But when the battles were over, Israel prevailed, and even more land was added to the Jewish homeland than had been apportioned by the United Nations.

When we celebrate Yom Ha'atzmaut, we share the excitement, pride, and national spirit that fills Israelis on this day of celebration. Yet subduing the joy and national sense of triumph this holiday brings is the sobering knowledge that peace is more hope than reality, even today.

Despite its statehood, Israel remains an embattled nation, plagued by terrorists and living under constant threat of attack. Everyone living there has someone to remember, someone who lost his or her life fighting for the country's independence. For those whose memories begin after 1948, Israel is a given, a fact of life, an established nation among nations. But for those who knew the time before, it is nothing short of a miracle.

Why We Celebrate the Holiday

With the rebirth of the state of Israel, Judaism exists both in its homeland and in the Diaspora. This holiday makes us think about our relationship with the Jewish homeland. The celebration of Yom Ha'atzmaut recognizes the beginning of a new time for the Jewish people, marking a cultural and spiritual renaissance that draws strength from the relationship between the State of Israel and Jews everywhere in the world.

While we are watching parades, enjoying Jewish performers, singing, dancing, and dining together in honor of Independence Day, what we are truly celebrating is the miraculous return of the Jewish people to our homeland and the unbreakable bond between Jews living in Israel and those living outside.

10

Lag b'Omer: An Island of Song

And from the day you bring the sheaf of wave offering, you shall count off seven weeks.

—Leviticus 23:15

A Spring Fling in Solemn Times

DURING ANCIENT TIMES, when people lived by the unremitting rhythms of the agricultural calendar, special ceremonies were created to help guarantee the harvest from beginning to end. To ensure that crops would be sufficient to support life for another year, the seedlings in the fields needed care and attention during the early planting. But our ancestors also believed that the people caring for them needed to show restraint and live without frivolity during this crucial time period each year, when the food they needed to sustain themselves would either take root and flourish—or die.

Jubilation in May

The holiday of Lag b'Omer falls in the spring, usually in May, and always on the thirty-third day of the forty-nine-day period between Passover and Shavuot. This is the time in the agricultural calendar just before the spring harvest and the crucial beginning of the farming year. During the seven-week period between Passover and Shavuot, while the new crops were establishing themselves, people were not permitted to wear new clothes, listen to music, marry, or even get their hair cut. That is, except on Lag b'Omer, when all the restrictions were lifted, and picnics, barbecues, singing, dancing, and bonfires were the order of the day. The forty-nine days of restraint mark a period that symbolizes concerns about the growth of the crops, and many cultures have this type of ritual built into their traditions. The guiding principle is that if one waits for the fullness of the season to be assured, normal life can go on again with assurances of survival for yet another year.

Counting the Omer

The Hebrew word *omer* means a measure or sheaf of grain equivalent to about one tenth of a bushel. On the second day of the Passover pilgrimage festival, it is commanded in Leviticus that the Israelites celebrate the beginning of the grain harvest and bring an *omer* (or measure) of barley, the first of the winter grains to ripen, to the temple priest to show their gratitude. In a vivid and colorful ceremony, the priest would wave the *omer* sideways, forward and back, up, down, and around. The ritual was meant as a prayer to God to protect the coming harvest from failure due to bad weather or pestilence.

For forty-nine days thereafter, a measure of grain was to be brought to the temple and each day was counted until the fiftieth day, which is Shavuot. This marks the beginning of the spring harvest, and on this day two loaves of bread are baked from the first wheat and offered in thanksgiving, and the *omer* cycle ends.

The Magic of Thirty-three

The period between Passover and Shavuot has come to be called the *omer*. Lag b'Omer, on the thirty-third day, gets its name from a numerical abbreviation. The word *lag* is a combination of the Hebrew letters *lamed* and *gimmel*, joined together phonetically. In addition to standing for a particular sound, every letter of the Hebrew alphabet has a numerical meaning. *Lamed* means thirty and *gimmel* means three. Joined together, they form the number thirty-three. Lag b'Omer means the thirty-third day of the counting of the *omer*, and has become a shorthand way of naming this day, the eighteenth day of the month of Iyar.

Although its origins are uncertain, Lag b'Omer, celebrated on the thirty-third day of the counting, has become a joyous festival day. Israeli schoolchildren get the day off from class. Many couples marry on this day, and in Israel people plant trees. The youngest of the Jewish festivals, it has become an island of happiness in a sea of solemn weeks. It is a day when all inhibitions are relaxed, and a festive break in a time of restraint is allowed.

How to Celebrate the Holiday

It wouldn't be a Jewish holiday without a good meal, of course, and on Lag b'Omer what makes the difference is the venue. Celebrations take place out of doors—in the backyard or on the patio, in the woods, at a park, at a lake, or at the ocean. Because it is spring and the weather has a good chance of being nice, the important element here is to be out in nature.

Picnics, hikes, and barbecues are most likely to mark the occasion. Any time of day is acceptable for a gathering, even morning. Families and friends might gather around a nighttime bonfire and tell stories of the brave heroes whose lives are commemorated on Lag b'Omer. Often singing and dancing take place, and the hora is a perennial favorite. Sometimes families gather at a festival of Jewish music. Many people like to eat Middle Eastern food, in honor of the origins of the holiday. You can barbecue or serve a cold, cook-ahead picnic, as long as you enjoy the festivities, too.

In Israel it's traditional to sit around a roaring fire, roast onions and potatoes, and sing Jewish melodies. In the United States, many people enjoy the spring warmth which usually begins around Lag b'Omer by going camping. Some gatherings feature community cookouts with outdoor games and sporting competitions.

A Link Between Celebrations

When the temple in Jerusalem was destroyed in 70 C.E., the *omer* offering could no longer be observed in its original form, so the rabbis recast the counting and made it part of the daily liturgy. Thus, everyone began counting the *omer*, not just those who made the offering, and the practice continues and is still observed by many today. It creates a link between Passover, which celebrates the Exodus, and Shavuot, which celebrates receiving the Torah on Mount Sinai, and serves as a timely reminder that life is precious, and that we should count every day, for every day counts.

Jewish mystics see something beyond the historical bond between the two holidays, saying this period joins the Jewish people's physical and spiritual redemption as we move through the seasons from Passover to Shavuot. They believe the seven weeks between the two holidays to be a time of spiritual cleansing that is necessary to make the Jewish people ready to receive the Torah on Shavuot.

Each evening of the forty-nine days, traditional Jews say a blessing, recite a formula for counting, read a psalm, wave the grain in the air, and say a special prayer. This is the context in which the holiday of Lag b'Omer, on the thirty-third day, is celebrated.

Holiday Heroes

Nearly two thousand years ago, Israel was conquered by a Roman general named Titus, who destroyed the Second Temple of Jerusalem and closed the religious schools, forbidding the study of Torah. Because these actions threatened to destroy everything the Jewish people hold dear, people studied in secret and plotted and planned ways to free themselves from this tyranny. About sixty years later, in an effort to gain national independence, Rabbi Akiva, a highly respected Talmudic scholar of the day, met Simeon Bar Kochba, whom Akiva believed was the Messiah. They gathered their followers, many of whom were students, and led a ferocious revolt, which began at Passover.

At first, the revolt looked as though it would succeed, and hopes flew high for rebuilding the temple. But a great plague attacked the fighters, and thousands died. Nonetheless, on the thirty-third day, the plague suddenly ceased, the Romans lost several strategic battles, a temporary victory was declared, and a day of jubilation was named to mark the event. This is one story of the origin of Lag b'Omer.

Soon after, however, the Romans gained massive strength and crushed the rebellion, killing Bar Kochba. The beloved Talmudic scholar Rabbi Akiva survived the battle and continued to defy the ban on studying Torah, but was soon cruelly executed. The solemn, semi-mourning tone that marks the seven-week period is sometimes said to commemorate the sadness of these defeats and honor the memory of all who died at this time. As signs of grief, Jews do not cut their hair, marry, listen to music, or wear new clothes—all activities banned during the *omer*.

The Many Sides to Lag b'Omer

While its origin is an agricultural festival, Lag b'Omer has been given the added dimension of a historical event. With the uprising against the Romans and the deaths of the student fighters and their leaders, a significant human tragedy occurred after the ritual of counting the *omer* began and was already in place. Thus we memorialize their deaths and celebrate the end of the community's suffering at the same time we celebrate the life-giving crops being blessed in the field during this season.

The Scholar's Holiday

Many cultures honor an old folk custom of sending people to the woods on a set day to shoot bows and arrows in all directions in order to drive out any potential evil spirits hiding there and secure a fertile year. On Lag b'Omer, one of the events enjoyed at many picnics and barbecues is mock archery games, usually played by the children with various types of toy bows and arrows. One reason for this practice is to honor yet another Lag b'Omer hero, Rabbi Shimon bar Yochai, who, like Rabbi Akiva, defied the Romans' decrees forbidding Jews to study Torah.

Bar Yochai courageously continued to teach his students, though he did so under cover, hiding in a cave in Galilee for thirteen years and making his students visit him dressed up as Roman soldiers on a training mission. In order not to be detected for what they were—Jews on the way to a study session—the young students took along bows and arrows and pretended to shoot them at one another in mock battles.

The rabbi died on Lag b'Omer, and asked that his death be commemorated in happiness and not mourning. Often this includes picnics, Jewish songs, and storytelling around a campfire and mock bow-and-arrow battles in his honor. Even Israeli soldiers have marksmanship contests on Lag b'Omer.

Bar Kochba, who is buried on Mount Meron in Israel near the town of Safed, is another scholar honored on Lag b'Omer. On that day the building erected to commemorate his memory is lit with thousands of candles and lamps, and people come from all over the country to sing, dance, and play drums, violins, and flutes in his honor. At midnight a huge bonfire is lit, and some people throw in their fine embroidery work, silken scarves, and handkerchiefs, and tell stories about the great rabbi. Others pitch tents, chant psalms, and study.

The use of bonfires to honor these martyred scholars has spread throughout Israel, and children enjoy a national holiday, play in the fields, and tell stories at night around the fire. Lag b'Omer is sometimes called the Scholars' Day, for the brave heroes who gave their lives for the freedom of the Jewish people and the study of Torah.

A Visit to the Hairdresser

An old custom among traditional Jews is not to allow boys to get their hair cut until the age of three. There are differing explanations for this. One says that it is reminiscent of the custom of not taking the fruit from a tree until it is three years old. Another says it is to honor a rite of passage from babyhood to childhood. Still another says that because Abraham and Sarah's son Isaac, the first child to be Jewish from birth, was weaned at three, this is the traditional age for a child to move into the first level of responsibility to obey the commandments.

In any case, on Lag b'Omer, many three-year-olds receive their first haircut. The seven-week-long prohibition against cutting hair during the *omer* is lifted on this day of celebration, and it has become a custom in Israel to clip these locks for the first time. Often the newly cut hair is tossed into the midnight bonfire, feeding the flames and supposedly making them even more beautiful.

You can honor this tradition with your family and friends by getting a haircut together on Lag b'Omer, or even a perm or a dye job. This fun activity can help connect your family life to the Jewish calendar.

Lag b'Omer and May Day

The ancient Anglo-Saxons chose May 1, right around the time of Lag b'Omer, to go into the woods and shoot arrows at the demons they believed were particularly dangerous at this time of year. The Celtic and Swedish people honored customs of lighting May Day bonfires that were designed to frighten these same demons away. Each culture has its particular cluster of legends that are acted out at this time of year. In Israel, on Lag b'Omer, some believe the bonfires are lit in honor of a wedding festival uniting heaven and earth. Many couples choose this day to marry, believing it ensures a happy life together.

Making the Holiday Meaningful

To honor the holiday and its role in sustaining life, you might consider having your children give *tzedakah* to reflect the importance of the numbers in the *omer* count. For example, your contribution could be the exact number of that night's count—one cent, two cents, three—all the way to forty-nine—until the seven weeks are over. You could save the pennies (or dollars) in a box and donate them all at once on Shavuot, or send a contribution daily for the time period of the *omer* counting.

A Special Way to Celebrate

If you have a home garden, you might want to consider planting winter rye in the fall during Sukkot. Rye germinates within ten days and begins to grow quickly. While it is mostly dormant during the winter months, once spring comes it continues growing before anything else can even be planted. The steady development of the grain is dramatic and exciting to watch.

When the *omer* counting begins at Passover, cut a handful of rye each night for numbering. Take a bunch of the lengthening stalks, bind them into sheaves, and perform the act of waving that the old rabbis used to do. This will give you a renewed sense of the wondrous and life-sustaining power of the grain cycle, a central seasonal theme of the seven weeks between Passover and Shavuot.

Our holidays are celebrated based on the climate of Israel, where it doesn't rain at this time of year, so outdoor parties and outings are always a success there. In other climates, however, where rain is always a possibility, it's still fun to plan a picnic or barbecue and a few outdoor games for the children.

Many parks have covered areas where you can cook out even during a downpour, and if you have the party in your backyard, you can always move the festivities indoors without losing any of the flavor of the celebration.

Food and Fixings for a Fun Event

From the beginning of the *omer* to the end, we go from the sumptuous meal at Passover to the simple meal of Shavuot, which is traditionally dairy, taking us on a gastronomical journey from physical pleasure to spiritual joy. Food at Lag b'Omer, about two-thirds of the way through, should emphasize grains as a reflection of the wheat harvest at the core of the celebration. Good dishes feature beans, salads, tabouleh (a mix of bulgar wheat and vegetables), and many types of breads.

It is also fitting to have sprouts, which are especially appropriate if you are planning a grain-cycle ceremonial, including waving the wheat shaft or counting the days from Passover to Shavuot. It is not hard to sprout beans if you start about a week ahead of your planned picnic. Just keep them damp, either wrapped in paper towel or immersed in about a quarter-inch of water in a shallow dish. Remember to change the water or wet the paper towel daily.

Many people eat carob on Lag b'Omer in honor of the legendary carob tree that grew outside the cave of Rabbi bar Yochai and sustained him for the thirteen years he studied there in secret. Carob is a tasty, non-caffeinated substitute for chocolate that can be used in brownies, fudge, and many types of cookies.

If Lag b'Omer falls on Shabbat, you can prepare a challah in the shape of a key and sprinkle sesame seeds on it as a reminder that manna began to fall during the month of Iyar while the Jewish people were wandering through the desert.

Sample Menus

For a cold, cook-ahead picnic, prepare these dishes and serve on paper plates:

Cold Fried Chicken
Fruited Chicken Salad
Balabusta Bread
Tabbouleh
Cole Slaw Supreme
Carob Fudge
Iced Tea With Orange Slices

Or if there is a barbecue area available to you and it would be fun to cook out, serve:

Kibbutz Kebabs
Marinated Chicken on Sticks
Scallion Potato Salad
Israeli Triple Salad
Rich Carob Brownies
Lemonade

Picnic Planning

To make the seating festive at your Lag b'Omer celebration, take along one red-and-white-checked picnic tablecloth for every six people who will be eating dinner. If there are picnic tables, spread the cloths over them. You might find yourself dining on a smooth expanse of lawn—if so, set out the cloths in a line as though you had a long dining room table, or group them in clusters to put the children together and near but not with the adults.

Fruited Chicken Salad

Add color and variety to your cold meat salads with tasty fruits of the season, like strawberries and grapes. Serve this curious concoction cold with crusty bread for a good dose of healthful vitamin C. You can make it ahead of time and chill it overnight in the refrigerator.

2 pounds cooked chicken breast	2 tablespoons mayonnaise
½ cup chicken stock	8 ounces grapes
½ cup diced celery	8 ounces sliced strawberries
1 large cucumber	

1. Cut the chicken in ½-inch pieces and pour the chicken stock over them.
2. Dice the celery and cucumber and mix together with the chicken.
3. Add the mayonnaise and stir.
4. Mix in the grapes and strawberries. Chill and serve.

Yield: 8 servings

Hopefully, it will not rain, but if you are forced inside, lay the cloths out on the floor and let the guests pretend they are in a clearing in the woods. If you have any music that mimics the sounds of nature, play it in the background.

If you expect to be outdoors on bumpy ground, take along a bed tray, the kind that stands on fold-out legs. Put it in the center of the tablecloth and use it as a stable area for flower vases, candles, tippy jars, bowls of sauce, and drinks. Sand and ants can spoil a picnic, but so can liquids spilled on unsuspecting laps.

Balabusta Bread

This hearty bread combines wheat, rye, and oats in a crusty combination that makes a most flavorful bread for your picnic or barbecue. Mixed-grain breads like this one have a nutty flavor and provide a distinctive taste and texture that goes well with spicy meat dishes.

¼ ounce package of yeast
¼ teaspoon sugar
¼ cup warm water
12 ounces whole wheat flour
6 ounces rye flour

6 ounces medium oatmeal
3 teaspoons salt
2 tablespoons safflower oil
8 ounces water

1. Dissolve the yeast and sugar in ¼ cup warm water.
2. Mix all the flour, oatmeal, and salt in the bowl of an electric beater.
3. Add the oil and the water and yeast mixture and blend with a dough hook for 4 minutes, or mix by hand until a soft, non-sticky dough is formed.
4. Place in a large bowl, lightly oiled, and cover with plastic wrap. Let rise until it doubles in size, which takes about 1½ hours.
5. Preheat oven to 425°F.
6. Divide the dough in half and knead each part for 1 minute, then shape into two loaves.
7. Let rise for about 30 minutes.
8. Bake at 425°F for 40 minutes, or until brown.

Yield: two 1-pound loaves

Passover

The youngest person present at the seder has the duty to ask the Four Questions, the answers to which form the story of the Exodus. Because of the Jewish emphasis on learning, guests are often encouraged to bring a question about Passover to the seder. Dissenting responses can lead to a lively discussion.

Every year at the seder the story of Passover is read from the Haggadah, which literally means "retelling." We hear once again the tale of our flight from slavery in Egypt to freedom in the Promised Land, complete with songs and poems, four glasses of wine, and nibbles of ritual foods from the seder plate.

The Passover table is set with wine, three matzohs and the five ceremonial foods traditional to the holiday: a roasted lamb bone, a roasted egg, bitter herbs (usually horseradish), a green vegetable (usually parsley), and haroset, a mixture of chopped apples, nuts, and wine.

PHOTOS © BILL ARON

Shavuot

Many people think of Shavuot as the wedding anniversary of the Jewish people, with the Torah as the marriage certificate between the Jews and God. Each Torah is individually hand-lettered according to prescribed rules and regulations handed down through the generations.

אשר דהיה דדלינעס

The holiday celebrates the giving of the Torah to the Israelites, who gathered in awe at the foot of Mount Sinai as Moses came down carrying the tablets. The Torah, which literally means both teaching and law, contains the rules, codes, and ethical teachings of Judaism, and accounts of early Jewish history.

Shabbat

Several rituals welcome Shabbat, including lighting the candles at sundown on Friday and reciting the kiddush, the blessing over the wine. In addition, we bless the challah and enjoy a leisurely meal with friends, family, and guests. *Shabbat* means "rest" in Hebrew.

Shabbat, the oldest of all the Jewish holidays, is a day set apart from the frenetic work week to bring us peace, harmony, and tranquility. This time of renewal begins on Friday at twilight and ends when three stars can be seen in the sky on Saturday evening.

Kibbutz Kebabs

This favorite outdoor grilling food can be flavored with garlic or made more exotic with marjoram or oregano instead. Kebabs make a hearty meat dish for any picnic or barbecue. You can substitute ground lamb for beef and onion for garlic in order to create a different taste for the same filling dish. If it is more convenient, mix the ingredients the night before and refrigerate the mixture, wrapped. This will allow the spices to permeate the meat. Enjoy the kebabs inside pita or with any crusty bread.

2 pounds ground beef
¼ cup dried parsley leaves
½ teaspoon salt
¼ teaspoon pepper

4 cloves garlic, mashed
½ teaspoon paprika
½ cup water

1. Mix all the ingredients together and form into 10 patties.
2. Grill over hot coals or on a hot gas grill for 10 minutes, turning halfway through.
3. Serve hot.

Yield: 5 servings

As a special touch, serve the meal on paper plates in blue and white for the colors of Israel. Use matching napkins and paper cups.

If you want to get the whole group involved in the food preparation, consider custom-made sandwiches for the main course. Prepare the makings for open-faced sandwiches on a sampler tray and let your guests decide which ingredients to use. Set up a tray with varied buns and rolls, a platter of iced raw vegetables and plates of relishes and garnishes for individual selection. Your guests will enjoy the experience and you won't feel oppressed by too many serving duties.

Israeli Triple Salad

Israel is famous for its wonderful vegetables, and farm-fresh produce appears on the dinner table every day (and often the lunch and breakfast tables as well). The key to success with this dish is finding succulent vegetables to use in the salad and then dicing them dramatically and perfectly. To keep the flavor at its peak, prepare the salad and then serve immediately. If you absolutely must make it ahead of time, refrigerate with a damp paper towel on top of the bowl.

3 large cucumbers	3 carrots
3 large tomatoes	3 radishes
3 scallions	3 tablespoons olive oil
3 green peppers	3 tablespoons fresh lemon juice

1. Dice all the vegetables and toss them together.
2. Mix the oil and lemon juice in a bowl and pour over the salad.
3. Serve with pita bread or as a side dish.

Yield: 6 servings

Holiday Crafts

A few days before the picnic, tell children the story of the brave Israelis who lost their lives fighting to free themselves from the oppression of the Romans, and introduce the idea of making Roman soldiers they can use for a game at the outing. All materials are easy to find, and if you are thirsty you will find they even come with a bonus snack inside that you can enjoy while making the craft project.

Another way to prepare for the picnic or barbecue and get children excited about the event is to help them weave simple baskets ahead of time to carry the food and utensils. The baskets are easy and fun to make

Rich Carob Brownies

This delicious non-chocolate chocolate confection can be made ahead of time and kept fresh in tins for two or three days. You can find carob powder, which is caffeine free, at health food stores.

¼ cup sweet butter

1 cup sugar (see note)

1 large egg

1 teaspoon vanilla

½ cup flour

½ teaspoon salt

1 teaspoon baking powder

3 tablespoons carob powder

Note: Either brown or white sugar can be used. Brown sugar will make a more flavorful, molasses-type brownie; white a lighter, more delicate-tasting one.

1. Preheat the oven to 350°F.
2. Melt the butter and mix in the sugar until it is dissolved.
3. Beat together the egg and vanilla and add to the butter and sugar mixture.
4. Sift together the flour, salt, and baking powder and add to the mixture.
5. Mix in the carob powder.
6. Bake about 25 minutes in an 8 × 8-inch baking pan.
7. Cool and cut into squares.

Yield: 8 brownies

(see sidebar) and you will find them useful at the celebration itself. All materials can be found around the house or purchased for pennies at a neighborhood craft or variety store.

If you are making several baskets, decorate them with different colors and line them with festive dishcloths to make each one look unique and handmade.

Woven Picnic Basket

Materials Needed

Scissors
One large piece of sturdy cardboard (about 14 × 14 inches) for each basket
Pencil
Ruler
Heavy string, jute cord, or plastic lacing (the kind you would use to make a lariat)
Duct tape or cloth craft tape in any color
Handkerchief or dish cloth

Directions

1. Cut the cardboard so that it is square. Then use the pencil and the ruler to draw a smaller square in the middle of the large one. The smaller square will be the base of your basket and should be about eight inches across.
2. Mark wide strips on the cardboard coming out from the small square to the edges of the large one.
3. Cut away the four new squares at the corners and fold the strips up to form a box shape.
4. Take your string and tape one end of it at the bottom of one of the strips.
5. Weave the string in and out between the strips about halfway up. Then reverse directions and weave the other way.
6. When you reach the top, cut the string and tape it inside the box where it doesn't show.
7. To seal off the top of the basket and make a pretty edge, cut a piece of tape long enough to go from one wall of the basket to the other. Crease it down the middle the long way and tape it along the top edge. Do this for all four edges.
8. Now you are ready to make the handle. Cut two pieces of string, each about ten inches long. Loop them through the woven strips on opposite sides, and tie the ends together inside the basket wall where the knot can't be seen.
9. Line the basket with a handkerchief or dishcloth, fill with goodies, and go on to your picnic.

The Game of b'Omer Bowling

To add to the fun of the picnic for children while they wait for dessert or after the meal is over, try organizing this game for them. It works for children of a wide variety of ages if the older ones can slow down to the level of the little ones, or you can have several same-age groups operating at once if you make enough Roman soldier bowling pins (see sidebar). You will need ten pins for each game plus a ball.

First, find a flat spot and mark off an area about four feet wide by twenty feet long. Set up ten soldiers in the traditional triangular bowling pin pattern of 4, 3, 2, 1 and let the children take turns rolling the ball to knock them over. Give them each two tries to knock down all ten.

You can use a large ball like a volleyball for young children ages two to seven, and a tennis ball for kids eight and up. When using the smaller ball, shorten the rolling area to about fifteen feet and move the pins closer together. As the children become more adept at the game, widen and lengthen the distance to add more challenge.

It's often best to have the children play in teams. Have two scorekeepers, one for each team, to ensure fairness. Games can be played by adding up the pins knocked over or counting only strikes and spares. Play to a score of eighteen, and explain the meaning of *chai* to younger children.

If it rains and your picnic has to move inside, this game can move inside with it. Indoors or out, make sure the children know they have to roll the ball and not throw it.

Soldiers for b'Omer Bowling

Materials Needed

10 narrow plastic water bottles, about 10 inches high
Construction paper in several colors
Cellophane tape
Paper cups
Markers
Small pieces of felt
Yarn

Directions

1. Empty the water bottles partway, leaving about half the water for stability. If the bottles are already empty, they can be partially filled with sand.
2. Wrap the bottles in construction paper and tape the paper securely.
3. Invert paper cups on top of the bottless to make hats. Secure with tape.
4. Use markers to draw faces on the soldiers.
5. Tape on bits of felt for features and decorate the hats with pieces of construction paper.
6. Tape on strands of yarn for hair and moustaches.
7. To create beard stubble, coat facial area with glue and sprinkle on sand.
8. Draw arms and hands and clothing, and don't forget details like jacket buttons and a whole array of medals on each soldier's chest.
9. Stage a mock battle training session among the soldiers while you are awaiting your turn at b'Omer Bowling.

11

Shavuot: Festival of Weeks

Ask me not to leave you, for wherever you go, I will go; wherever you live, I will live. Your people shall be my people and your God, my God.

—Ruth 1:16

Three Celebrations in One

A JOYOUS AND FESTIVE HOLIDAY, Shavuot is considered by many rabbis to be the most pleasant of all Jewish festival days. It is a triple holiday, commemorating the harvesting of wheat in the Holy Land, the ripening of the first fruits in Israel, and the giving of the Torah on Mount Sinai.

Shavuot is celebrated on the sixth day of the month of Sivan and falls in late May or early June, exactly seven weeks after Passover. Shavuot literally means "weeks," and one of its names is the Festival of Weeks because there is no prescribed calendar date for its celebration, only its relationship to the time of Passover, measured in weeks. Two of its other names are the Holiday of the Harvest and the Day of the First Fruits, reflecting the dominant motif of agricultural celebration and thanksgiving.

It is probably best known as the Time of the Giving of Our Torah, linking it to the Exodus and the journey to the Promised Land. It is also called, with a touch of well-loved Jewish humor, the Cheesecake Holiday, in deference to the fact that it is traditional to eat a dairy meal in celebration.

First, A Pilgrimage Festival

For Reform and Reconstructionist Jews in the United States and everyone in Israel, the celebration lasts one day. Conservative and Orthodox Jews outside of Israel celebrate Shavuot for two days, on the sixth and seventh of Sivan.

Along with Sukkot and Passover, Shavuot began as one of the three major pilgrimage festivals, holidays during which the Jewish population traveled to Jerusalem in ancient times to make a prescribed offering at the temple in thanksgiving for the success of the harvest. For Shavuot, the gift was two loaves of bread baked from the first wheat of the season and samples of the first fruits of the harvest: figs, dates, pomegranates, grapes, olives, barley, and wheat. These are the seven crops for which Israel is famous.

The Giving of the Torah

While Shavuot is mentioned in the Bible only as an agricultural festival, an event of enormous historical significance was later linked to the holiday and, in modern times, has largely eclipsed the holiday's harvest origins.

After the destruction of the Second Temple by the Romans in 70 C.E., rabbinic scholars determined that it took exactly seven weeks for our ancestors to travel from Egypt to Mount Sinai, and that the revelation at Mount Sinai, when God appeared to Moses with the Ten Commandments and gave the Torah to the children of Israel, occurred on Shavuot.

The Torah, which literally means both "teaching" and "law," lays down the rules, code of laws, and ethical teachings of Judaism, in addition to recounting the early history of the Jews. It consists of the Five Books of Moses (Genesis, Exodus, Leviticus, Numbers, and Deuteronomy), and the rest of the Hebrew Bible, the Prophets, the Psalms, and the Megillot, plus the oral law and interpretations contained in the Talmud (the Mishnah and the Gemara).

During Passover, the Jews broke free from slavery, but they needed to learn to live good lives before they could be good human beings. Their acceptance of the Torah transformed this tribe of ex-slaves into a cohesive group with a set of laws. In this way Shavuot celebrates the birthday of our religion, just as Passover symbolizes the birthday or independence of the Jewish people.

Because there is no prescribed ritual to honor the holiday, such as lighting candles at Hanukkah or reading the Haggadah at Passover, Shavuot has become one of the less commonly observed holidays in the Jewish calendar. But why let it stay that way? The fact that celebrations are scant makes Shavuot an especially enjoyable holiday to honor in your home, particularly if you are new at hosting and not entirely sure of yourself yet. The truth is you can't make a mistake on this one. You can choose from the numerous customs and traditions that have grown up over the years and tailor them to suit your tastes, instead of secretly worrying that you might not be correctly following a preordained pattern of celebration in a more traditionally celebrated holiday.

Celebrations of Love and Education

Today many people see Shavuot as a holiday that affirms Jewish study and education. One old tradition is to start children on their studies of Hebrew and the Torah on Shavuot. If you have young children at home, you might plan a family dinner on the evening before Shavuot, and introduce your children to the learning of the Hebrew alphabet. In order to show that studying is sweet, the ancient rabbis would write young children's first letters on a slate, coat it with honey, and let them lick it off. You might reward your child's first efforts at reading Hebrew with a specially baked honey cake or fruit dipped in honey.

It has also become a custom for synagogues to offer a confirmation service for teenagers at the end of their formal Jewish education, usually at around the age of sixteen, when they pledge themselves publicly to lead lives based on the Torah. You might consider having a Shavuot dinner party in honor of a child in your family or a close friend who has studied for two or three years beyond bar or bat mitzvah age.

Shavuot is also a day to honor converts to Judaism. The holiday is a renewal of commitment to the Torah and our covenant with God and a celebration of the faith and loyalty of Ruth, the first convert. If someone in your family has converted to Judaism, a Shavuot dinner in his or her honor would be a warm way to say "Welcome."

At any of these celebrations, have guests recall their own Jewish education with anecdotes, pictures, and stories from the heart.

A Torah Celebration Party

Thousands of years ago, when civilizations flourished at different times in Jerusalem, Athens, and Rome, no one would have predicted that the only civilization to continue into the modern world would be Judaism. But Judaism still remains, stronger than ever, based on the law given on Mount Sinai.

You could host an original and unique Shavuot dinner honoring the Torah. As a centerpiece, build a model of Mount Sinai by covering a styrofoam cone with aluminum foil, then spearing slices of fruit on toothpicks and covering your mountain with them. For symbolism, select ten different fruits, one to commemorate each of the Ten Commandments.

An alternative centerpiece could be miniature flowerpots set in a circle, one for each guest to take home, or sheaves of wheat from a florist to recall the wheat offering at the temple in ancient times. Or you could make a family-tree centerpiece (see sidebar).

A Real Family-Tree Centerpiece

Materials Needed

Pencil
Cardboard (like the kind in shirt packages)
Colored paper
Scissors
Markers
Glue
A tree branch, with smaller branches coming off it
A small sturdy box
Enough sand to fill the box

Directions

1. With the pencil, draw a leaf about 3 inches high on a piece of cardboard.
2. Cut it out to use as a template.
3. Trace the leaf on colored paper, one leaf for each member of your family.
4. Cut out all the leaves and, using the markers, write one family member's name on each one. Write a few words to describe the person, his or her relationship to you, and why you like this person.
5. Glue the leaves onto the tree branches.
6. Fill the box with sand and put in your tree branch so it can stand up.
7. Decorate the box with markers and place in the center of the dining table.

For placecards, make small Torah scrolls from pieces of paper wrapped around toothpicks or matchsticks and tied with ribbon. You can even wrap the silverware to look like a Torah scroll if you lay the utensils, handles up, on a folded cloth napkin, roll inward from the outside edges, and tie with a gold ribbon.

Written invitations are always a nice prelude to a dinner party. Make yours from heavy paper in the shape of the Tablets of the Law for a special touch. For dessert, serve ice cream molded into the shape of the tablets, or a cone-shaped cake resembling Mount Sinai.

How to Decorate Your Home for the Holiday

One beautiful tradition closely associated with Shavuot is filling your house with fragrant flowers and plants. There are several explanations given for this. Some say you should spread sweet-smelling grasses on the floor to commemorate the pasture at the bottom of Mount Sinai. Others say we celebrate with flowers because the desert around Mount Sinai burst into bloom on the day the Ten Commandments were given. Still others believe the mountain was dressed with lush foliage and fresh flowers and so we decorate our homes the same way in remembrance.

Children could make garlands of fresh flowers and wear them at your Shavuot celebration. And each guest as he or she arrives could be given a flower for the hair or to place in a handy buttonhole.

Decorate your home with great gorgeous blooms in the front hall, the dining room, and the living room. Deck the fireplace with vines and garlands. You can't overdo it. When the holiday is over, plant the flowers in your garden, in pots lining your patio or walkway, on the terrace, or in window boxes.

When to Have Your Party

On the first night of the festival, evening services at the synagogue are delayed until three stars appear in the sky. In late May or early June, when Shavuot occurs, dusk falls late in the day. This gives you time for a leisurely dinner plus a craft or two, and time for the adults to tell stories before leaving for services.

Hosting a Study Session

Many Jews stay up all night on the eve of Shavuot, a practice begun by the Mystics of the sixteenth century. They study all through the night, symbolizing their commitment to the Torah. Often they read a special book that contains parts of the beginnings and endings of each book in the Bible, the Talmud, and the mystical literature. In the morning they greet the dawn, bleary-eyed yet filled with new knowledge, and attend Shavuot morning services with a new perspective and a heightened sense of spirituality.

A fanciful reason given for this practice is that the children of Israel prepared for three days and three nights to receive the Torah on Mount Sinai, but when the time finally came, they were all so deeply asleep from their exhausting efforts they did not immediately hear the call. Today, in an attempt to make up for this laxity, Jews around the world stay up all night to be ready and alert for the first light of day on Shavuot.

Dairy Traditions

As with all Jewish festivals, feasting is a part of the holiday celebration. Traditionally a dairy meal is served, with cheesecake, cheese blintzes, and noodle pudding predominating.

There are almost as many opinions about why a dairy meal is served as there are cheesecake recipes. Some people think it is because the children of Israel abstained from eating meat on the three days before being given the Torah as they underwent a ritual of purification, which included killing no animals. Others say it is due to the season of the year, as Shavuot occurs at the time when farm animals give birth and produce an abundance of milk. In pastoral societies all over the world, May and June are traditionally the time when milk and cheese dishes are plentiful, and churning and cheesemaking are common features at spring harvest festivals.

It has also been said that the whiteness of milk is symbolic of the purity of Torah, and that because God promised the Jews the land of milk and honey, they eat dairy dishes on Shavuot.

Another possible reason is that the Israelites first learned about kosher laws when they were given the Torah, and then found they could not use their old cooking utensils; hence a simple dairy meal sufficed until sufficient cleaning could take place.

What to Serve at Your Shavuot Party

Many people start the meal with a cold fruit soup to honor the first fruits of the harvest. Raspberry or cherry soups are not hard to make and are popular with cooks and guests alike.

Traditional Jews serve two challahs on Shavuot, one for each of the Tablets of the Law. Some serve one extra-long challah to symbolize the fact that the law is broad and deep.

Always include a platter of fresh and dried fruits to recall Shavuot's origins as a harvest festival. Strawberries, nectarines, watermelon, dried apricots, dates, and figs are good examples of fruits to serve.

If you like traditional cheese blintzes with sour cream, that can be a wonderful main course. But if you want a continental variation, you can do just as well with the Italian and French counterparts, manicotti and crepes.

Cook Ahead for Convenience

Shavuot is traditionally a cooking holiday, but you can prepare much of the food in advance, if that suits you. For example, you can make blintz wraps ahead of time and stack them between sheets of waxed paper. Put them in a plastic storage bag and refrigerate for up to three days or freeze for up to two weeks.

If you want to try something a little different, consider a macaroni and cheese casserole, vegetable lasagne, herring in cream sauce, or onion soup. These dishes are especially well suited to buffets. If you choose to serve dinner this way, place the dishes on a table decorated with seasonal greenery, interspersed with fruit baskets and bunches of fresh flowers.

Traditional Shavuot Recipes

Here are menu suggestions to help your guests enjoy a Shavuot feast in a mélange of flavors you will enjoy serving:

Tel Aviv Fruit Soup
Spinach Salad With Croutons
Spiced Bowtie Pasta
Barley-Cheese Kugel
Vegetable Blintzes
Chantilly Cheesecake

Something Special for the Children

Few of us think about where the items on the grocery store shelves came from or how they got there, but children will enjoy learning firsthand that butter was sweet cream before it became their favorite spread and that mixing up the cream in a special way makes it change form.

You might explain to children that there is lots of grass at this time of year for cows to eat, so they are very productive. Dairy workers put out a

Tel Aviv Fruit Soup

This elegant chilled soup makes a delicious beginning for a Shavuot meal, celebrating the first fruits of the harvest. You can use fresh or canned fruit, and use the sour cream as an optional garnish.

1 cup pitted sour red cherries   ¼ teaspoon salt
1 cup pitted plums   ½ teaspoon cinnamon
1 cup sliced peaches   ½ teaspoon cloves
6 cups water   1 tablespoon cornstarch
¼ cup sugar   7 tablespoons sour cream (optional)
½ cup sweet red wine or cream sherry

1. Combine the fruit, water, sugar, wine, salt, and spices in a saucepan and bring to a boil.
2. Cover and simmer for 10 minutes.
3. For extra smoothness, pour the soup mixture through a large sieve and mash the fruit, then return the mixture to the saucepan.
4. Stir the cornstarch into a quarter cup of water until it dissolves completely.
5. Add to liquid and cook another 10 minutes.
6. Chill and garnish with sour cream, if desired.

Yield: 8–10 servings

lot of effort collecting the milk twice a day. Many cows have calves in the spring, and that keeps the milk flowing.

You can make butter from scratch if you follow these simple directions. For a quarter-cup of butter, you will need one-half cup of heavy cream and a jar with a well-fitting lid. Simply pour the cream into the jar, cover it tightly and shake, shake, shake.

Barley-Cheese Kugel

This hearty casserole can be used as a main dish for a vegetarian meal or as a substitute for potatoes in a more traditional dinner. Filling and tasty, it makes a good Shavuot side dish for a buffet table or as a main course at a sit-down dinner. Barley is in high season at this time of the year, so it is a perfect time to incorporate it into a kugel.

4 cups water	2 tablespoons butter
2 teaspoons salt	2 onions
½ teaspoon pepper	½ pound chopped mushrooms
1 cup pearl barley	2 cups grated Cheddar or Monterey
2 large eggs	Jack cheese, grated

1. Preheat the oven to 350°F.
2. Set the water to boil and sprinkle in the salt and pepper
3. Cook the barley in the boiling water for 45 minutes.
4. Beat the eggs and add to the barley.
5. Heat the butter in a skillet and brown the onions and mushrooms. Add to the barley.
6. Grease a casserole dish and turn the mixture into it.
7. Sprinkle the cheese on top and bake for 40 minutes or until browned.

Yield: 6 servings

Soon you will notice the cream beginning to separate into butter, whey, and watery liquid. Shake, shake, shake! When you get tired, give the jar to a friend, and have that friend shake some more! When most of the cream has solidified, open the jar and pour off the whey and excess liquid. Make some toast and spread the fresh butter on it. Mmm! Save some to serve at your Shavuot dinner, and be sure to tell the guests you made it yourself.

Chantilly Cheesecake

This delicate dessert has held a place among the glories of Jewish cuisine for centuries, probably as far back as the Greek occupation of Palestine in the second century B.C.E. Today most cheesecakes are variations on the original Greek recipe—curd cheese, eggs, and sweetener, baked in a protective crust. This variation freezes particularly well, with no loss of flavor, so you can prepare it well in advance.

CRUST
2 cups all-purpose flour
¼ teaspoon salt
½ cup butter, chilled
4 tablespoons cool water

FILLING
3 eggs, separated
12 ounces low-fat soft cheese
2 tablespoons sweet butter, softened
2 ounces sugar
2 teaspoons lemon juice
½ teaspoon vanilla extract

1. To make the pastry crust, sift the flour and salt together, then use a pastry blender to gradually work in the butter.
2. When these are blended, sprinkle the water over the dough and knead together no more than 10 turns.
3. Cool for 30 minutes, then roll out to ⅛-inch thickness and fit into a 10-inch pan.
4. Preheat the oven to 350°F.
5. To make the filling, mix the egg yolks and all the remaining ingredients in a large bowl.
6. In a smaller bowl, beat the whites until they peak and then fold into the egg mixture.
7. Pour into pastry crust.
8. Bake for 40 minutes, then lower the oven temperature to 325°F and bake for another 30 minutes.
9. The cake is ready when it is a light golden color and feels firm at the edges.

Yield: 6–8 servings

Vegetable Cheese Blintzes

Blintzes are one of the mainstays of Jewish cooking and can be a main course, a dessert, an appetizer, or even a cocktail-party snack. Fillings vary from sweet to savory to tart, but they are always pleasing to eat and to make.

BLINTZ BATTER

1 cup whole milk	2 tablespoons safflower oil
3 eggs	¾ cups sifted flour
½ teaspoon salt	2 tablespoons butter

1. Beat the milk, eggs, salt, and oil together.
2. Stir in the flour.
3. Heat a small amount of the butter in a frying pan or skillet.
4. Pour in about 2 tablespoons of batter, swiveling the pan to coat the bottom.
5. Let the pancake brown slightly on the bottom, then flip it over.
6. Cook for 10 seconds, then stack on a plate.
7. Repeat steps 3 through 6 until all the batter is used up.

VEGETABLE FILLING

¾ cup onions, finely diced	¼ cup cooked rice
2 tablespoons oil	½ cup cottage cheese
½ cup green peppers, thinly sliced	½ teaspoon salt
½ cup carrots, grated	

1. Brown the onions in the oil and add the green peppers and carrots.
2. Add rice, cottage cheese, and salt, and stir.
3. Spread a heaping tablespoon of the vegetable-cheese mixture onto each pancake.
4. Fold closed and fry in oil in skillet.

Yield: about 18 blintzes, or 6–8 servings

Wine for Dinner

What kind of wine goes best with dairy and vegetarian meals? You can count on the fruity taste of a good Riesling, or select a Chenin Blanc or Sauvignon Blanc to accompany your blintzes, noodle puddings, and other dairy dishes. If these are hard to locate, you can do equally well serving a chilled Chardonnay to please your guests.

How to Enhance the Holiday

Because of the emphasis on Jewish education inherent in this holiday, Shavuot is the perfect time to register for a Hebrew class, Bible study group, or religious philosophy course. This is the season that honors learning and the law, and your immersion in them can add immensely to your enjoyment of the holiday cycle.

Arrange for your children to plant something new in your garden or window box. Plants and flowers are an important part of the Shavuot celebration, not only to honor Mount Sinai but to add beauty to your home and synagogue and remind us that Shavuot was originally a nature festival.

Learn about the flowers in Israel. The many varieties that have been coaxed out of the desert soil will astound you.

Try a new fruit for dessert or for a snack. What about yellow cherries? How about blackberries in natural syrup? This is an especially good time to introduce reluctant children to new foods in the hope that a tiny taste will open up a new range of nourishing foods.

Today in Israel long lines of children fill the street as they march with baskets of fruit and beautifully decorated floats in honor of Shavuot. The fruits are sold for the benefit of the Jewish National Fund. You might consider making a donation to the fund in honor of a child who has just begun studying Torah or one who has recently been confirmed.

Pretty Paper Cut-Outs

Materials Needed

Pencil
Plain white typing paper
Plastic margarine container
Sewing scissors
About 6 inches of yarn
Dab of glue
Small piece of tape

Directions

1. Draw a circle in pencil on the paper using the margarine container as a guide, adding about $\frac{1}{2}$ inch to the diameter all around.
2. Cut out the circle.
3. Fold in half and in half again.
4. Cut away most of the edge of the margarine container so only the rim remains to serve as a frame.
5. Tie a short length of yarn through the circle to make a loop.
6. With the scissors, cut out small snips from the folded paper. Unfold the paper and admire your design.
7. Glue the paper to the margarine container rim.
8. Hang in the window with tape.

Start a new family tradition by having children fill baskets of fruit and donating them to worthy causes such as nursing homes and hospitals in your community.

Honoring the Commandments

One special way to give a Shavuot party is to honor your parents by making the Fifth Commandment the central theme of your gathering. Send your parents a handmade invitation with the words from the Torah: "Honor your father and your mother so that your days will be long upon the land that your God is giving to you."

Have your siblings and your children each write a small poem or tribute to the parents and grandparents, recalling a time of special kindness or closeness. Ideally everyone at the table should read his or her contribution, but if children are too shy you could make a scrapbook with all the tributes neatly pasted in for your parents to take home. Add some family pictures, and it will surely be among their most treasured possessions.

Enlarge a photo of your parents—a recent one or even their wedding picture—frame it, and display it prominently near the table. Seat them at the place of honor and serve as many of their favorite foods as you can make. Take a photo of everyone at the table as a memento of a day they will always want to remember.

Holiday Roses

In Eastern Europe a tradition developed during the eighteenth century in which Jews decorated their homes for Shavuot with paper cut-outs called *shavuoslech,* literally little Shavuots, or *raizelech,* little roses. Some rabbis felt the flower decorations that were so beloved were too pagan, so paper cut-outs took their place. They quickly developed into a popular artform (see the sidebar), and the ability to cut them and frame them so they would be suitable to hang in windows was highly prized.

Today in Israel this folk craft is highly developed.

Shavuot Practices

Your Shavuot dinner can open with the candle blessing, a recitation of the Shehecheyanu, kiddush over the wine and a *ha-motzi* over the challah. (See appendix A for the blessings.) Then the festival meal can begin, followed by evening services in the synagogue. If you have a second-night dinner, it is traditional to light a Yahrzeit candle for King David, who was born and died on the sixth of Sivan, Shavuot, and who is considered a model for the Messiah and also a forebear. After dinner, you might sing or recite some psalms, which are attributed to King David, and later in the evening read from the Book of Ruth. (David is a descendant of Ruth's.)

In the synagogue the Ten Commandments are traditionally recited during the reading of the Torah portion, and the entire congregation stands. But if you are hosting a dinner that will not be followed by services, you may want to read them in your home. The Ten Commandments are almost universally accepted; thus the holiday has wide-reaching significance, not only for Jews but for people of all religions, nations, and cultures.

While scholars and theologians may fairly debate what actually occurred on Mount Sinai, the simple statements of the Ten Commandments are central to Judaism. Through the Commandments and the Torah, we are taught to care about the people around us, our community, and the world.

The Ten Commandments can be found in the Book of Exodus, beginning with chapter 20. Assign the task to someone with a solemn voice, or go around the table taking turns in a serious tone.

The Book of Ruth

We read the Book of Ruth because it takes place during the summer harvest in Israel, ushered in by Shavuot. Its theme is faith and loyalty, fitting ideals for a holiday that celebrates the covenant made between God and the children of Israel at Mount Sinai. Rabbinic scholars see a parallel between Ruth's willing acceptance of Judaism and the Jewish people's acceptance of Torah. In addition, the Book of Ruth reminds us of King David, her great-grandson. It is one of the five scrolls, or Megillot, read on special holidays. (The Book of Esther, the other well-known Megillah, is read on Purim.)

In the story, a woman named Naomi and her husband and two sons leave Bethlehem in Judah to escape a famine. In Moab, where they settle, her husband dies and her two sons grow up and marry Moabite women, one named Orpah, the other Ruth. Years later, before either couple has children, the two sons die and Naomi decides to return to Judah. She tells each of her daughters-in-law to return to the homes of their mothers.

Orpah does so, but Ruth insists on staying with Naomi, saying, "Ask me not to leave you, for wherever you go, I will go; wherever you live, I will live. Your people will be my people, and your God, my God." Thus Ruth becomes the first convert to Judaism, and she sets off toward Judah with her mother-in-law and finds a place to settle there.

Ruth takes care of Naomi, gathering that part of the harvest left for the poor—the corners of the field—as it is stated in Jewish law. Boaz, the owner of the field, and a distant relative of Naomi's, falls in love with Ruth and they marry. Their child, Obed, becomes the grandfather of David, the much-beloved second king of Israel.

Shavuot in Israel

Some traditional temples in Israel light 150 candles on Shavuot, one for each of the 150 psalms, thus memorializing King David. In addition to being an expression of loyalty and devotion, it is a commemoration of

Tiny Ruth and Naomi Dolls

Materials Needed

Glue
Yarn
2 clothespins
Pipe cleaners
Scissors
String
Markers
Fabric, assorted small pieces
2 tiny stalks of wheat from the florist, or dried weeds from your
    garden or the park

Directions

1. Glue yarn to tops of clothespins to make hair. To make each
   doll distinctive, give Ruth long hair and Naomi a short yellow
   ponytail.
2. Wind a pipe cleaner around each clothespin to make arms
   coming out at the sides.
3. Cut out strips of fabric in different patterns. Tie around the
   clothespin bodies with string.
4. Make one doll fatter than the other by layering the fabric.
5. Cut holes for the pipe cleaner arms.
6. Tie a sash around Ruth's waist, and put a shawl over Naomi's
   shoulders. Experiment with giving each an apron and a
   kerchief to match their outfits.
7. With the markers, draw faces on the two dolls.
8. Place the wheat or dried weeds between the clothes and the
   body of each doll, so it looks as though it is being carried.
9. Put the two dolls shoulder to shoulder and attach the ends of
   the pipe cleaners so they are holding hands.

the formal act of conversion to Judaism, which the children of Israel performed at Mount Sinai.

Jews from all parts of Israel make Shavuot pilgrimages to Mount Zion, where King David's tomb is located. There they read psalms and think of the day when the Messiah will come and the peace and justice envisioned in the Torah will become a reality.

Some say Shavuot is the wedding anniversary of the Jewish people, and the Torah is the marriage certificate between the Jews and God. In Israel some Shavuot feasts are dedicated to celebrating the Torah as a repository of wisdom and the Jewish people's constitution, a symbol of commitment to living an ethical life.

12

Shabbat: A Day of Rest and Retreat

Let my home glow with the beauty of our heritage. Let my doors be opened wide to wisdom and righteousness.

—V'ahavta Prayer

A Home-Centered Holiday

THERE IS A TALMUDIC LEGEND that says that Jews have two souls on Shabbat, the one they always have and an extra one to celebrate the most important holiday of the year, the golden seventh day that comes every week after six hard days of work. It is the day that commemorates the rest God took after six days of labor creating the universe, and a time for Jews to honor the importance of rest, tranquillity, peace, revitalization, and love.

Shabbat begins each Friday at twilight and ends at sundown on Saturday evening. Ideally the holiday will bring peace to the household, along with three good meals, one or two visits to the synagogue, visits with family and friends, a long walk outdoors, and a deep sense of rejuvenation.

The weekly holiday of Shabbat—a respite from work, competition, and the pursuit of wealth and power—is considered to be a uniquely valuable Jewish contribution to our civilization, introduced into practice among Jews long before it became a mainstay in other cultures. The Shabbat rules, in fact, include everyone in the household, even children, and extend to animals, which are not permitted to plow the field on Shabbat, and to the field itself, which is also recognized as being in need of periodic rest.

The Shape of the Shabbat

Because no work is allowed on Shabbat, an entire cuisine had to be created that allowed all the food to be cooked in advance, a difficult task with the main holiday meal requiring the inclusion of wine, two challahs, salt, and either fish or meat.

In ancient times, when toil and poverty were the rule, Jews ate only two meals per day, and often scrimped on their rations to have enough food for their Shabbat celebrations, most often sharing what little they had with guests. Imagine how helpful it was toward fulfilling their labors to be able, as the week moved on toward its end, to look forward to a day of rest, peace, no work, and three full meals.

Although the holiday was created by the Fourth Commandment: "Remember the Sabbath and keep it holy," Shabbat observance only began in earnest when the prophet Ezra, returning from exile in Babylonia in 459 B.C.E., enacted laws telling everyone—farmers, workers, scholars—they were mandated to observe its laws. In biblical times people were called to the holiday by shofar; in Israel today officials use air raid sirens on Friday evenings to tell everyone to cease their work and go home. Government offices are closed all day Saturday, buses don't run, and business in the country essentially comes to a standstill.

Changing the World

Many people today feel Shabbat is an obligation that is also a gift. On this one day a week we attempt to recreate the moment after Creation when there was peace and harmony everywhere and God rested. Six days a week we try to make the world a better place through our actions; on the seventh day we model a transformed world through mere existence. The Talmud describes the Messianic era as a time of eternal Shabbat, and the holiday is meant to provide us with a foretaste of the peace and glory of the world to come.

Shabbat, which means "rest" in Hebrew, is a religious activity and a gastronomic experience all at once, the oldest of all the Jewish holidays and understandably the one most honored. In the Hebrew calendar, Saturday is the last day of the week, a day set aside from all others, meant to be a haven from the tension and troubles of the work week. There is an old Jewish adage that states, "More than the Jews kept the Sabbath, the Sabbath has kept the Jews."

Cooking for Shabbat

Many dishes for Shabbat are slow-cooked, as in ancient times tradition made it necessary to begin cooking over a heavy fire, then let the embers keep the pot warm when the sun went down. In old eastern European villages every family would mark their pot with chalk and set it in the town baker's oven on Friday afternoon to be picked up after synagogue on Saturday. Most dishes were made with potatoes, buckwheat groats, and beans, with a meat bone added for flavoring along with a handful of onions.

Today this dish is known as *cholent*. The name comes from the medieval French words *chauld,* meaning "hot," and *lent,* meaning "slow." It cooks on the stove or in the oven at a very low heat and sometimes contains boneless brisket, along with carrots, potatoes, and kasha, a commonly available type of buckwheat. *Cholent* is most likely to show up at a midday meal on Saturday, having been slow-cooked since late Friday afternoon until the flavors have melded and the ingredients have softened to perfection.

Shabbat evening calls for an elaborate dinner to set it apart from the other evening meals of the week. In many families dessert is served only on Friday nights, and the meal should be both leisurely and long, meant to inspire a feeling of gratitude for the good food, beautiful service, and warm company.

The Bread of Abundance

Central to the Shabbat dinner are the two loaves of challah that play an important role in the festivities. *Challah* means "dough" in Hebrew. In ancient times, plain, everyday bread was coarse, chewy, and dark. This was in sharp contrast to the holiday bread, which was yellow-white, fluffy, and sweet, made with the family's precious white flour and eggs.

Two loaves always grace the Shabbat table. This is in honor of the manna that fell from heaven during the forty years the Jews wandered through the Sinai desert on their way from Egypt to the Promised Land. The sages tell us that every day one portion of manna fell to feed each person, but on Friday a double portion came down, so the Israelites could rest the next day and observe the laws of Shabbat completely by not having to gather or prepare their food. Another reason given for the two loaves on Shabbat is that they express the feeling of abundance, a good holiday feeling of fullness and hope for the future.

Traditional Friday night challahs are braided into long ovals. Challah braids are usually made with four strands of dough, which look nicer and rise higher than three. Some experienced bakers use six, but this is hard to achieve in the home kitchen. The warm, plump loaves appear on every holiday table except Passover and sooner or later become a staple in the culinary repertoire of every Jewish cook.

Originally the word *challah* did not refer to the loaf itself, but to a small piece of raw dough removed from each large batch of bread by the baker as an offering to God, as mandated in the Torah. Bakers in ancient times symbolically carried out this offering by burning the small piece in the oven while saying a Hebrew blessing. Today the entire bread is called the challah.

Yellow-colored egg challahs are heavier than the more contemporary eggless water challahs that have sprung up among more cholesterol-conscious cooks. Many people use just a dash of egg yolk in a glaze for the surface of the challah that enables sprinkled-on poppy or sesame seeds to stick. If you want to leave out the eggs but keep the yellow color, consider adding a few drops of yellow food coloring to the dough before baking.

To make use of leftover challah, try making French toast or bread pudding, or let the challah dry out for two days and make it into bread crumbs in the food processor.

Lighting the Shabbat Candles

Shabbat has become a mainstay in Jewish life largely because it is a warm, friendly, personal holiday that is easy to celebrate at home. It is an old custom to sing table songs called *zemirot* between courses of the slow, unhurried meal on Friday evening, lending an air of festivity and family cohesiveness to the event.

Many families try to invite a newcomer in the community or an old friend who is alone to the Shabbat evening meal, and some begin the holiday by putting a few coins into the Jewish National Fund or Torah Fund box at home or pledging to support other Jewish philanthropic endeavors. To greet the Sabbath, we say, *"Shabbat shalom,"* meaning, "A peaceful Sabbath."

To begin the Shabbat celebration, the table should be set with the best linen, china, silver, and glassware, the candlesticks polished and the kiddush cup and wine decanter set in their place next to the two challahs, which are covered with a decorated cloth or napkin. The first task to welcome Shabbat is to light the candles.

Candlelight bathes the home in warmth and peace, suffusing it with unity, holiness, and harmony. Some people set out ten candles for the Ten Commandments; others have one for each member of the household; most simply have two candles. Tradition calls for the candles to be white, and they should be long enough to burn for several hours.

The correct time to light the candles is eighteen minutes before sundown, a time that can be determined from looking at the listing in a local Jewish weekly. The number eighteen is important because the word in Hebrew corresponding to the number eighteen, *chai,* means "life." But more important than lighting the candles at exactly the right time is the act itself, and in many families accommodations are made to allow it to occur a little earlier, a little later, or even more than a little later when necessary.

Traditionally it is the woman of the house who lights the candles, but in today's egalitarian society it is fine for anyone who wants to do so to do it. If children have their own candles, they might light them themselves. Everyone who lights a candle joins the worldwide Jewish family, which is doing the same thing for the same purpose in countries all over the globe.

The candlelighting ceremony is different from other blessings, because here we do the act first, then say the blessing. In all other cases the opposite is true. The reason we do the act first is that we can't light a flame after Shabbat begins. So we strike the match, light the candles, then cover our eyes so we don't derive benefit from the flame until after we have blessed it.

Next, we move our hands around the flames several times and bring them toward the face. This gesture welcomes Shabbat into the home. Next we say the blessing (see appendix A), concluding a simple ceremony that marks the beginning of the holiday. The candles are made to burn down to the end, so don't blow them out.

Family Rituals

Probably the most moving part of the Shabbat home service is the one that is the least honored in these fast-moving times: blessing the children with the traditional threefold benediction. After the candles are lit, parents put a gentle hand on each child's head and say, "May God bless you and care for you. May God's light shine on you and be gracious to you. May God's face be lifted upon you and give you peace." For boys they add, "May God make you like Ephraim and Menashe," and for girls, "May God make you like Sarah, Rebecca, Rachel, and Leah."

The blessing of the children goes all the way back to Jacob, who never expected to see his beloved son Joseph again after Joseph was sold into slavery by his brothers. Many years later they were reunited, and when Jacob was on his deathbed Joseph brought his two sons, Ephraim and Menashe, to see him. Jacob cried out his love and blessed the two children. Today we do the same every week on Shabbat and additionally once a year on the eve of Yom Kippur.

Sometimes parents bless each other also, reading a few lines from their *ketubah,* or marriage contract, if they have one. Others read each other special psalms or sections from the Proverbs. Eshet Hayil, A Woman of Worth, is a popular verse to read, and can be found in Proverbs 31:30–31. In some families this is the time for each member to say a few words of gratitude toward those who have done good things for them in the past week.

Blessing the Wine and the Challah

Next comes the blessing of the wine, called the kiddush. It is a good idea to use a kosher wine, but if that is not possible any wine made from grapes or even grape juice will do nicely, as the blessing calls for the "fruit of the vine" but does not specify more than that. Simply raise the kiddush cup, say the appropriate blessing alone or with the entire family

Braided Napkin Rings

Materials Needed

2 cups flour
$^1/_2$ cup salt
$^3/_4$ cup water
Large bowl
Paintbrush
Yellow watercolor paint
Clear lacquer

Directions

1. Mix together the flour, salt, and water in a large bowl until firm and doughlike.
2. Scoop out a small handful and roll into a ball about the size of a golfball.
3. Divide the ball into three equal pieces. Roll each piece into a rope, about 6 inches long.
4. Attach the three ropes at one end and gently braid them, then attach the two ends of the braid together, making a ring about 2 inches in diameter.
5. Let dry for about 2 hours in a warm place or bake in a 350°F oven for 45 minutes.
6. Brush with yellow paint to make it look like a mini-challah braid.
7. When dry, coat with clear lacquer.
8. Repeat steps 2 through 7 for each napkin ring you want to make.
9. When you set the table, gently put each napkin through its ring, fan out the ends and set on a plate.

joining in (see appendix A), take a sip, and pass the cup around for everyone to drink from.

Wine is a symbol of joy and life in Judaism. While it is not biblically mandated to have wine on Shabbat, the rabbis decided it was a good idea because wine is so special. The word *kiddush* means "sanctification," and comes from the same Hebrew root as *kadosh,* which means "holy." Reciting the kiddush over the wine is a way of sanctifying Shabbat. Many families have special silver kiddush cups, but any cup or glass can be used, as long as it is capable of holding 3.3 ounces of wine, the amount required for the ceremony.

The next part of the ceremony is the blessing of the challah. Up to now the challahs have been covered with a specially designed challah cloth, symbolizing the dew that covered the manna and kept it fresh during the forty years of wandering in the Mount Sinai desert. Remove the covering now, pick up the two challahs and hold them together, and recite the blessing (see appendix A), known as *ha-motzi.*

Some Jews place a knife next to the challah to slice it; others feel a knife is a weapon of war and has no place at the table on a holiday that is about peace and love, and they use their hands to tear the challah apart. In either case, it is important to give each person present a piece of the delicious golden bread so they can share in the service and feel the beautiful sense of belonging generated by the Shabbat ceremony.

Time for Dinner

While any dishes that are family favorites are perfectly acceptable for Shabbat dinner, far and away the most popular fare for Friday evening is roast chicken with noodle pudding as a side dish. There is an old saying that Jews eat noodle dishes because we are like noodles ourselves—so entangled with one another that we can never be separated. Some may see this as exemplifying the unity of the Jewish people.

In ancient times chicken was a luxury saved for Shabbat dinners, and serving a poultry main course today honors that time in our history. During the Middle Ages it was a common belief that eating chicken aided in human fertility, and in some communities Jews were forbidden to raise or purchase chickens for exactly this reason.

It is also traditional to serve fish for Shabbat dinner. Jewish lore promises that when the Messiah comes, we will all feast on the leviathan. Thus Shabbat, which is a foretaste of the Messianic Age, is an appropriate time to eat fish. An old Yiddish saying tells us that a Shabbat without fish is akin to a wedding without dancing.

To combine both traditions, many cooks serve a fish appetizer and a chicken main dish. A very popular way to do this is to serve herring or gefilte fish to start, followed by roast or boiled chicken as the entrée.

On every Shabbat table is a salt shaker, because tradition tells us to eat salt with the challah. In ancient times, salt was always present in the Second Temple to be used for ritual sacrifices, and in time salt came to represent the covenant between God and the Jews. Thus, our first taste of challah on Shabbat is always accompanied by a pinch or two of salt.

Dessert on Shabbat is generally a simple affair, usually consisting of some type of coffee cake or mixed fruit. The meal is meant to be lavish without being fancy, creating a sense of abundance but not wastefulness.

A full menu for Friday night dinner might contain the following:

Shabbat Challah
Vegetable Soup With Tiny Knaidlach
Herring in Cream Sauce
Roast Lemon-Apricot Chicken
Fancy Noodle Pudding
Peas and Carrots With Mushrooms
Orange Sherbet With Pineapple Sauce

Shabbat Challah

The art and craft of challah-making has been refined through the ages more lovingly than just about any other technique in the Jewish gallery of culinary achievement. Challah is so much more than just a special holiday bread; it's a gift from the kitchen, a common thread in all our celebrations, and a link between the generations.

1 package (¼ ounce) dry yeast
1 cup tepid (not hot) water
½ teaspoon salt
¼ cup sugar
4 eggs

¼ cup oil or margarine
4 cups white or whole wheat flour
    plus 2 tablespoons
¼ cup caraway or poppyseeds
    (optional)

1. Dissolve the yeast in the water.
2. Add the salt and sugar and stir until the mixture is smooth.
3. Beat three of the eggs, then add to the mixture along with the oil or margarine.
4. Slowly add the 4 cups of flour, stirring with a spoon until everything is mixed well.
5. Sprinkle 1 tablespoon of flour on a cutting board and turn out the dough onto it.
6. Knead for a few minutes, then form the dough into a ball, put it back into the bowl, and cover it with a damp dishtowel.
7. Put in a warm place and let rise for 2 hours.
8. When the dough has doubled in size, punch it down, then sprinkle the remaining tablespoon of flour onto the cutting board and put the dough on it.
9. Divide it into four equal sections, then divide each section into three pieces.
10. Roll each piece into a rope.
11. Braid the three large strands together, pinching the ends and turning them under.
12. Braid the three small strands and put the smaller braid on top of the larger one.

(continued on next page)

13. Place the challah on a greased baking pan. Cover with a dishtowel and put in a warm place to rise for about 2 hours.
14. Preheat the oven to 350°F.
15. Break the fourth egg and separate the white from the yolk.
16. Stir the yolk, then use a pastry brush to paint the egg on the top of the challah.
17. Sprinkle with the seeds, if desired.
18. Bake for 35–40 minutes.
19. Remove from oven when golden brown. A thump on the bottom of the challah should produce a hollow sound to let you know it is done.

Yield: 1 double loaf

Holiday Activities

After dinner, it is customary to say the *birkat ha-mazon,* the grace after meals, thanking God for the generous gift of food. Many families also sing songs at this time. A nice way to involve children in the Shabbat festivities is to have them collect songs during the week. You might want to put together a booklet of songsheets and make copies for each guest.

Another way to involve children in Shabbat is to have a family member read the beginning verses of Genesis, telling the story of how God created the world and then rested on Shabbat, the seventh day. There are several good summaries available in children's Jewish holiday literature, or you could just read the verses directly from the Bible. Doing so makes the purpose of the holiday much more immediate and reminds children of the rhythms of the week, from work to rest and back again.

Many families go to synagogue after the Friday night meal, but others stay home and play games, tell stories, or have a family discussion about plans for the week to come or events from the week that has just ended.

Herring in Cream Sauce

Herring are small, soft, brownish-blue fish found in cold waters throughout the world. Because they are flavorful and have a high fat content, they are sought-after delicacies most often served in small portions, making them perfect for appetizers. Herring are generally enjoyed smoked or pickled in either cream or wine sauce.

1 cup cold water	2 teaspoons pickling spice
1 tablespoon wine vinegar	¼ teaspoon salt
4 large herring fillets	¼ teaspoon whole peppercorns
1 cup red onions, thinly sliced	2 bay leaves
1 cup scallions, thinly sliced	2 lemons
2 teaspoons sugar	½ cup warm water
1 cup balsamic vinegar	2 pints sour cream

1. Combine 1 cup cold water and 1 tablespoon wine vinegar in a ceramic or glass bowl and soak herring fillets for about an hour.
2. Drain and pat dry.
3. Cut the herring into bite-sized pieces and layer in a glass baking dish or bowl, alternating levels with the onions and the scallions.
4. In a saucepan mix together the sugar, vinegar, pickling spices, salt, peppercorns, and bay leaves with ½ cup water and the juice of one lemon.
5. Bring to a boil, let cool, and pour over the herring.
6. Cover with aluminum foil, shake gently, and refrigerate for 6 hours.
7. When cool, remove the herring and drain the liquid into a bowl through a sieve.
8. Mix the sour cream into the liquid, then add the herring and stir together.
9. Slice the remaining lemon and arrange the cream-coated herring on a platter surrounded by the lemon slices.

Yield: 6–8 servings

Roast Lemon-Apricot Chicken

Simple poultry dishes that grace the Shabbat table with elegance and flair fill family and friends with a sense of satisfaction and peace that can carry over to the holiday itself. Lightly spiced fare is most welcome at a celebration that honors the gentle feelings of love and kindness, a day on which we look to refreshment and rejuvenation as our twin goals.

1 fresh roasting chicken, about 5–6 pounds	¼ teaspoon paprika
¼ teaspoon salt	¼ cup warm water
⅛ teaspoon ground black pepper	2 large lemons
	1 bag dried apricots

1. Preheat oven to 400°F.
2. Rinse the chicken both inside and out and pat dry with a paper towel.
3. Lightly rub the chicken skin with salt, pepper, and paprika.
4. Wash one lemon and prick it about ten different places. Cut off both ends so the inside is exposed.
5. Place the lemon in the cavity of the chicken along with 12–15 apricots.
6. Put the chicken on a rack in the roasting pan and place in oven.
7. Immediately turn the oven down to 350°F and roast for 20 minutes per pound, about 3 hours.
8. Remove the chicken and add the warm water and the juice of the remaining lemon to the pan.
9. Pour the liquid into a gravy boat and heat in microwave for 1 minute.
10. Cut up the chicken and serve on a warmed platter, surrounded by several uncooked apricots and a few slices of lemon.

Yield: 5–6 servings

Old-World Cholent

A rich stew simmering overnight is guaranteed to fill the house with wonderful aromas and produce an avid interest in the midday Saturday meal. Traditionally served halfway through the Shabbat day yet tasty and appropriate for any evening meal, cholent blends old-world taste and texture with modern-day convenience and comfort.

1 brisket, about 3 pounds	1 clove garlic, minced
2 tablespoons butter or margarine	¼ teaspoon caraway seeds
1 large onion, sliced	¼ teaspoon peppercorns
6 potatoes	1 teaspoon salt
½ cup kasha or buckwheat groats	2 or 3 beef bones
½ pound lima beans	1 cup warm water
1 bay leaf	1 cup beef or chicken stock
½ teaspoon paprika	

1. Preheat the oven to 200°F.
2. In a sauté pan, melt 1 tablespoon of butter and brown the brisket. Then place brisket in a shallow roasting pan.
3. Melt remaining butter in sauté pan and brown the onions. Sprinkle them over the meat.
4. Peel and slice the potatoes and place them around the meat.
5. Add the kasha and lima beans.
6. Mix the spices together and sprinkle over the meat.
7. Place the beef bones in roasting pan.
8. Pour in 1 cup of warm water and 1 cup of stock.
9. Cover tightly with foil and place in slow oven.
10. Bake overnight.

Yield: 6–8 servings

If families honor the mandates not to work, write, tear, or build on Shabbat, children's games can be scored by placing a marker in a book with the page number corresponding to the number of points won or lost.

On Saturday, a day of leisure in which we use our time to study, reflect, and rest, it is a time-honored tradition to take family walks together, looking at the sky, the flowers, and the trees, and actually calming down enough to hear the birds. Many family members like to nap; others to visit friends. The goal of the day is *shalom bayit,* peace in the house.

In the synagogue on Saturday morning, the Torah portion for the week is read, uniting Jews around the world who are reading the same words and discussing the same meanings at the same time. In Israel everything is closed on Saturdays. Shabbat is more than a private holiday inside your own home; it is a specially acknowledged public holy day celebrated inside the home and also out on the streets throughout the country.

While the midday meal on Saturday is usually some variety of *cholent,* which has been cooking since before sundown on Friday, many Jews also have a special late Saturday afternoon meal as Shabbat is coming to a close. The meal is usually meatless and served cold, and contains bread, eggs, noodle kugel, smoked or pickled fish, and tea. This meal, the third and final meal on Shabbat, came about because of a legend in biblical times. King David was told by a prophet that he would die on the Sabbath, but he was not told which Sabbath. So at the end of each Shabbat he gave a feast in celebration of the fact that he would live another week.

Shabbat is the only holiday on which it is considered a *mitzvah* to eat three main meals. According to the Talmud, those who do so will receive favorable judgment in the world to come.

Saying Goodbye With Havdalah

While Shabbat begins with the kiddush blessing to sanctify it, it ends with a ceremony of separation that marks the difference between it and the other days of the week. The ceremony is called Havdalah, and it centers around a prayer giving thanks for the rhythms of time and life.

Havdalah Candle

Materials Needed

Heating pad
4 candles (each 14–16 inches long) in different colors
3 dishtowels
Smooth plastic work board
Utility knife
Pins

Directions

1. Warm up the heating pad to the high setting.
2. Wrap each candle in a dishtowel and place on the heating pad. Fold the pad around the candles.
3. Apply heat for one minute. Unwrap the pad and check to see how much the candles have softened.
4. Rewrap and apply heat for one more minute. Repeat until the wax is soft and pliable.
5. When the candles have softened sufficiently for you to be able to work them, unwrap them and place them together on the plastic work board.
6. Pinch together the wide ends. If necessary, slice off the bottoms of the merged candles with the utility knife to create a finished edge.
7. Braid the four strands together, overlapping them loosely, taking care not to put too much pressure on the delicate wax.
8. As you reach the tops of the candles, make the last crossover about ½ inch from the top, so the wicks meet but do not join. This will allow the flames to merge when the wicks are lit.
9. Prick little holes up and down the candles with the pins to make a tiny pattern for a fancy, textured look.
10. Set in a cool place to allow the wax to harden, then store safely until your Havdalah service.

Havdalah literally means "division" or "separation" in Hebrew. To hold the service, you will need a cup of wine with a saucer, a box of specially blended aromatic spices called a *besamin,* and a braided candle.

After sunset, when three stars are visible in the sky, friends and family gather at home for the brief ceremony, which can take place anytime after nightfall. There is a five-part ritual that defines the service.

First, Hebrew readings that praise God are read, then we read the same blessing over the wine that we recited on Friday night (see appendix A), which fulfills the biblical injunction to remember Shabbat. We fill the wine cup to overflowing to try to bring about a week that will overflow with blessings. (This is one reason the Havdalah wine cup needs a saucer.)

Next comes the blessing over the spices (see appendix A), usually a mixture of cloves, nutmeg, cinnamon, and a bay leaf. We pass around the spice box and inhale the fragrance as we wish for a week as sweet as this aroma. Moses Maimonides, the Jewish philosopher and physician of twelfth-century Spain, believed the good fragrance of the spices would refresh the soul and make up for the extra spiritual strength that has departed with Shabbat, bringing joy to a soul saddened by the holiday's end.

The Lights of Hope

After the spices, we light a long, multicolored, braided candle, held in the hands of the youngest child present, and say the blessing (see appendix A). Most Havdalah candles have four wicks and are woven in colorful strands. The candle is braided so the wicks are joined in a single flame.

We honor light as the symbol of God's presence and the divine potential we all possess. The Torah tells us that God's first creation was separating light from darkness, so it is fitting that making light is our first act as a new week begins.

Everyone at the Havdalah service comes close to the colorful candle, so different from the simple white candles that begin Shabbat, and all

Spice Box

Materials Needed

Plastic margarine container with lid
Small Phillips-head screwdriver
Hammer
Felt-tip markers in several colors
Dried spices: cinnamon, nutmeg, cloves, bay leaf

Directions

1. Wash and dry the plastic container.
2. With the screwdriver tip and hammer, punch ten small evenly spaced holes in the top.
3. Remove the top of the container and, with a marker, draw a large Star of David on it.
4. On the sides of the container draw four evenly spaced candles with flames, alternating with four drawings of kiddush cups.
5. Put a teaspoon of each of the spices into the margarine container and replace the lid.
6. Store in a cool place until Havdalah, then bring out your box of fragrant spices for the blessing. Be sure to pass it around so all the guests can enjoy the aroma.

take turns cupping its flame in their hands, casting great shadows on the ceiling and making the distinction for themselves between light and dark.

The candle, once blessed, is extinguished in wine poured in the saucer. The candle is saved and used again the following week. Guests wish each other a good week by saying, *"Shavua tov,"* then sing "Eliyah Hanavi" ("Elijah the Prophet"), in hopes of bringing forth the herald of the Messiah. Thus ends another warm and sheltering Shabbat.

Shabbat Crafts

Getting kids excited about Shabbat isn't hard to do with a little advance planning and a bagful of craft ideas. Because it is customary to give *tzedakah* on Shabbat, you might have children make a special box to hold coins they will want to contribute to honor the holiday. Simply take an empty metal Band-Aid box, make a slot on the top by hammering the end of a screwdriver placed in the center of the top, and cover the box with colorful construction paper. Write *"Tzedakah"* on the sides in English or in Hebrew, and place the box in the kitchen where it is easily seen.

Candles are an intrinsic part of the holiday, and there are many ways to make lovely and practical candle holders. One easy way is to make a base out of clay or commercial or homemade play dough. Roll it into a ball about three inches in diameter, then use a Shabbat candle to make an indentation about half an inch deep. Cover the ball with aluminum foil and stud it with sequins held on by pins stuck into the clay. Two of these made with matching decorations will look nice on the Shabbat table.

Another way is to purchase plain wooden candle holders from a craft or fabric store. Tear several sheets of aluminum foil into strips, roll the strips into ropes, and wrap them around the candleholders, securing them with transparent craft clue.

For simple candle holders, save two screw-off tops from soda bottles, push them into two balled-up, two-foot-square pieces of aluminum foil, and glue them in place. Flatten the bottoms of the foil balls to make them able to sit without rocking. Most short tapers will fit quite nicely into the bottle tops. Empty spice bottles filled with colored sand or salt make stable bases for candles, too.

To make a spice box, or *besamin,* for a home Havdalah service, cut 2 contiguous egg cups from a paper egg carton and fold so that one half serves as the bottom of the box, the fold as a "hinge," and the other half as the top. Fill the bottom half with cloves, allspice, cinnamon, and nutmeg; and tape closed. Poke holes in the top, color with markers, and pass around at the ceremony. You can also use an orange studded with cloves, which makes a very fragrant natural spice "box" that is pleasant to hold and pass around.

The Spirit of the Day

All Jewish living involves learning and discovery, and the celebration of Shabbat is no exception. Busy as we are, we all need reminders to momentarily step out of our hectic lives and take a look at the meaning of what we are doing.

The weekly celebration of Shabbat provides just that reminder, and structuring the day according to its traditional form provides the break we so often need. With today's quickly shifting moral ground, the ceremonies and rituals of Shabbat have a way of anchoring us in the values of centuries of Jewish life. And the reconnection with our own thoughts and feelings can often give us that elusive sense of renewal so necessary for our lives to feel whole.

For many, Shabbat is the most important holiday in the Jewish calendar; it brings us back to our roots and thus adds a layer of meaning to every other holiday in the annual cycle. Easy as it is to celebrate, it is even easier to enjoy.

Blessings for Shabbat and the Festivals

Candle Lighting

On the eve of Shabbat

Blessed are you, Adonai our God, ruler of the universe, who makes us holy with your commandments, and commands us to kindle the Sabbath lights.

Baruch atah Adonai Eloheinu melech ha'olam, asher kidshanu b'mitzvotav v'tzivanu l'hadlik ner shel Shabbat.

On the eve of Yom Kippur

Blessed are you, Adonai our God, ruler of the universe, who makes us holy with your commandments, and commands us to kindle the Yom Kippur lights.

Baruch atah Adonai Eloheinu melech ha'olam, asher kidshanu b'mitzvotav v'tzivanu l'hadlik ner shel yom ha-kippurim.

On all other festivals

Blessed are you, Adonai our God, ruler of the universe, who makes us holy with your commandments, and commands us to kindle the festival lights.

Baruch atah Adonai Eloheinu melech ha'olam, asher kidshanu b'mitzvotav v'tzivanu l'hadlik ner shel yom tov.

On kindling the Hanukkah lights

Blessed are you, Adonai our God, ruler of the universe, who makes us holy with your commandments, and commands us to kindle the Hanukkah lights.

Baruch atah Adonai Eloheinu melech ha'olam, asher kidshanu b'mitzvotav v'tzivanu l'hadlik ner shel Hanukkah.

Blessed are you, Adonai our God, ruler of the universe, who has performed miracles for our fathers and mothers in days of old at this season.

Baruch atah Adonai Eloheinu melech ha'olam, she'asa nissim la'avoteinu l'imoteinu bayamin hahem bazeman hazeh.

Shehecheyanu, for a First-Time Event

Blessed are you, Adonai our God, ruler of the universe, who has kept us in life, preserved us, and enabled us to reach this season.

Baruch atah Adonai Eloheinu melech ha'olam, shehecheyanu vekiyemanu vehigiyanu lazeman hazeh.

Kiddush Over the Wine

Blessed are you, Adonai our God, ruler of the universe, creator of the fruit of the vine.

Baruch atah Adonai Eloheinu melech ha'olam, borei peri ha'gafen.

Ha-Motzi Over the Challah

Blessed are you, Adonai our God, ruler of the universe, who brings forth bread from the earth.

Baruch atah Adonai Eloheinu melech ha'olam, ha-motzi lecham min ha-aretz.

For Apples and Honey on Rosh Hashanah

Blessed are you, Adonai our God, ruler of the universe, creator of the fruit of the tree. Our God and God of our people, may this new year be good for us, and sweet.

Baruch atah Adonai Eloheinu melech ha'olam, borei peri ha-eitz.

On Sukkot

To bless the sukkah

Blessed are you, Adonai our God, ruler of the universe, who makes us holy with your commandments and commands us to sit in the sukkah.

Baruch atah Adonai Eloheinu melech ha'olam, asher kidshanu b'mitzvotav v'tzivanu leishev b'sukkah.

To bless the lulav and etrog

Blessed are you, Adonai our God, ruler of the universe, who makes us holy with your commandments and commands us concerning the waving of the palm branch.

Baruch atah Adonai Eloheinu melech ha'olam, asher kidshanu b'mitzvotav v'tzivanu al n'teelat lulav.

On Tu b'Shevat

Blessed are you, Adonai our God, ruler of the universe, creator of the fruit of the tree.

Baruch atah Adonai Eloheinu melech ha'olam, borei peri ha-eitz.

For Havdalah

Candle lighting

Blessed are you, Adonai our God, ruler of the universe, creator of the lights of fire.

Baruch atah Adonai Eloheinu melech ha'olam, borei meorei ha'eish.

For the spices

Blessed are you, Adonai our God, ruler of the universe, who creates varieties of fragrant spices.

Baruch atah Adonai Eloheinu melech ha'olam, borei menei v'samim.

Blessing of separation

Blessed are you, Adonai our God, ruler of the universe, who separates the holy from the ordinary, light from darkness.

Baruch atah Adonai Eloheinu melech ha'olam, ha-mavdil bein kodesh lechol, bein or le'choshech.

To extinguish the candle

May God, who separates the sacred from the profane, forgive our sins and make us secure and as numerous as the sands on the shore of the sea and the stars of night.

Hamavdil bein kodesh lechol, chatoteinu hu yimchol, zareinu v'chaspeinu yarbeh ka-chol, vecha-kochavim b'laila.

Secular Dates of the Major Holidays

The Hebrew calendar is complicated because it is both lunar and solar at the same time. The months are determined by the moon, while the year is measured by the sun, and the numbers do not match. The sages realized that a way had to be found to keep the Jewish holidays in their proper seasons, so rabbinic authorities added an additional "leap" month in certain years to adjust for the extra eleven days in each annual rotation around the sun.

This is the reason the Jewish holidays fall on different dates each year. This is also the reason it is impossible to figure out when a Jewish holiday will occur without consulting a chart specifically made to reconcile the civil and Hebrew calendars.

Here are the upcoming dates of the major holidays for the next several years to assist you in planning your celebrations:

2001–02
Rosh Hashanah, Sept. 18; Yom Kippur, Sept. 27; Sukkot, Oct. 2; Simchat Torah, Oct. 9; Hanukkah, Dec. 10; Tu b'Shevat, Jan. 28; Purim, Feb. 26; Passover, March 28; Yom Ha'atzmaut, April 17; Lag b'Omer, April 30; Shavuot, May 17.

2002–03
Rosh Hashanah, Sept. 7; Yom Kippur, Sept. 16; Sukkot, Sept. 21; Simchat Torah, Sept. 28; Hanukkah, Nov. 30; Tu b'Shevat, Jan. 18; Purim, March 18; Passover, April 17; Yom Ha'atzmaut, May 7; Lag b'Omer, May 20; Shavuot, June 6.

2003–04
Rosh Hashanah, Sept. 27; Yom Kippur, Oct. 6; Sukkot, Oct. 11; Simchat Torah, Oct. 18; Hanukkah, Dec. 20; Tu b'Shevat, Feb. 7;

Purim, March 7; Passover, April 6; Yom Ha'atzmaut, April 26; Lag b'Omer, May 9; Shavuot, May 26.

2004–05

Rosh Hashanah, Sept. 16; Yom Kippur, Sept. 25; Sukkot, Sept. 30; Simchat Torah, Oct. 7; Hanukkah, Dec. 8; Tu b'Shevat, Jan. 25; Purim, March 25; Passover, April 24; Yom Ha'atzmaut, May 12; Lag b'Omer, May 27; Shavuot, June 13.

2005–06

Rosh Hashanah, Oct. 4; Yom Kippur, Oct. 13; Sukkot, Oct. 18; Simchat Torah, Oct. 25; Hanukkah, Dec. 26; Tu b'Shevat, Feb. 13; Purim, March 14; Passover, April 13; Yom Ha'atzmaut, May 3; Lag b'Omer, May 16; Shavuot, June 2.

2006–07

Rosh Hashanah, Sept. 23; Yom Kippur, Oct. 2; Sukkot, Oct. 7; Simchat Torah, Oct. 14; Hanukkah, Dec. 16; Tu b'Shevat, Feb. 3; Purim, March 4; Passover, April 3; Yom Ha'atzmaut, April 23; Lag b'Omer, May 6; Shavuot, May 23.

2007–08

Rosh Hashanah, Sept. 13; Yom Kippur, Sept. 22; Sukkot, Sept. 27; Simchat Torah, Oct. 4; Hanukkah, Dec. 5; Tu b'Shevat, Jan. 22; Purim, March 21; Passover, April 20; Yom Ha'atzmaut, May 8; Lag b'Omer, May 23; Shavuot, June 9.

2008–09

Rosh Hashanah, Sept. 30; Yom Kippur, Oct. 9; Sukkot, Oct. 14; Simchat Torah, Oct. 21; Hanukkah, Dec. 22; Tu b'Shevat, Feb. 9; Purim, March 10; Passover, April 9; Yom Ha'atzmaut, April 29; Lag b'Omer, May 12; Shavuot, May 29.

Glossary

Adonai A name for God.

Afikomen Literally means "dessert." The piece of matzoh broken early in the Passover seder and then hidden. The children search for it and ransom it back to the adults and it is eaten at the end of the meal. The word is of Greek origin.

Ahasuerus The King of Persia at the time of Esther.

Al hanisim Literally means "for the miracles." A prayer of Thanksgiving added to the service on Purim and Hanukkah.

Ashkenazim Jews from Central and Eastern European countries, including those who speak Yiddish, and their descendants.

B.C.E. "Before the Common Era," referring to the time non-Jews call B.C. (Before Christ).

Besamin The spices used for the Havdalah service.

Bimah The raised platform in the front of the sanctuary, where the rabbi stands to lead services. The ark is kept there with the Torah inside.

Birkat hamazon Prayers recited after a meal, sometimes called grace. Literally means "blessing of the meal."

Blintzes Thin pancakes served rolled up with a filling of cheese, jam, sour cream, or fruit, often eaten on Shavuot.

Bochser The fruit of the carob tree, eaten on Tu b'Shevat.

C.E. "The Common Era." Non-Jews use A.D. for *Anno Domini*, which means literally "in the year of the Lord."

Challah Special holiday bread for Shabbat and festivities.

Chametz Literally means "vinegar." Refers to leavened grain products. The category of food that is not kosher for Passover.

Charoset A mixture of chopped apples, nuts, and wine used at the Passover seder to signify the mortar used by the Israelite slaves in Egypt.

Cholent A slow-cooked dish made for Shabbat. Usually a stew of beans, potatoes, and sometimes meat.

Citron A lemonlike fruit from one of the four plant species gathered on Sukkot.

Confirmation A group ceremony held near the time of Shavuot as a commitment by teenagers to follow the teachings of Judaism.

Consecration A ceremony for children entering Hebrew school, held at the time of Simchat Torah.

Days of Awe The ten days between Rosh Hashanah and Yom Kippur during which Jews pray, meditate, reflect, and cross-examine themselves about their acts of the previous year.

Dayenu A part of the Passover seder. Literally means "It would have been enough for us."

Diaspora The widespread network of Jewish communities made up of Jews living outside Israel.

Dreidel A spinning top with four sides containing the Hebrew letters *nun, gimmel, hay,* and *shin.* Used to play a betting game at Hanukkah.

Elijah The prophet for whom we open the door on Passover; he who is destined to announce the coming of the Messiah.

Eloheinu God.

Elul The sixth month of the Hebrew calendar, and the month before Tishri.

Eshet hayyil Literally, "a woman of valor," the first words of a poem at the end of the Book of Proverbs, and an expression used to praise a worthy woman.

Esther The heroine of the Book of Esther, read on Purim. Also known as Hadassah. Her actions prevented Haman from destroying the Jews of Persia.

Etrog Hebrew word for citron, used in ceremonies on Sukkot.

Etz hayyim Literally means "tree of life." Name for the wooden handles at the ends of the Torah scroll.

Falafel Middle Eastern food made of mashed chickpeas and spices.

Gefilte fish A mixture of chopped fresh-water fish blended with eggs and matzoh meal and boiled in fish stock. A common holiday appetizer.

Gelt Coins given as gifts during Hanukkah. The Yiddish word for money.

Gemara A vast body of rabbinic commentary and a part of the Talmud, edited in the fifth century C.E.

Gimmel The third letter of the Hebrew alphabet. One of the four letters on the sides of the dreidel.

Grogger A noisemaker used to drown out the name of Haman each time it is read from the Book of Esther during Purim.

Hadassah Esther's Hebrew name, which means "myrtle," one of the four plant species used at Sukkot.

Haftarah Literally means "conclusion." A section of the books from the Bible about the prophets, read on Shabbat and holidays after the Torah reading.

Haggadah Literally means "telling" or "narrative." The book used for the Passover seder telling the story of the Exodus from Egypt.

Hakafot One joyous circle around the synagogue with the Torah on Simchat Torah.

Haman The official in the court of King Ahasuerus who ordered the annihilation of the Jews in the Book of Esther.

Hamantaschen Three-cornered pastry filled with poppy seeds, apricot jam, or prunes, eaten on Purim to make fun of Haman's hat.

Ha-motzi The prayer said before eating. Literally means "the one who brings forth bread."

Ha-navi Literally means "the prophet," and refers to Elijah in the Havdalah service.

Ha-olam Literally means "the world."

Hanukkiyah A candelabrum with nine branches used at Hanukkah.

Hanukkah The Festival of Lights. Means literally "dedication." Begins on the twenty-fifth of Kislev and lasts for eight days. Celebrates the victory of Judah Maccabee and the rededication of the Temple in Jerusalem.

Havdalah The ceremony of separation at the end of Shabbat.

Hay The fifth letter of the Hebrew alphabet. One of four Hebrew letters on the sides of the dreidel used at Hanukkah.

Holy Temple The building dedicated to worship in Jerusalem. The religious and cultural center of life in ancient Israel.

Hora An Eastern European folk dance associated with modern Israel.

Kaddish The mourners' prayer.

Kapparot The symbolic ceremony on the eve of Yom Kippur where Jews spin a chicken over their heads to expiate their sins.

Karpas The parsley on the seder plate as a symbol of spring or hope.

Kasha A grain, also the mush made from cooking it. Refers to buckwheat, millet, barley, or wheat.

Ketubah The Jewish marriage contract.

Kiddush Literally means "sanctification." The blessing recited over the wine at Shabbat and holidays.

Knaidlach Matzoh balls.

Kol Nidre The prayer chanted at services on the eve of Yom Kippur.

Kosher According to Jewish dietary laws.

Kreplach Triangular pockets of dough filled with meat or cheese, boiled and served with soup, or fried and eaten as a side dish.

Kugel A baked sweet noodle or potato pudding.

Lag b'Omer The thirty-third day of the counting of the *omer*, falling on the eighteenth day of Iyar, between Passover and Shavuot.

Latkes Potato pancakes traditionally eaten during Hanukkah.

L'shanah tovah tikatevu Literally means "May you be inscribed for a good year." A greeting at Rosh Hashanah.

Lox Smoked salmon.

Lulav A palm branch. One of the four plant species gathered at Sukkot. Also refers to the combination of the palm, myrtle, and willow branches that are bound and waved together.

Maccabees The band of farmers who defeated the Syrian Greek army under the leadership of Judah Maccabee and rededicated the Temple in Jerusalem in 168 B.C.E We recall their deeds at Hanukkah. Literally means "hammers."

Mah nishtanah The opening words of the four questions asked by the youngest child at the Passover seder.

Mahzor The prayer book used at festivals. Literally means "cycle" in Hebrew.

Manna The food that fell from heaven to feed the Israelites during their forty years of wandering in the Sinai Desert after the Exodus from Egypt.

"Ma'oz Tsur" A favorite song at Hanukkah.

Maror Bitter herbs used at the Passover seder.

Matzoh The unleavened bread eaten at Passover, the bread of affliction and of freedom.

Matzoh balls Balls made of matzoh meal and egg whites and served in soup on Passover.

Mazel tov Literally means "good luck." Generally used to mean congratulations.

Megillah Scroll, such as the Scroll of Esther.

Menorah Originally the religious candelabrum with seven branches used in the Temple in Jerusalem. Today it refers to the nine-branched hanukkiyah used at Hanukkah.

Messiah The redeemer, or savior, who will come and make the world perfect.

Mishnah A part of the Talmud, codifying Jewish oral tradition, completed about 200 C.E.

Mitzvah Plural of *mitzvot*, literally "commandment" or "religious obligation." It is generally considered to mean a good deed.

Mordechai The cousin of Esther, who lived in Shushan in Persia during the reign of Ahasuerus from 486–465 B.C.E.

Moses The leader of the Exodus out of Egypt who received the Torah from God on Mount Sinai.

Motzi The blessing recited over the bread.

Myrtle One of the four plant species gathered on Sukkot.

Ner tamid The eternal light over the Torah ark.

Nes gadol haya shem "A great miracle happened there." Each of the letters on the dreidel stands for a word in this sentence.

Nisan The first month of the Jewish calendar.

Nun One of the four Hebrew letters found on the dreidel.

Omer Originally a measure of grain, now applied to the counting of the forty-nine days between Passover and Shavuot.

Oneg Shabbat Literally, "the delight of the Sabbath." Refers to the social gatherings after services on Shabbat evening.

Palm One of the four plant species gathered on Sukkot.

Parasha The weekly Torah portion read in the synagogue every Shabbat morning.

Passover The spring festival beginning on the fifteenth of Nisan and lasting for seven days that commemorates the Israelites' Exodus from Egypt with the concept of freedom as the main theme.

Pilgrimage festivals The holidays of Passover, Shavuot, and Sukkot, during which Jews came from all around Israel to bring offerings to the Temple in Jerusalem.

Purim The somewhat raucous holiday commemorating Esther's saving of the Jews from destruction in ancient Persia.

Purim spiel A play produced for Purim, usually a parody or a humorous performance.

Rabbis The generations of Jewish scholars and teachers; the sages.

Rosh Hashanah The New Year in the Jewish calendar. Literally means "head of the year." A day of judgment for all people.

Rosh Hodesh The new moon; the beginning of each month. Literally means "head of the month."

Sabra A native Israeli; literally, "prickly pear."

Sages The Torah scholars or rabbis of the Talmudic period.

Schnapps Whiskey, especially a sweet liqueur enjoyed by Jews.

Seder Literally, "order" or "arrangement"; the family service and meal at Passover.

Sephardim Literally, "Spaniards." Refers to Jews who derive their heritage from Spain, and the heritage of tradition of Jews who come from Africa, the Middle East, southern Europe, and Asia.

Sevivon The Hebrew word for dreidel.

Shabbat The seventh day of the week; the day of rest and spiritual refreshment, the Sabbath.

Shalach mones Literally means "sending of portions." Refers to the baskets of pastries Jews prepare and give to each other on Purim.

Shalom "Hello" or "peace and harmony" in Hebrew. Word used in greeting on arrival or departure.

Shalom bayit Literally means "peace in the house"; the value of harmony in a family, the goal of Shabbat.

Shammash Literally means "servant" or "attendant." Refers to the candle on the Hanukkah menorah that lights all the others and to the sexton of a synagogue.

Shavua tov A greeting for the end of Shabbat that means "Have a good week."

Shavuot The festival celebrated on the sixth day of Sivan, seven weeks after Passover. Also called the Harvest Festival, the Festival of First Fruits, and the Season of the Giving of the Torah. Literally means "weeks."

Shehecheyanu The key word in the blessing of gratitude recited when something new has been done. Literally means "Who has kept us alive."

Shevarim One of the sounds produced by the shofar, the alternation of high and low notes. Literally means "broken sounds."

Shevat The eleventh month of the Hebrew calendar.

Shin One of the four Hebrew letters on the side of a dreidel.

Shofar The ram's horn blown on Rosh Hashanah and Yom Kippur.

Shtetl Yiddish word for a Jewish village in Eastern Europe.

Simcha Hebrew word meaning "joy."

Simchat Torah The festival marking the annual end and beginning of the Torah-reading cycle in the synagogue. Literally means "rejoicing in the Torah."

Sivan The third month of the Jewish calendar.

Sufganiya Hebrew word for doughnut. Usually refers to a jelly doughnut served on Hanukkah.

Sukkah The booth erected for the festival of Sukkot.

Sukkot Literally means "booths" or "tabernacles." Refers to the fall festival beginning on the fifteenth of Tishri and ending on the twenty-second of the month with Simchat Torah. It honors the sukkahs in which the Israelites lived while they wandered in the desert after the Exodus from Egypt.

Taiglach Small pieces of dough cooked in honey and served as Rosh Hashanah treats.

Tallit A prayer shawl used in synagogue services.

Talmud The major repository of post-Biblical Jewish law and tradition. Consists of the Mishnah and the Gemara. Literally means "study" or "learning."

Talmud Torah The study of Torah; also the mitzvah of Jewish study.

Tashlich A ceremony on the afternoon of Rosh Hashanah when Jews empty their pockets and throw crumbs into the river to cast their sins away. Literally means "thou shalt cast."

Techiah One of the types of blasts of the shofar; a glissando that begins on a lower note and rises into a higher one.

Ten Commandments The major obligations between people and God and among people themselves, given to Moses on Mount Sinai.

Teruach Nine short, fast blasts blown on the shofar on Rosh Hashanah. Literally means "alarm."

Teshuvah Literally means "return." Biblical repentance, a resolve to refrain from evil made on Yom Kippur; self-examination, a return to God.

Tikkun olam Repairing the world; the goal of Jewish action.

Tisha b'Av The ninth day of the month of Av, a day of mourning commemorating the destruction of the first and second Temples in Jerusalem.

Tishri The Hebrew month in which Rosh Hashanah and Yom Kippur occur.

Torah The five Books of Moses; the Bible; the totality of Jewish learning, law, and tradition; also called the Tree of Life.

Tree of Knowledge, Tree of Life Two trees in the Garden of Eden; eating from the first provides the ability to discern good from evil; eating from the second imparts eternal life.

Tu b'Shevat The holiday on the fifteenth day of Shevat that is the New Year of Trees, a holiday celebrating nature.

Tzedakah The giving of charity; a gift given as an act of justice; giving to those in need. Literally means "justice."

Tzimmes A baked combination of vegetables and meat, often with dried fruit, honey, raisins, and usually carrots.

Willow One of the four plant species gathered at Sukkot.

Yahrzeit candle A twenty-four-hour memorial candle lit on the anniversary of the death of a loved one.

Yiddish A language of medieval origin developed by Ashkenazi Jews and derived from German and Eastern European dialects.

Yom The Hebrew word for "day."

Yom Ha-Atzmaut Israeli Independence Day, celebrated on the fifth of Iyar.

Yom Ha-Shoah Holocaust Memorial Day, commemorated on the twenty-seventh day of Nisan.

Yom Kippur The Day of Atonement, a solemn day of fasting, prayer, and repentance, concluding the ten Days of Awe that began at Rosh Hashanah. The most important day of the Jewish year.

Yom Yerushalayim Jerusalem Day, celebrated on the twenty-eighth of Iyar, the day in the Six Day War when the Israeli Defense Forces captured East Jerusalem and the city was once again united.

Zemirot Literally means "songs"; refers to the collection of musical selections sung at the table on Shabbat.

Zion An ancient name for Israel.

Recommendations for Further Reading

Agnon, S.Y. *Days of Awe*. New York: Schocken Books, 1965.

Antonelli, Judith S. *In the Image of God: A Feminist Commentary on the Torah*. New York: Jason Aronson, 1995.

Apisdorf, Shimon. *Passover Survival Kit*. New York: Leviathan Press, 1994.

Banin, Israela. *Entertaining on the Jewish Holidays*. New York: SPI Books, 1992.

Diamant, Anita. *Choosing a Jewish Life*. New York: Schocken Books, 1977.

Donin, Rabbi Hayim Halevy. *To Pray as a Jew*. New York: Basic Books, 1980.

Donin, Hayim Halevy. *To Be a Jew: A Guide to Jewish Observance in Contemporary Life*. New York: Basic Books, 1991.

Falk, Marcia. *The Book of Blessings*. New York: HarperCollins, 1996.

Fiszer, Louise, and Jeanette Ferrary. *Jewish Holiday Feasts*. San Francisco: Chronicle Books, 1995

Frankel, Ellen. *The Five Books of Miriam*. New York: Grosset/Putnam, 1996.

Friedland, Susan R. *The Passover Table*. New York: Harper Perennial, 1994.

Gold, Avie, Hersh Goldwurm and Noson Scherman. *Rosh Hashanah: Its Significance, Laws and Prayers*. New York: Mesorah Publications, 1983.

Goodman, Philip. *The Yom Kippur Anthology*. Philadelphia: Jewish Publication Society, 1971.

Hertzberg, Arthur. *Judaism*. New York: George Braziller, 1961.

Gordis, Rabbi Daniel. *God Was Not in the Fire*. New York: Charles Scribner's Sons, 1995.

Greenberg, Rabbi Irving. *The Jewish Way: Living the Holidays*. New York: Touchstone Publishers, 1985.

Kitov, Eliyahu. *The Book of Our Heritage*. New York: Feldheim Publishers, 1968.

Kushner, Rabbi Harold S. *To Life!* New York: Little, Brown & Co., 1993.

Lerner, Michael. *Jewish Renewal.* New York: Grosset/Putnam, 1994.

Palatnik, Lori. *Friday Night and Beyond: The Shabbat Experience Step-by-Step.* New York: Jason Aronson, 1994.

Petsonk, Judy. *Taking Judaism Personally.* Boston: The Free Press, 1996.

Plaut, Gunther T. *The Torah: A Modern Commentary.* New York: Union of American Hebrew Congregations, 1981.

Renberg, Dalia Hardof. *The Family Guide to the Jewish Holidays.* New York: Adama Books, 1985.

Schauss, Hayyim. *The Jewish Festivals.* New York: Schocken Books, 1962.

Silver, Abba Hillel. *Where Judaism Differed: An Inquiry Into the Distinctiveness of Judaism.* New York: Jason Aronson, 1987.

Telushkin, Rabbi Joseph. *Jewish Literacy.* New York: William Morrow & Co., 1991.

Trepp, Leo. *The Complete Book of Jewish Observances.* New York: Behrman House, 1980.

Wolpe, Rabbi David J. *Teaching Your Children About God.* New York: Harper Perennial, 1993.

Zeidler, Judy. *The Gourmet Jewish Cookbook.* New York: William Morrow, 1988.

Acknowledgments

Gratitude is like water; you can't see its shape until you pour it into the right container. This book contains my deep appreciation for those who helped me shape *Jewish Holiday Traditions* exactly the way I envisioned it, only better:

For nourishing my Jewish soul, I thank Rabbi Bonnie Steinberg of Temple Beth-El in Huntington, Long Island, and Rabbi Ted Tsuruoka of Temple Isaiah of Great Neck.

I am most grateful to my daughters, Katie and Amy Burghardt, for providing a living laboratory for me to continually refine my Jewish ideals.

For imbuing me with a deep love of Judaism, I thank my parents, Hilda and Fred Feuerberg, who survived the Holocaust, and their parents, who did not.

I am indebted to Don MacGillis of the *Boston Globe,* whose publishing of my early writing in the *Berkshire Eagle* paved the way to longer and deeper works.

For consistent cheers of encouragement, I thank my friends and colleagues Loretta Schorr, Elizabeth Wissner-Gross, Charlotte Lee, and Bobbie Preiser.

I am grateful to Margaret Wolf for her devoted attention to the manuscript as she turned a box of pages into a finished book, and to Bruce Bender and the rest of his staff at Kensington Publishing Corp. for their efforts.

For her meticulous editing of the manuscript, I thank Carrie Cantor; and for her excellent eye for design, I am grateful to Anne Ricigliano.

For her tireless advocacy on my behalf, I thank my agent Sheree Bykofsky of Sheree Bykofsky Associates. And for his sensitive and evocative photographs of Jewish holiday celebrations, I offer my appreciation to Bill Aron.

Finally, with much love, I express my gratitude to my husband, David Burghardt, whose courage and conviction to choose Judaism enabled me to pour my heart into this project and finally begin to see its shape.

Index

Abraham, 22, 78, 211
Adam, 127
Adloyada (Tel Aviv), 147
Afikomen, 176
Ahasuerus, 145
Akiva, Rabbi, 209
Al Het, 54
Aliyah, 89, 94
"Aliyot" (symphony piece), 158
Almond-Orange Muffins, 138
"Ani Purim" (song), 159
Anthology of Jewish Song (Schwartz), 194
Antiochus, 12–13, 105, 106
Apple(s)
    Dish Placemat (craft project), 28
    serving on Rosh Hashanah, 21, 26, 29,
        36, 267
    Walnut Strudel, 67
Applesauce, Pink, 116
Apricot-Lemon Chicken, Roast, 256
Arbor Day. *See* Tu b'Shevat
Archery games, on Lag b'Omer, 210
Avocado and Chickpea Salad, 155

Baked Salmon in Cream Sauce, 30
Baked Stuffed Zucchini, 92
Baklava, Turkish, 93
Balabusta Bread, 216
"Banner of the Jews, The" (Lazarus), 111
Bar Kochba, 209, 210
Barley-Cheese Kugel, 233
Barley Stuffing, Roast Chicken With, 52
Baskets, 218–19
    shalach manot, on Purim, 149, 161
    Woven Picnic Baskets (craft project), 220
Bee Mobile (craft project), 37
Ben-Gurion, David, 203
Benjamin, 86
Besamin (spice box), 260, 261, 262
Betzah, 180

Bible Quiz, 189
Birkat ha-mazon, 254
Blessings for holidays, 265–68
Blintzes, Vegetable Cheese, 235
"Blowin' in the Wind" (song), 179
Bonfires, on Lag b'Omer, 210–12
Bowling, on Lag b'Omer, 221
    Soldiers for (craft project), 222
Bracelet, Friendship (craft project), 55
Braided Napkin Rings (craft project), 250
Braised Parsnips and Carrots, 53
Bread(s). *See also* Challah; Pita bread
    Balabusta, 216
    Citron Poppy Quickbread, 64
Break-the-fast foods, on Yom Kippur,
        56–57
Brisket à la Modin, 114
Brownies, Rich Carob, 219
Butter, making from scratch, 232–33

Cabbage in Tomato Sauce, Stuffed, 66
Candle, Havdalah, 260–61
    craft project, 259
Candle-Holder Boxes, Passover (craft
        project), 181
Candle holders, making for Shabbat, 262
Candles, lighting, on Shabbat, 247–48,
        260–61, 265, 268
Candy Garden (craft project), 132
"Cantorial Masterpieces" (song), 133
Car Antenna Flag (craft project), 88
Carob
    Brownies, Rich, 219
    serving on Lag b'Omer, 213
Carrots and Parsnips, Braised, 53
Centerpieces (table decorations)
    for Hanukkah, 108–9
    for Passover, 180
    for Purim, 157–58
    Real Family-Tree (craft project), 227

for Shabbat, 248
for Shavuot, 226, 227, 228
for Sukkot, 69, 71
Torah Mobile (craft project), 96–97
for Tu b'Shevat, 133
"Chad Gad Ya" (song), 179
Challah(s), 137, 246–47
  leftover, using up, 247
  recipe for (Shabbat), 253–54
  serving on Lag b'Omer, 213
  serving on Purim, 146, 152
  serving on Rosh Hashanah, 34–35
  serving on Shabbat, 246–47, 249, 251, 266
  serving on Shavuot, 230
  serving on Yom Kippur, 48, 54
  yellow-colored, making, 247
Challah cover, 36
Chametz, 175
Chantilly Cheesecake, 234
Charitable giving *(tzedakah)*
  on Lag b'Omer, 212
  on Passover, 177
  on Purim, 147
  on Shabbat, 247, 262
  on Shavuot, 236, 238
  on Tu b'Shevat, 128
  on Yom Ha'atzmaut, 191
  on Yom Kippur, 41, 43
Cheese
  -Barley Kugel, 233
  Vegetable Blintzes, 235
Cheesecake, Chantilly, 234
Cheesecake Holiday, 224. *See also* Shavuot
Chicken. *See also* Chicken Soup *below*
  Breasts, Old-Fashioned Orange, 154
  Roast Lemon-Apricot, 256
  Roast, With Barley Stuffing, 52
  Salad, Fruited, 215
  Schnitzel, Lemon, 139
  serving on Shabbat, 252
  serving on Yom Kippur, 48
Chicken Soup
  Herbed, 172
  serving on Passover, 168, 170
  Yom Tov Lemon, 51
Chickpea and Avocado Salad, 155
Children. *See also* Craft projects
  blessing the, on Shabbat, 249
  blessing the, on Yom Kippur, 45

Lag b'Omer activities, 218–19, 221
Passover activities, 176
Purim activities, 157–58, 159, 161
Shabbat activities, 254, 258
Shavuot activities, 228, 231–33, 236, 238
Simchat Torah activities, 89, 94
Sukkot activities, 71, 73, 75
Tu b'Shevat activities, 135, 143
Yom Ha'atzmaut activities, 201
Chocolate Torte, Viennese, 174
Cholent, 245–46, 258
  Old-World, recipe for, 257
Chumash, 82. *See also* Torah
Chupah, 128
Citron Poppy Quickbread, 64
Classic Potato Latkes, 115
Cold storage, for foods, 7
Collins, Judy, 136
Cookie Sukkah (craft project), 71, 72
Copland, Aaron, 133
Corn Pudding, Holiday, 91
Costumes, on Purim, 146, 158
Craft projects. *See also specific craft projects*
  on Lag b'Omer, 218–19
  on Purim, 159, 161
  on Rosh Hashanah, 36–37
  on Shabbat, 262
Cream Sauce
  Baked Salmon in, 30
  Herring in, 255
cummings, e. e., 136
Cup for Elijah (craft project), 178

Dairy traditions, on Shavuot, 229–30, 231–32
Dan, 86
Dancing. *See* Folk dancing
Dates, of major holidays, 269–70
David, King. *See* King David
"Dayenu" (song), 179
Day of Atonement. *See* Yom Kippur
Day of the First Fruits. *See* Shavuot
Day of the Sounding of the Ram's Horn (Yom Teruah), 20, 22–24
Debates, on Purim, 162
Decoupage Boxes, Israeli (craft project), 192

Deuteronomy, 12, 82, 95, 128, 135, 165, 168
Dina, 86
Dreidels, 117, 120
    Simple Paper (craft project), 118

Earth Day. *See* Tu b'Shevat
Ecclesiastes, 60, 136
Education, Shavuot and, 225–26, 229, 236
Eggplant, Sliced Spiced, 199
Eggs, on Passover, 168
Elijah, 176, 182
    Cup for (craft project), 178
Entrées. *See also* Menus; *and specific entrées*
    determining serving amounts, 5
    for Passover, 170
    serving two, 7
    for Sukkot, 61
Eshet Hayil, A Woman of Worth, 249
Esther, 13, 144–47, 149–50, 153
Etrog, 77, 130–31, 267
Exodus, 14, 104, 163, 165, 168, 208, 239
Ezra, 244

Falafel, 194
    Fancy, recipe for, 198
Family-Tree Centerpiece (craft project), 227
Fancy Falafel, 198
Fancy Fig Squares, 140
Fancy Gefilte Fishlets, 171
Fasting, on Yom Kippur, 40, 41, 44, 48
Festival of Lights, 103, 106–7
Festival of Weeks, 223. *See also* Shavuot
Fifth Commandment, 238
Fig Squares, Fancy, 140
Fish
    determining serving amounts, 5
    Fancy Gefilte Fishlets, 171
    Herring in Cream Sauce, 255
    serving on Rosh Hashanah, 21
    serving on Shabbat, 252
    serving on Yom Kippur, 48
Flag(s), 89
    for the Torah Procession (craft project), 85
    Welcome, for the Sukkah (craft project), 70
    for Your Car Antenna (craft project), 88

Flowers, on Shavuot, 228, 236
Folk dancing
    on Simchat Torah, 94–95
    on Yom Ha'atzmaut, 194
Folk songs. *See* Music, for parties
Food. *See also* Menus; Recipes
    servings, determining amounts, 5
Forest of the Martyrs, 128
Forgiveness, on Yom Kippur, 46–47
Four Questions, on Passover, 176, 179
Four species, Sukkot and, 76–77
Fourth Commandment, 244
Freezing foods, in advance, 7
Friendship Bracelet (craft project), 55
Fruit(s). *See also specific fruits*
    Hang-Ups, Sukkah (craft project), 62
    serving on Shavuot, 224, 230, 236, 238
    serving on Tu b'Shevat, 124–25, 133, 134–35
    Soup, Tel Aviv, 232
    Tzimmes With Biblical, 90
Fruit of the Goodly Tree, 125
Fruited Chicken Salad, 215
Fruit trees, 127, 130

Game plan, 4–5
Gauchoff, Maurice, 133
Gefilte Fishlets, Fancy, 171
Gemara, 83, 106
Genesis, 98, 134, 135–36, 254
Gift Paper, Hanukkah (craft project), 121
Gifts
    on Hanukkah, 109, 120, 122
    on Rosh Hashanah, 35–36
Gimmel (ganz), dreidel game and, 118
Glossary of terms, 271–79
Goat, on Yom Kippur, 54
"Go Down, Moses" (song), 179
Greeting cards, on Rosh Hashanah, 24, 26
    Star of David New Year's Cards (craft project), 25
Greetings
    on Rosh Hashanah, 35
    on Shabbat, 247
    on Simchat Torah, 84
    on Yom Kippur, 43
Groggers, 159
    Homemade (craft project), 151–52
Guest lists, 6, 8

Hadassah, 150
Haggadahs, 14, 135–36, 164–65, 168, 176–77, 179, 180
Hag ha-Aviv, 163. *See also* Passover
Hag ha-Matzot, 165. *See also* Passover
Haircuts, on Lag b'Omer, 211
Haman, 13, 146, 147, 149–50, 153
Hamantaschen, 146, 159
  Heavenly, recipe for, 156
Ha-motzi, 239, 251, 266
Hanukkah, 12–13, 101–22, 144–45. *See also* Menorah
  blessings, 266
  dreidel game, 118–20
  foods for the holiday, 111–13
  Gift Paper (craft project), 121
  gifts on, 109, 120, 122
  hosting your celebration, 108–9
  in Israel, 107–8
  miracle of the oil, 106–7
  origins of, 102–3, 105–6
  party activities, 109–11
  sharing with family and friends, 108
Hanukkah gelt, 118, 120, 122
Haroset, 180, 182
Harvest
  Lag b'Omer and, 206, 212, 213
  Shavuot and, 223, 224, 230
  Simchat Torah and, 88
  Sukkot and, 59, 61, 63, 68–69
Harvest Vegetable Soup, 65
Hasmoneans, 106
"Hatikvah" (song), 14, 193, 201
"Havah Nagila" (song), 194
Havdalah, 258, 260
  blessings, 268
  Candle, 259, 260–61
Hay (halb), dreidel game and, 118
Heavenly Hamantaschen, 156
Hebrew University (Tel Aviv), 190
Herbed Chicken Soup, 172
Herring in Cream Sauce, 255
Herzl, Theodor, 193, 201, 203
Hiring help, 8
History of Israel, 201, 203–4
Holiday Corn Pudding, 91
Holiday of the Harvest. *See* Shavuot
Holiday prayer book *(machzor)*, 36
Holocaust, 107, 128, 203

Holofernes, 112
Homemade Groggers (craft project), 151–52
Honey
  Cake, King David, 32
  at Rosh Hashanah celebrations, 21, 29, 36
  Taiglach, Sweet, 33
Honey Plate (craft project), 28
Hoshanah Rabbah, 68
Hummus on Spinach Leaves, Mild, 50

Imber, Naphtali Herz, 193
Independence Day, 187–88, 191, 193, 195. *See also* Yom Ha'atzmaut
  Picnic Cloth (craft project), 202
  "In Shu, Shu, Shushan" (song), 159
  "In the Beginning" (song), 133
  Invitations, for parties
  for Hanukkah, 108
  for Purim, 157
  for Rosh Hashanah, 29
  for Shavuot, 228
  for Simchat Torah, 84
  for Sukkot, 69
  for Tu b'Shevat, 133
Isaac, 22, 211
Israel Day Parade, 191
Israeli Decoupage Boxes (craft project), 192
Israeli Jelly Doughnuts, 117
Israeli Triple Salad, 218
Israel's Independence Day. *See* Yom Ha'atzmaut
"I thank God for this most amazing day" (cummings), 136
Iyar, 14. *See also* Yom Ha'atzmaut

Jacob, 86, 249
Jelly Doughnuts, Israeli, 117
Jeremiah 31:7, 187
Jerusalem, 59–60, 107–8, 125, 165, 195, 208
Jewish Arbor Day, 126. *See also* Tu b'Shevat
Jewish National Fund, 126, 128, 191
Jonah, 54–56
Joseph, 86, 249
Joshua, 22
Judah, 106
Judith, 112

Kapparot, 49, 54
Karpas, 182
Kebabs. *See* Shish kebabs
Ketubah, 249
Kibbutz Kebabs, 217
Kiddush Cups (children's chorus), 158
Kiddush, on Shabbat, 249, 251, 266
Kids. *See* Children
Kilmer, Joyce, 136
King David, 240, 242
    Honey Cake, recipe for, 32
Kislev, 106
Klezmer music, 158
Knaidlach (matzoh balls), 168, 173
Kol Nidre services, on Yom Kippur,
        45–47
Kreplach, 48
Kugel
    Barley-Cheese, 233
    Shanah Tovah Noodle, 31

Lag b'Omer, 15, 205–22
    archery games on, 210
    celebrating the holiday, 207–8
    children's activities, 218–19, 221
    counting the Omer, 206
    craft projects, 218–19
    foods for, 213–14
    link between celebrations, 208
    May Day and, 211–12
    origin of holiday, 207, 208–9
    picnic planning, 214–15, 217
    special celebrations for, 212–13
    visiting the hairdresser, 211
Latkes, 108, 111, 112–13
    Classic Potato, 115
Lazarus, Emma, 111
Leafy Picture Frames (craft project), 142
Leah, 86
Leeks, serving on Rosh Hashanah, 35
Lemon
    -Apricot Chicken, Roast, 256
    Chicken Schnitzel, 139
    Chicken Soup, Yom Tov, 51
Levi, 86
Leviticus, 19, 39, 58, 60, 76, 136, 205, 206
Liberation, Passover and, 166
Lighting, for parties, 9
Lillith, 83

Lorax, the (Dr. Seuss), 143
Lulav, 68, 71, 76–77, 267

Maccabees, 101–2, 105–8, 120
Machzor, 36
Maimonides, 22, 48
"Ma'oz Tsur" (song), 109
Marinated Shashlik on Sticks, 196
Maror, 180, 182
Marranos, 47
Marriage trees, 128
Martha Schlamme Sings Jewish Folk Songs,
        194
Masks, Purim (craft project), 148, 159
Mattathias, 106
Matzoh, 167–68, 182, 183
    Cover (craft project), 169
    making, tips for, 168
    Traditional Matzoh Balls, 173
May Day, Lag b'Omer parallels with,
        211–12
May 14 (Independence Day). *See* Yom
        Ha'atzmaut
Megillah (Megillot), 147, 149–50, 240
Memorial Yahrzeit Candle and Holder
        (craft project), 42
Menorah(s), 102, 109
    lighting of, 103–4, 105, 266
    making your own (craft project), 110
    modern alternatives, 104
    ritual of, 105
Menus, 7. *See also* Recipes
    determining serving amounts, 5
    for Hanukkah, 113
    for Lag b'Omer, 214
    for Passover, 170
    for Purim, 153
    for Rosh Hashanah, 29
    for Shabbat, 252
    for Shavuot, 230, 231
    for Simchat Torah, 88–89
    for Sukkot, 60, 63
    for Tu b'Shevat, 137
    for Yom Ha'atzmaut, 195
    for Yom Kippur, 48–49, 57
Micah, Book of, 27
Midrash, 83
Mild Hummus on Spinach Leaves, 50
Miracle of the oil, at Hanukkah, 106–7

Mishloach manot, 147, 161
Mishnah, 83
Mobiles
   Bee (craft project), 37
   Centerpiece Torah (craft project), 96–97
Modin, 106, 107, 108
Modzitser Melave Malke Melodies, 194
Mordechai, 13, 145
Moses, 40, 165–66, 224
Mount Herzl (Jerusalem), 195
Mount Meron (near Safed), 210
Mount Sinai, 22, 40, 208, 224, 226, 239
Mount Zion, 107, 242
Muffins, Orange-Almond, 138
Music (folk songs), for parties, 9. *See also*
      specific songs
   on Passover, 179
   on Purim, 158, 159
   on Tu b'Shevat, 133
   on Yom Ha'atzmaut, 193–94

Naomi, 240, 241
Napkin Rings, Braided (craft project), 250
Nehemiah, Book of, 24
Neilah, 56–57
Ner tamid, 107
New clothes
   on Rosh Hashanah, 27
   on Yom Kippur, 43
New Year of Trees. *See* Tu b'Shevat
New Year's cards, 36–37
   Star of David (craft project), 25
Nisan, 126, 163
Noah, 21
Noisemakers. *See* Groggers
Noodle(s)
   Kugel, Shanah Tovah, 31
   serving on Shabbat, 251
Notebook, for planning parties, 4–5, 6
Nun (nichts), dreidel game and, 118

Old-Fashioned Orange Chicken Breasts,
      154
Old-World Cholent, 257
Omer, 206, 207. *See also* Lag b'Omer
Orange-Almond Muffins, 138
Orange Chicken Breasts, Old-Fashioned,
      154
Orpah, 240

Outdoor parties (picnics; al fresco dining),
      7
   on Lag b'Omer, 207–8, 214–15, 217,
      218–19
   on Yom Ha'atzmaut, 193, 195, 201

Palestine, 203
Paper Cut-Outs, 238–39
   Pretty (craft project), 237
Papier Mâché Puppet Heads (craft project),
      160
Parades, on Yom Ha'atzmaut, 188, 190
Parashot, 82
Parsley Planter (craft project), 129
Parsnips and Carrots, Braised, 53
Passover, 14, 163–83, 208, 224. *See also*
      Passover seder *below*
   birth of the Jewish people, 163–64
   Candle-Holder Boxes (craft project), 181
   children's activities, 176
   enhancing the holiday, 176–77
   experiencing the holiday, 164–65
   food traditions on, 167–68, 170
   rules and customs, 175
   services for, 167
   story of, 165–66
Passover seder, 164–65, 166, 175, 176–77
   ceremonial foods and their role at, 180,
      182
   food traditions for, 167–68, 170
   plate, 177, 182
   preparations for, 179, 180
   symbols of, 180
   tips for a successful, 182–83
Peri Etz Hadar, 125
Philo, 175
Picnic Baskets, Woven (craft project), 220
Picnic Cloth, Independence Day (craft
      project), 202
Picnics. *See* Outdoor parties
Picture Frames, Leafy (craft project), 142
Pilgrimages
   to Israel, for Yom Ha'atzmaut, 200
   on Shavuot, 224, 242
   on Sukkot, 59–60, 224
Pink Applesauce, 116
Pita bread, 194–95, 197
   Pockets (recipe), 197
Placemat, Apple Dish (craft project), 28

Planning tips
  guest lists, 6, 8
  hiring help, 8
  menus, 7. *See also* Menus
  notebook for, 4–5, 6
  servings, determining amounts, 5
  timetables, 6
  timing of party, 9
Planter's Prayer, 136
Planting trees, on Tu b'Shevat, 126, 128,
  130, 143
Plants, on Shavuot, 228
Pomegranate seeds, project for Sukkot,
  73
Pomegranates, on Rosh Hashanah, 34
Poppy Quickbread, Citron, 64
Potatoes, 111–12. *See also* Latkes
Prayer book *(machzor)*, 36
Preserved foods, serving for Sukkot, 61
Pretty Paper Cut-Outs (craft project), 237
Proverbs, 79, 127, 249
Psalms, 23, 109, 136, 201
Pudding, Holiday Corn, 91
Puppets, for Purim, 157–58, 159, 161
  Papier Mâché Puppet Heads (craft
    project), 160
Purim, 13, 144–62
  Book of Esther, 149–50
  children's activities, 157–58, 159, 161
  costumes on, 146, 158
  favorite activities for, 159, 161, 162
  Hadassah and the story of, 150
  Masks (craft project), 148, 159
  music and folk songs, 158, 159
  planning dinner for, 152–53
  planning your celebration, 150, 157
  rituals, 147, 149
  shalach manot baskets for, 149, 161
  spiels, 146–47, 150, 159, 161, 162
  table decorations, 157–58
  typical foods for, 145–46
  wine on, 153, 157

Quickbread, Citron Poppy, 64

Rachel, 86
Raizelech, 237, 238–39
Ram's horn. *See* Shofar
Readings, recommended, 281–82

Real Family-Tree Centerpiece (craft
  project), 227
Recipes
  Apple Walnut Strudel, 67
  Baked Salmon in Cream Sauce, 30
  Baked Stuffed Zucchini, 92
  Balabusta Bread, 216
  Barley-Cheese Kugel, 233
  Braised Parsnips and Carrots, 53
  Brisket à la Modin, 114
  Chantilly Cheesecake, 234
  Chickpea and Avocado Salad, 155
  Citron Poppy Quickbread, 64
  Classic Potato Latkes, 115
  Fancy Falafel, 198
  Fancy Fig Squares, 140
  Fancy Gefilte Fishlets, 171
  Fruited Chicken Salad, 215
  Harvest Vegetable Soup, 65
  Heavenly Hamantaschen, 156
  Herbed Chicken Soup, 172
  Herring in Cream Sauce, 255
  Holiday Corn Pudding, 91
  Israeli Jelly Doughnuts, 117
  Israeli Triple Salad, 218
  Kibbutz Kebabs, 217
  King David Honey Cake, 32
  Lemon Chicken Schnitzel, 139
  Marinated Shashlik on Sticks, 196
  Mild Hummus on Spinach Leaves, 50
  Old-Fashioned Orange Chicken Breasts,
    154
  Old-World Cholent, 257
  Orange-Almond Muffins, 138
  Pink Applesauce, 116
  Pita Bread Pockets, 197
  Rich Carob Brownies, 219
  Roast Chicken With Barley Stuffing, 52
  Roast Lemon-Apricot Chicken, 256
  Shabbat Challah, 253–54
  Shanah Tovah Noodle Kugel, 31
  Sliced Spiced Eggplant, 199
  Stuffed Cabbage in Tomato Sauce, 66
  Sweet Honey Taiglach, 33
  Tabbouleh, 141
  Tel Aviv Fruit Soup, 232
  Traditional Matzoh Balls, 173
  Turkish Baklava, 93
  Tzimmes With Biblical Fruits, 90

Vegetable Cheese Blintzes, 235
Viennese Chocolate Torte, 174
Yom Tov Lemon Chicken Soup, 51
Recycling projects, on Tu b'Shevat, 131
Remembrance Day, 195
Resolutions, on Rosh Hashanah, 26–27
Rich Carob Brownies, 219
Ritual, role of, 6
Roast Chicken With Barley Stuffing, 52
Roast Lemon-Apricot Chicken, 256
Rosh Hashanah, 10–11, 19–38
    blessings, 24, 267
    celebrations, 21
    challah and, 34–35
    craft projects, 36–37
    diary for, 38
    festivities at home, 27, 29, 34
    guests at, 35–36
    introspection and prayer, 21–22
    making the most of the holiday, 24, 26
    origins of holiday, 20
    shofar and, 20, 22–24
    specialties, 35
    traditions, 26–27
    visit to flowing waters, 27
Ruth, 223, 226, 240
Ruth and Naomi Dolls (craft project),
    241
Rye, 212

Sabras, 200
Salad(s)
    Chickpea and Avocado, 155
    Fruited Chicken, 215
    Israeli Triple, 218
    Tabbouleh, 141
Salmon in Cream Sauce, Baked, 30
Salt shakers
    removing on Rosh Hashanah, 21
    on Shabbat, 252
Salt water, on Passover seder, 180, 182
Sauce(s)
    Baked Salmon in Cream, 30
    Herring in Cream, 255
    Stuffed Cabbage in Tomato, 66
Schnitzel, Lemon Chicken, 139
Schnecken, 137
Scholar's Day, 210–11
Secular dates, of major holidays, 269–70

Seder. See Passover seder; Tu b'Shevat
    seder
Seder plate, 177, 182
Seed vegetables, on Rosh Hashanah,
    35
Serving, determining amounts, 5
Shabbat, 16, 213, 243–63
    activities, 254, 258
    blessings, 265–68
    candles, lighting, 247–48
    challah on, 246–47, 249, 251, 266
    Challah, recipe for, 253–54
    cooking for, 245–46
    craft projects, 262
    family rituals, 249
    foods for, 251–52
    Havdalah, 258, 260–61
    origins of holiday, 244
Shalach manot, 149, 161
Shammash, 104
Shanah Tovah Noodle Kugel, 31
Sharona Aron Sings Israeli Songs, 194
Shashlik. See Shish kebabs
Shavuoslech, 237, 238–39
Shavuot, 15, 206, 208, 223–42
    as celebration of love and education,
        225–26
    children's activities, 228, 231–33, 236,
        238
    cooking ahead, 230–31
    dairy traditions, 229–30
    decorating your home, 228
    enhancing the holiday, 236, 238
    giving of the Torah, 224–25
    honoring the Commandments, 238
    in Israel, 240, 242
    practices on, 239
    serving suggestions, 230–31
    timing of party, 228–29
    Torah celebration party, 226, 228
    wine for dinner, 236
Shehecheyanu, 266
Shemini Atzeret, 60, 80, 81
Shevat, 13, 123–24, 126. See also Tu
    b'Shevat
Shin (shtell), dreidel game and, 118
Shish kebabs (shashlik), 195
    Kibbutz Kebabs, 217
    Marinated Shashlik on Sticks, 196

Shofars, 20, 22–24, 44
    Homemade (craft project), 46
Sidrot, 82
Simchat Torah, 12, 60, 79–98
    changes in, 80–81
    children's activities for, 89, 94
    dates for, 80
    dinner themes, 84, 86
    foods for the holiday, 88–89
    planning your party, 83–84
    reading beyond the Torah, 83
    traditions, 81, 94–95
Simple Paper Dreidel (craft project), 119
Singer, Isaac Bashevis, 111
Sing, Israel (Nathanson), 194
Sliced Spiced Eggplant, 199
Soldiers for b'Omer Bowling (craft
    project), 222
Song of Songs, 167
Soups
    Chicken, Herbed, 172
    Chicken, Yom Tov Lemon, 51
    Fruit, Tel Aviv, 232
    Vegetable, Harvest, 65
Spice Box (craft project), 261, 262
Spiced Eggplant, Sliced, 199
Spices, blessing the, on Shabbat, 260,
    268
Spinach Leaves, Mild Hummus, 50
Sprouts, on Lag b'Omer, 213
Star of David, 201
    New Year's Cards (craft project), 25
Strom, Yale, 158
Strudel, Apple Walnut, 67
Studying, on Shavuot, 225–26, 229
Stuffed Cabbage in Tomato Sauce, 66
Stuffed Zucchini, Baked, 92
Stuffing, Roast Chicken With Barley, 52
Sufganiyot, 108, 113, 117
Sukkah, 43, 59, 60, 68, 71, 73
    blessing the, 267
    building, 73–74
    Cookie (craft project), 71, 72
    decorating, 74
    enjoying the, 78
    Fruit Hang-Ups (craft project), 62
    lighting, 74
    origins and meaning of, 75–76
    Welcome Flag for (craft project), 70

Sukkot, 11–12, 58–78, 212, 224. *See also*
    Sukkah *above*
    blessings, 267
    celebrating harvest at, 58–59
    centerpieces, 69, 71
    children's activities for, 71, 73, 75
    food for the holiday, 61, 63
    four species, 76–77
    origins of holiday, 59–60, 75–76
    planning your party, 63, 68
    rituals and traditions, 73–74
    temple traditions, 60–61
    Thanksgiving parallels with, 68–69
    when to celebrate, 60
"Sung by the Pomegranate Tree" (song),
    133
Sweet Honey Taiglach, 33
Szold, Henrietta, 150

Tabbouleh, 141
Table decorations. *See* Centerpieces
Tahini, 50, 194
Taiglach, Sweet Honey, 33
Tal, 167
Talmud, 83, 229
Tashlich, 27
Tchernichowsky, Saul, 136
Tel Aviv Fruit Soup, 232
Ten Commandments, 40, 224, 238, 239
Thanksgiving, Sukkot parallels with, 68–69
Theodor Bikel Sings Yiddish Songs, 194
Tikkun olam, 130
Timetables, 6
Timing of party, 9
Tishri, 11, 19, 20, 40, 58, 80, 126
Titus, 208–9
Tomato Sauce, Stuffed Cabbage in, 66
Torah, 79–80, 81, 94–95, 208, 209. *See
    also* Simchat Torah
    celebration party, on Shavuot, 226, 228,
        240, 242
    Centerpiece Mobile (craft project), 96–97
    Flags for Procession (craft project), 85
    giving of, on Shavuot, 224–25
    study of, on Shavuot, 225–26, 229
    understanding, 82
Torte, Viennese Chocolate, 174
Traditional Matzoh Balls, 173
"Trees" (Kilmer), 136

Trees, on Tu b'Shevat, 126–28, 130–31
  planting of, 126, 128, 130, 143
Tu b'Shevat, 13, 123–43. *See also* Tu
    b'Shevat seder *below*
  blessings, 267
  celebrating the holiday, 128, 130
  children's activities, 135, 143
  commemorations, 130–31
  foods for, 136–37
  modern traditions, 126
  origins of holiday, 125
  planning your celebration, 131, 133
  reading the Haggadah, 135–36
  spring in Israel, 126–27
  as wine and fruit celebration, 124–25
Tu b'Shevat seder, 124, 125, 128, 131, 133,
    136
  activities for, 143
  leading the, 133–35
  story of, 131
Turkey, serving on Purim, 145
Turkish Baklava, 93
Turkish delight, 88
"Turn, Turn, Turn" (Collins), 136
Twelve Tribes, 84, 86
Tzedakah. See Charitable giving
Tzimmes, 61, 88
  With Biblical Fruits, 90

Vegetable(s). *See also specific vegetables*
  Cheese Blintzes, 235
  Israeli Triple Salad, 218
  serving on Rosh Hashanah, 35
  serving on Sukkot, 61
  Soup, Harvest, 65
Viennese Chocolate Torte, 174

Walnut Strudel, Apple, 67
"We Have a Day" (song), 159
Welcome Flag for the Sukkah (craft
    project), 70
Welcoming guests, 8–9. *See also* Greetings
White clothes, on Yom Kippur, 43
"Wicked Man, A" (song), 159
Wine(s)
  blessing of, on Shabbat, 249, 251, 260
  on Hanukkah, 113

on Passover seder, 170
on Purim, 153, 157
on Shavuot, 237
on Simchat Torah, 89
on Tu b'Shevat, 124–25, 133, 134–35
oven Picnic Baskets (craft project), 220

Yahrzeit candles, 41, 239
  Memorial Yahrzeit Candle and Holder
    (craft project), 42
Yizkor, 54
Yochai, Rabbi Shimon bar, 210, 213
Yom Ha'atzmaut, 14, 187–204
  celebrating the holiday, 190–91, 204
  children's activities, 201
  before the festivities, 195
  history of Israel, 201, 203–4
  music for, 193–94
  pilgrimage to Israel for, 200
  temple services, 200–201
  traditional foods for, 194–95
  traditions in Israel, 188, 190, 191, 193
Yom Ha'zikaron, 195
Yom Kippur, 11, 26, 39–57
  ancient rites and modern practice, 49, 54
  blessings, 265
  blessing the children, 45
  break-the-fast foods for, 56–57
  culinary customs, 48–49
  day of observance, 44
  feast for the spirit, 40–41
  honoring the holiday, 41, 43
  Kol Nidre services, 45–47
  story of Jonah, 54–56
  toward a better future, 39–40
  traditions, 41, 43
Yom Teruah, 20. *See also* Rosh Hashanah
Yom Tov Lemon Chicken Soup, 51
"Yom Tov Purim" (song), 159

Zebulun, 86
Zemirot, 247
Zeroah, 180
Zionism, 201, 203
"Zlateh the Goat" (Singer), 111
Zohar, 125
Zucchini, Baked Stuffed, 92